DATE DUE			
Mar 24 '75			

WINGS OVER THE WORLD

WINGS OVER THE WORLD

The Life of George Jackson Mead

by
Cary Hoge Mead

The Swannet Press
Wauwatosa, Wisconsin

Library of Congress Catalog Card Number: 74-141967.

Printed in the United States of America.

The Swannet Press
P.O. Box 7499
Wauwatosa, Wisconsin 53213

To the memory of my husband
George Jackson Mead
and to our children and their families
this book is lovingly dedicated

Contents

Preface

My childhood and youth were spent in Louisville, Kentucky, where my father, Dr. Peyton H. Hoge, was minister of the Warren Memorial Church. When my ninth birthday was approaching, my mother asked what gift I would like. I told her the one thing I really wanted was a pair of wings. She said there was no place to get wings. I answered that I was sure she could make me a pair out of light, strong material stretched over frames, with straps I could slip my arms through. I could see them plainly in my mind's eye. I could also envision myself flapping around above the house and the trees. Birds did it; why not I? In vain, Mamma explained that arms were located much higher up on our bodies than birds' wings were, so that spoiled the balance. Furthermore, our bodies were proportionately heavier, so our arms wouldn't be strong enough. And anyway, there was just not any possible way to get the materials to make the wings. I was sure, though, that if she really set her mind to it, she could somehow produce the wings; and I was also sure that if I had them, I'd figure out a way to fly with them.

Little did I dream that most of my adult life would have wings and the power that lifted them as one of its prime interests and concerns. They were a gift to me from my husband.

On December 17, 1903, in Kittyhawk, North Carolina, Orville and Wilbur Wright flew 852 feet in 59 seconds in what their neighbors called their contraption, thus proving that it was possible for man to fly in a machine heavier than air.

On July 20, 1969, man walked on the moon.

During the 66 years that elapsed between the first brief flight in a fragile plane powered by a small homemade engine and the miraculous achievement of July 1969, life for mankind took on a new dimension. We were no longer earthbound but could first soar into the wide blue yonder and then go on to explore the vast reaches of outer space.

Many people contributed their ideas, their work, their courage, and often their lives to the tremendous development in aviation which took place in those years of constant experimentation. For many years I have been wanting to make a record of the life of one of those great men—George Jackson Mead, my husband. More than any other one man, it was he who put safety into aviation. It was primarily from his mind that the Wasp and Hornet airplane engines became a reality. And he was deeply involved in the development of the Pratt & Whitney Aircraft Corporation as well as the United Aircraft Corporation.

Perhaps this book should have been written by someone whose technical knowledge would make it possible to give a clearer picture of his work from an engineering standpoint. For such data I have referred to published material in various automotive and aeronautical magazines, and to some of his own writings. But I wanted this to be an account of his life as well as his work—to set forth his character and his personality. He was not only a skilled engineer but an outstanding person.

Cary Hoge Mead
Hartford, Conn.
May 30, 1970

WINGS OVER THE WORLD

George Jackson Mead

Chapter I

A Life and An Epoch Begin

On December 27, 1891, in Everett, Massachusetts, a boy was born to Dr. George Nathaniel Plumer Mead and his wife, Jennie Henrietta Matilda LeMann Mead. He was named George for his father and for his grandfather LeMann, and Jackson for his grandfather Mead. Loving arms were eagerly awaiting this not too robust little boy with the fine head, delicate features, and brilliant dark eyes; but it is doubtful if even those whose lives were most closely wrapped up in his had any conception of the scope of the contributions to aviation that were to mark his future.

On his mother's side there was fine British stock mingled with Swiss and a touch of Austrian. Jennie's father, George Keene LeMann, a British merchant for whose ancestors Lake LeMann, now Lake Geneva, was named, had, on one of his trips to Russia, met Jennie Strauch whose mother was lady in waiting to the Austrian-born Czarina. He fell deeply in love with her, and in due time they were married. There were three children, Jennie, Neva, and Charles.

On his father's side, Jack, as he was called by his family, came from pioneer New England stock. His paternal grandfather, Nathaniel Jackson Mead, was one of seven brothers. With their parents, they hewed a road through virgin forest, from what passed for a highway in the township of New Hampton, New Hampshire, so that they could build their house on top of a hill, from which on clear days they could see Mount Washington. They were a hard-working family, each sharing in the toil of clearing the land and wresting a farm from that rugged country. It was Nathaniel, though, who devised many ways to save his mother unnecessary labor. In a day when no one dreamed of any modern conveniences, he built a pipeline of hollowed logs from the spring to the house so that by means of a rather primitive faucet, she could have running water right at hand. I mention this, not because of its importance, but because it exemplifies one facet of his character.

Nathaniel developed into a gifted, able and shrewd New England business man with great ingenuity and considerable engineering ability. He had a contracting business in Concord, New Hampshire. On one occasion, when the town fathers had decided to move the barracks from one end of town to the other, his bid was much lower than the others. His competitors gleefully waited for him to lose his shirt. However, he fooled them. Instead of the elaborate and costly house-moving arrangements they planned, he simply had a blacksmith make him some long saws, sawed the barracks into sections that would fit on big sleds, hauled them to the new location during the winter, and put them back together on their new foundations, as neat as could be.

Yet all through his successful life, he was never too busy for the thoughtful kindnesses that had endeared him to those who were closest to him from early boyhood. He was especially gentle with little children and even wanted to round off the corners of the furniture so small heads would not get bumped. He must have been a very dear and wonderful man, and I have always felt a real sorrow that he died long before I could have met him.

This was the family background which nurtured George Jackson Mead. His parents had been married by Phillips Brooks four years before his birth, and it was natural that they should want this great Christian minister to baptize their son. A letter from him dated March 23, 1892, says in part, "My dear Mrs. Mead, I thank you for your kind note and shall be very glad indeed to accept your invitation when I visit Everett on the 13th of May. I shall be glad also, at the same time, to baptize your little child. . . . Meanwhile, with all best wishes for you and your husband, I am Faithfully your friend, Phillips Brooks."

The earliest picture of Jack was taken when he was six months old. It shows a slender but well-muscled baby in whose sensitive face lay the promise of brilliance and sweetness which was to characterize his whole life. It is necessary to depend on memory for the story of the next few years, as very little was ever written down. Probably his mother wrote many letters about him to her sister, aunts and cousins in England, and to her brother Charles in Australia, but those letters are not available. However, during our many talks through the years after Jack and I were married in May 1921, I learned much of his childhood and have in my mind a vivid picture of him as a baby, little boy, and youth.

From his infancy, the Mead family spent their summers at Holderness, New Hampshire, in a bungalow on White Oak Pond, near Squam Lake. The majesty of the mountains and the incredible beauty of the lake and its surroundings seemed to have been taken into Jack's being along with the pure air he breathed. Throughout his whole life, this region was, to him, something more than the most beautiful spot on earth. The mountains brought him rest when he was weary, strength when he was overburdened, health when he was ill, and refreshment at all times.

Babyhood passed into little boyhood. The spun-gold curls were cropped, and along with the short hair and short pants came a boy's independence of spirit. Jack's mother used to tell me how, when he was determined to do something she forbade, he would clap his hands over his ears, to shut out her voice, and run as fast as he could. He must have run fast indeed if she failed to catch him, for though she was scarcely five feet tall, no one could ever cover the ground more swiftly than she. One day they missed him, and when he was found, he had been visiting a neighbor's calf. He had loved the calf, and unfortunately the calf had loved *him,* and expressed its affection by licking his face so thoroughly with its rough little tongue that there was almost no skin left.

On his fourth birthday, his mother took him to lunch at the Old Parker House in Boston. She allowed him to choose what he would eat, and the old colored waiter was intrigued when he ordered quail. As they waited a long time for this unusual meal for a four-year old, Jack remarked, "It seems as if they must be out shootin' dem birds."

When Jack was three and a half, his sister Doris was born, and there was rejoicing in the family. Her pictures show an adorable baby, and by all accounts she must surely have been a precious child. As Doris got bigger, she and Jack had happy times together. Some snapshots of them playing in the bungalow in Holderness are rather faint but are priceless, because they are a record of that period. There is also a delightful picture of them in a typically 19th century pose. However, those days of a little sister's companionship were all too short. In the spring before she was four, she fell from a rope swing, and as she was picking herself up, the seat returned and struck her in the back of the head. At first, it did not seem serious; but during the summer she began to sicken, and on November 14, 1900, she died of a brain tumor. Although her parents accepted this blow with quiet and heroic courage, they never really recovered from this sorrow. No more little children came to bless their home, and all their hopes were centered on Jack.

In 1897 the family had moved from Everett to Winchester, Massachusetts, where Dr. Mead had a big practice as a surgeon and family doctor. Their house was at 27 Church Street across Dix Street from the Congregational church. The common was to the east, and beyond that were the railroad tracks and station. Jack was fascinated by the trains and spent as much time investigating them as possible. The train crews made a great pet of him and sometimes took him for a short ride in the cab. On one memorable occasion he was allowed to run the engine for a short distance.

One summer, around 1898 probably, Jack became very patriotic and was suddenly distressed that his mother was flying the British flag from the flagpole on the bungalow. So he took the American flag and climbed to the ridgepole, where he fastened it *above the British flag.* That bit of spirit always gave me a big kick, as it did his parents. Thereafter, the Stars and Stripes were fastened to the flagpole above the Union Jack, and there was peace between the nations.

In 1899 Dr. and Mrs. Mead took the children to England to show them off to her family. It was on this trip that they first met Captain Jago, who became a cherished friend of the family. The meeting was unusual. Jack had been intrigued as he watched the sailors running up the rope rigging to the crow's nest, and he cherished a desire to get up there too. One day, though he knew it was forbidden, the longing got the better of him, and he climbed nimbly up, feeling very triumphant until he got almost to the crow's nest. Then he began to notice how the added height multiplied the heretofore gentle motion of the ship. It had not looked nearly so high from below, and as the mast seemed to sway out over the ocean, he was terrified and clung to the ladder, not daring to budge. The captain spotted him and sent a sailor aloft to bring him down—a wiser little boy. Captain Jago did not reprimand him; he knew he had already been punished enough, and they were fast friends from that day on.

In England that summer of '99, there was a family reunion at Fortin Chard, the home of Jack's aunt Neva and her husband, Eric James. Uncle Charles and his wife and son were also home from Australia; and with the four James children, Heather, Phil, Winsome, and Sonia, they had some wonderful times. Heather was nearest Jack's age, and she had all the spunk and spirit of her Aunt Jennie and led him a merry chase. Visits were infrequent between the families, but they always kept close and are still close to me.

Dr. Mead's office was right in the house, since that part of Church Street was about as centrally located as one could wish. He had a coachman named Aaron who took care of the three horses that were required for his thirty or more calls a day. At that time, soon after the turn of the century, there was no hospital in Winchester. All babies were born at home, and if time or circumstances made it inadvisable to take surgical patients into a Boston hospital, operations were performed on kitchen or dining room tables, sometimes by lamplight. It was a grueling life for the doctor, with little sleep, irregular meals, and almost no time with his family.

Jack attended the public school in Winchester. After hours, in winter, he enjoyed coasting and became quite a skating expert. This was, of course, before the days of movies; but in any case his Spartan mother would have seen to it that he lived outdoors as much as possible, so he could toughen his body and develop into a strong man.

Always he drew. First he concentrated on locomotives; later these gave way to cars. Some of the drawings were rare and wonderful, but gradually they began to take on an accuracy and precision that showed an insight and understanding far beyond a child's spontaneous interest in a new form of locomotion.

One day when he was about nine, Jack was stricken with appendicitis. People at that time were not on the alert for this trouble; and it was long before the days of blood counts. However, Dr. Mead was convinced that this was no ordinary digestive upset, and late in the day he summoned a Dr. Richardson from Boston. Together the two surgeons and Mrs. Mead, who had trained as a nurse, struggled with their problem. It was getting dark. It was not very safe to operate by lamplight. They dared not subject the boy to a jostling trip to Boston. If they could wait until morning, there would be a better chance of saving him. But dared they wait? It was the surgeon's skill and judgment weighed in the balance with the life of a child.

As the night wore on and Jack grew more desperately ill, Dr. Richardson said, "If he were my son, I'd operate now." All was in readiness, and the three went into action immediately with the child's mother acting as nurse and anaesthetist and his father assisting Dr. Richardson. They were not a moment too soon, for the appendix broke just as they were removing it. I do not know enough of the technicalities to explain why a somewhat more extensive operation enabled them to save him from peritonitis, which would have been fatal in a day of no antibiotics; but save him they did. The long ugly wound had to be kept open with drains for almost a year. The daily dressings were an agonizing performance. Even simply being in bed all that time would have been stern discipline for a normally active boy. I have often wondered what his parents' thoughts must have been all those long months. Dr. Mead said to me once: "I have heard that suffering develops character, but I hope I'll never again have to see a child's character developed that way."

It was probably during Jack's convalescence that he started

making scrapbooks of early automobiles. They are real museum items. There are pictures of early models—the first racing cars and their drivers; there are ladies in huge hats swathed in veils, sitting high in the horseless carriages. There are also cartoons of nursemaids with baby carriages, fleeing to safety, or of horses running away or climbing trees at the sight and sound and smell of the snorting monsters.

At last Jack was well again, but a whole year of school had been lost; and although a young teacher named Miss Lettie Kimball had tutored him when he was well enough, it was not like going to school, and he was somewhat behind. His parents were determined that he should have a good education, no matter how difficult it was for them to manage. So they persuaded Lettie to come to Holderness and tutor him in the summer of 1902.

It so happened that there was a widower named Frank Smith, some years Lettie's senior, camping nearby. Lettie's teaching duties left her considerable free time, and—well—moonlight on a lake, in a canoe, with mountains as a backdrop against a starry sky, coupled with some leisure time, made an unbeatable combination, so that not only did Jack find himself scholastically that summer, but she found her happiness; and she and Mr. Smith were married in the fall. Twenty years later, when I met these two dear people, it was heartwarming to sense their love for my husband. There was the teacher's pride in a student who had fulfilled the promise which he had shown as a ten-year old. There was evident the response of a warm-hearted woman to a lovable child, and of course there was the gratitude they both felt toward the one who had brought them together.

Meantime, Dr. Mead felt that his practice was too hard on the horses. Also, maintaining three was too expensive. So he bought an automobile—a single-cylinder Cadillac. His was not a mechanical mind, his father's engineering ability having quite definitely skipped a generation. The family stories of this period are semi-humorous, semi-rueful. Now Jack's gift with motors began to flower. But, all was not joyous. Cars being what they were in those days, and Dr. Mead's driving skill—or lack of it—being what it was, there were some tense moments. He would come to the erstwhile carriage house to get the car and set forth on his calls only to find the auto in some hopeless stage of disassembly and with many of its parts in various stages of repair.

Fortunately the Meads still had one horse and buggy, and "Tommy" became the car's most important spare part. One day the doctor was driving along in his car, which had a steering lever instead of a wheel. He saw that his bag was about to fall out and leaned over to catch it. Unfortunately he leaned on the steering lever, and the next thing he knew he was lying in a lady's yard under his overturned car, with the owner of the yard standing over him. While the engine chugged and the wheels turned aimlessly, she told him irately just what she thought of people who drove those horrid contraptions onto people's lawns and spoiled the grass. Dr. Mead was a redhead, and he thought of a few things to say himself; but instead he submitted meekly to her tirade. When she ran down, he asked if she would get word to Jack and Aaron to extricate him, so that he and the car could remove themselves from her premises.

I think the training Jack got from disassembling, repairing, reassembling, and tuning up his father's cars of those years probably was the equivalent of going through any automobile manufacturer's service school today. What he lacked in teaching and supervision, he gained in ingenuity and perception as to what made them tick. That, combined with an indefinable "feel" and insight into the harmony of the laws of mechanics, made him an invaluable help to his father, while putting him far ahead of his age in all things pertaining to internal combustion engines.

In a written statement when applying for his first job, he says: "My experience with internal combustion engines dates back to 1900. I started at that time to experiment with automobiles and was the youngest person in Massachusetts to obtain a professional chauffeur's license when the law requiring this first went into effect."

All of Jack's spare time until he went to college in 1911 was spent working and experimenting with various types of automobiles. He carried on a good deal of original work in his own shop.

Before Jack was twelve, he began working on a device to improve the working of the automobile clutch. He made a wooden model, and his father took him to the Patent Office in Washington. The device really did make it much easier to shift gears smoothly, and those in the Patent Office looked with favor on Jack's model until they realized that it was he, a boy of thirteen, who had made it. They then decided that because of his age, they could not issue a patent. If only they had had more vision, how many thousands of gears could have been shifted quietly in the course of the many years that were to pass before transmissions were improved!

Jack showed me his model once when we were visiting his parents. I would have loved to take it home with us where I could have studied it, and we could have kept it with other special treasures; but we did not like to take it away from them. I regret to say that later someone cleaning the attic threw it away. However, in going over Jack's boyhood drawings, I discovered the following description titled simply "The Transmission."

> It is a mechanical transmission of the selective type, of three speeds forward, and one reverse. The gears are composed of but seven pinions, that is, counting the bevel gear. As they are very compact, taking about half the space usually necessary, they are carried in the bevel gear housing on the rear axle. They are run in oil on four very liberal Hess Bright ball bearings. The housing in which they are carried is aluminum. No dog clutch is employed on the main shaft. No pinions are in mesh when not in the act of transmitting power. In any speed, the drive is direct, reverse included. When a change of gears is necessary, the pinion is all that is moved. The number of pinions in ordinary transmissions of three speeds forward, and one reverse, is from ten to twelve, as compared to the seven of this one. Being small and compact, it weighs very little, and as it is small, the cost is also greatly reduced. The gears can be shifted quickly without noise or labor. Combined with the quadrant is a small piece of mechanism by which it is impossible to make the gears shift without first releasing the clutch. The change speed lever is absolutely locked in position when the clutch is in. The release of the clutch causes the instant release of the lever.

Jack's struggles with his father's cars inspired him to plan to build one himself. This car was to be quite free from the faults that had plagued them to date. There are beautiful, careful, precision drawings during the years from 1904 on, showing very careful consideration of the throws on crankshafts, the stroke and bore of cylinders, the size and number of pinions or teeth on the gears, the strength of the drive shaft, the rear axle, and so on. Even the bolts are carefully drawn in; and polished surfaces are indicated by hundreds of fine lines.

In the summer of 1905 Jack attended Camp Algonquin. The life there was meat and drink to him, because it gave him a closer, more intimate knowledge of the lake and mountains he loved. He had always been able to swim; but now he learned form and attained speed and endurance. His diving became something more than just going into the water head first. He learned to paddle a canoe in true Indian style without lifting the paddle from the water. Never have I known anyone who could paddle a canoe so swiftly, and so absolutely silently. One of the delights we used to enjoy together in later years was going out on the lake in the canoe at dusk, and silently approaching the loon family that lived near us. Because of his silent paddling and the fact that the loons were used to us, we could come quite close to them and watch them teaching their baby to dive and stay under water. One time we witnessed a delightful bit of loon housekeeping. The father loon dove down and caught a nice fat fish. The mother ate one end, and the baby the other; then the father swallowed the middle. No dishes to wash, no garbage, no fuss!

One of the big undertakings at Camp Algonquin that year was cutting a new trail to the summit of Sandwich Dome from Sandwich Notch. Jack and Ted Main were especially interested in this project and saw it through to completion. This must have awakened in Jack a desire to make trails, because always, throughout his life, he not only loved to climb mountains but loved to clear old trails and make new ones. There is a trail on Mount Israel now which bears his name. Because of the 1938 hurricane, as well as some lumbering operations, Jack had to relocate that particular trail at least twice; but there were such glorious views from it—whence you could see the other mountains, and lakes and farms in the distance—that he was determined not to allow it to be lost. Later he bought the land through which the trail ran, to save it from being lumbered. I knew he wanted it to be a part of the National Forest, so in 1950 I turned it over to the trustees of the forest; they then named the trail he had built for him.

When Jack was ready for high school, Mrs. Mead, with her British background, felt that a good boarding school was of prime importance for him. She forthwith entered him at St. George's at Newport, Rhode Island. This was not, however, the wisest choice. The school was one which prepared for a liberal arts career, but Jack's gifts lay quite obviously in the engineering field. Learning that George Clare St. John, a well-known educator, was soon to become headmaster at the Choate School in Wallingford, Connecticut, Jack persuaded his mother to allow him to transfer; and in 1907 he entered Choate which, though small and rather "young," was already noted for its high standards of scholarship and character development.

The influence of Dr. and Mrs. St. John on the lives of the boys and the atmosphere of encouraging, and of bringing out all that was in each boy, made his life there the most significant period of his whole youth. They helped in molding his character and in developing the remarkable gifts which came to full fruition in early manhood. It is amazing in looking through the memory book of his years at Choate to see how self-evident his capabilities and qualities of leadership were to his fellow students. Because of poor eyesight and the grim necessity of wearing glasses at all times, it was impossible for him to participate in sports like football and basketball, but he was unanimously elected manager of both teams in 1909 and 1910 and was awarded his "letter" by the Athletic Association for his excellent work as manager, though a letter had never before been awarded to the manager of teams. He was captain of the hockey team and was "The Marshal" on Field Day in 1910 and 1911. His extra-curricular activities were not confined to athletics, however, for there is a note in the Choate News saying, "Great credit is due to Jack Mead and Ralph Cross for their excellent stage management, which sent the play 'Private Secretary' through without a hitch." Another note mentions that, "The dance committee members were Webster Knight 2nd, George Jackson Mead, Kirkland Hart Day, and Amory Standish Sperry." It is evident that in speaking of dances, "The News" also "went formal," with full names and no abbreviations!

Jack's name first appears on Choate's Honors List in December 1908 and again in February 1909. He was elected a prefect in 1910, and the note in "The News" is very revealing: "While the prefects are not chosen directly by the fellows, it is quite evident that Case and Mead would have been unanimously elected if this had been true. The News extends to them its heartiest congratulations." He received the prize for penmanship, which was naturally a fine fountain pen. His distinguished and legible handwriting characterized his whole life.

He gave the valedictory address at graduation in 1911, and at that time received the highest honor the school could give—the School Seal Prize. This prize is treasured among the other medals which came to him as the years went on. To me, that medal is symbolic of the reason for calling graduation "commencement." Throughout his life, he made a point, as he had in school, of giving to every task that came to hand the utmost of which he was capable. The medals were valuable to him only insofar as they showed that he really had given his best to each enterprise.

During Jack's high school years, the summers spent on Squam Lake had developed his interest in boats. His knowledge of every cove in the lake was intimate and thorough. He and Ted Main had taken a canoe trip in which they were determined to explore all indentations. Since the lake, though but nine miles long, had a ninety-mile shoreline, this was quite an undertaking. It took them a week, and when they completed their "tour," it is probable that they knew more about the locations of rocks and shoals than all the crews who had the task of placing the buoys.

Jack longed for a motor boat and made three beautiful little models. He then started to build a full-size boat, but his money-making jobs interfered with its completion.

One summer he took a job with Frank G. Webster, Sr., who owned a great deal of property on Squam Lake and had several motor boats to be kept in perfect condition and, on occasion, driven. Jack's first concern in beginning this job was to clean the boathouse until the windows shone and the boards between the slips looked as if they had been "holy stoned." Cobwebs and bats found their accustomed spots untenable, and the whole place looked the way a boathouse should. Then Jack turned his attention to the boats, which also came into their own, their mahogany hulls polished, and their engines cleaned and oiled and shining. His knowledge of every cove and channel on the lake made him the ideal skipper, and his understanding and "feel" for all motors assured the perfect performance of the boats.

In the autumn of 1911, Jack entered the Massachusetts Institute of Technology, specializing, of course, in internal combustion engines and related subjects. Here, his mind, which was like good soil, well prepared by his struggles with the unreliabilities of early automobiles, and the intricacies and perversities of marine motors, was ready to receive the technical knowledge that was planted there. The superb theoretical and technical education he received at M.I.T. assuredly made possible the early fruition of his genius and helped him immeasurably to use the splendid gifts with which he had been endowed. He plunged into his college work with a delight which I could sense years later when he told me about his life there.

He lived at home, commuting to classes and labs on a motorcycle. This gave him more sleep and was less expensive, but it permitted no real college life. His father's patients were numerous and his work dedicated, but it was never a wealthy practice, and bills were often paid with personal possessions, if at all. For this reason, Jack was extra conscientious in striving to get all he could from the education, which meant a sacrifice for his parents. From early boyhood his eyes had always given trouble, and at one point during his college years, they gave out completely. Doctors advised him to give up all thought of a career that would involve any real use of his eyes; but he was not one to give up so easily. After consultation with his parents, he decided to spend a winter logging in the New Hampshire woods. He went to Plymouth, where he boarded with Curt Burleigh and his wife. The logging was done in Sandwich Notch. The wholesome out-of-door life of that winter, with the complete rest to his eyes, restored not only his sight but improved his health in all respects, and he returned to Tech the following year, completing as much of his course as was humanly possible in the year 1914–1915.

He was now twenty-three and felt that his father had supported him long enough, but his eyes had to have another period of rest after the year at Tech when he had tried to do two years' work in one, so he did not return to get his degree. It is interesting to note in this day of emphasis on degrees that the man who probably made the greatest contribution to aviation in its early days did not have even a B.S. degree.

Two of the summers during Jack's college years were spent in Michigan building and racing hydroplanes in order to familiarize himself with large engines. It was probably because of this unusual experience that, some years later, when Ned Webster, Frank Webster's older son, became interested in speedboats and had his first racing hydroplane built, it was Jack who was entrusted with the task of escorting her from her builders in Michigan to Squam Lake. This was an important trust for a youth, for it involved driving her in rough, unfamiliar waters, getting her shipped overland, and finally delivered safely to the Websters' boathouse.

Because of Jack's previous interest in marine engines, his first job was with the Sterling Engine Company of Buffalo, New York. His mother insisted that, whatever else he lacked, he should board where he would have good wholesome food. This he did, but his weekly wage was just one dollar more than the cost of his weekly board. Obviously there was not much opportunity here for the higher life; but he was doing the work he loved, and supporting himself, and was therefore happy. For well over a year he continued in this job, saving as much of the weekly extra dollar as he could, and because he had no bank account, he kept his savings pinned inside his coat pocket. The job, however, seemed to hold little promise; and his reading about the automotive industry focused his attention on Henry Crane, the builder of the Crane Simplex automobile. All that Jack read about this rare man attracted him. Learning that there was an opening for an experimental engineer, he took his meager savings and boarded the train for New Brunswick, New Jersey. Crane's and Jack's regard for each other seems to have been mutual from the first, because Jack was given the job and settled down happily to work for a man whom he could love and admire wholeheartedly, and who had the same integrity in his approach to his work that he had.

The Simplex automobile was built with the care and precision of a watch. Two years before I met Jack, I saw the chassis of one of these cars at the automobile show in New York, and even in my complete ignorance of the intricacies of internal combustion engines, the sheer beauty and perfection of its parts, the symmetry of its design, and the infinite care that one could sense in its assembly thrilled me to the core. I remarked to my brother-in-law, George Houston, that I thought it was by far the most beautiful car in the show. He laughed and told me he admired my taste, that it was indeed the finest car there, but that he hoped for my own sake I wouldn't aspire to one yet a while.

This was in 1917. The United States had entered World War I. All Jack's efforts to join the services were stymied, as no branch would accept a man who was completely dependent on his glasses. The Wright-Martin Aeronautical Corporation had acquired a license to build the famous Hispano-Suiza aviation engines; and since there was great need for well-trained, careful personnel, Mr. Crane agreed to turn over to Wright-Martin his company along with its highly trained machinists and engineers. This was Jack's first connection with aviation. Lives depended on the care and accuracy in building and the thoroughness of the testing of the motors. During tests on experimental motors, Jack never relied on his subordinates but stayed on the job to check them personally at each stage.

At the end of the war, Wright-Martin had 14,000 employees in two plants and had produced more aeronautical engines than any other company in the United States. Jack was in charge of the experimental division of the engineering department, under Crane, who was chief engineer. During the reorganization period in the aviation industry immediately following the Armistice, Jack was given the job of engineer in charge of the power plant laboratory of the United States Army at McCook Field, Dayton, Ohio.

This situation presented an opportunity to study all types of aeronautical engines which had been used in the war. Some of the "studying" was done in an extremely hair-raising manner. Jack was the observer for a tall lanky pilot known as "Shorty" Schroeder, a man of skill and daring. One of the "studies" was to find out how steeply a plane could climb. These tests fortunately were always made when the plane had reached an altitude which should allow a sufficient margin of safety. On one occasion, at least, when the pilot had attempted too steep a climb, the plane went into a spin and fell several thousand feet out of control, but Captain Schroeder managed to bring it out of the spin and landed safely. Standardized tests were made at McCook Field on the engines of all the countries that had participated in the war. Here indeed was the golden opportunity for Jack's inquiring mind. Here was the chance to see and evaluate the work to date of all those who had built engines under the stress and impetus of the war. Here was the real beginning of an era, for though men had flown in craft heavier than air since the famous experiments by the Wright brothers at Kitty Hawk in 1903, flying as a practical means of transportation had not progressed very far until the stark necessity of war had opened men's eyes to the possibilities of air travel.

Chapter II

A Short Review of Early Aeronautical Development

Here it would be well to glance back to see what had been accomplished thus far in aeronautical engineering all over the world. When one stops to think how vital were these first steps, and how much has been learned as a result of the courage of those who dared to fly, the somewhat dry facts come alive, and one cannot but feel a responsive thrill concerning all that their experiments have made possible. An article written by Jack, which was published in "Aviation" magazine, dated December 26, 1921, gives a clear account of the high spots. I quote from it extensively.

> Flying was quite a novelty in 1914. Races had been held in France, and engine competitions in Germany, both of which stimulated development and brought before military authorities the importance of aviation. At the opening of hostilities, we find that the armies used the very few planes they had entirely for recon-

naissance and observation. Gradually, the pilots began to carry shotguns and pistols, and finally pursuit aviation developed very fast single-seater ships, armed with machine guns. These guns were first fired through the propellers, unsynchronized. This, of course, resulted in tragic accidents and prompted the development of synchronizers which operated the guns so as to fire between the propeller blades. The object of these planes became very definite, namely, to obtain and maintain control of the air, thus permitting observation and bombing operations to go forward over the enemy's territory unhindered.

Pursuit aviation became a race, and it was soon apparent that the supremacy of the air depended on the speed and maneuverability of the pursuit ships. Great speed alone availed nothing without maneuverability, or the ability to climb rapidly, turn quickly, and dive at tremendous speed. These qualities required that the plane itself be of the smallest possible dimensions, particularly in wingspread. For these really small airplanes, the maximum power was required from the weight that could be allowed for the power plant. For maneuverability, the engine also had to be very compact. In the service, everything, even safety and the life span of the plane and engine, had to be sacrificed for speed and maneuverability.

In 1914, the French pinned their faith on rotary, air-cooled engines, such as the Gnome and Le Rhone. The ships equipped with these engines were quite maneuverable due to the compactness of the power plant and concentration of weights. . . . However, the French soon found that the rotaries which, due to their lightness, had more or less directly enabled successful flight in the early days, must be abandoned, since their power was limited by the speed of rotation. Incidentally, as rotary engines reached their maximum dimensions, their gyroscopic action proved more and more detrimental to maneuverability. This same factor was seriously impaired by the inability of these engines to be run at very high speeds. The ship's diving speed was thereby limited. Centrifugal force became the limiting factor, as, to prevent the cylinders leaving the crankcase, the pilot must not exceed the predetermined engine speed, which, in turn, limited the diving speed. The instrument boards on the "Nieports" carried this warning: "Maximum speed of revolution must not exceed 1400 r.p.m."

The war had, of course, put an end to the demand for high-priced motor cars, and many European designers therefore turned their attention to aviation. Among these was Marc Birkigt, a Swiss engineer, who had been unusually successful in developing a high-grade motor car, the Hispano-Suiza. Mr. Birkigt designed an aviation engine which proved to be the salvation of the allies in the air. It was called after the motor car produced by his company and turned out to be the first successful water-cooled engine, having a weight per horsepower *less* than that of rotaries. It was, moreover, almost as compact as they were. The French took up its manufacture in earnest, and at the end of the war, there were twenty-two plants engaged in producing it.

The German military authorities gave considerable attention to aviation prior to the war, and encouraged the development by their large automobile companies of aeronautical engines. In this way, they were able to bring to bear on this problem all their experience with high-speed internal combustion engines. It is interesting to note that the Mercedes racing cars, which won the Grand Prix in 1914, were really testing the type of engine, adopted as their standard aviation engine at the beginning of the war. The Hispano-Suiza in the famous Spad, held in reverence by all the Allies, upset their standard which was a six-cylinder vertical water-cooled engine. It was not until after the close of the war that it was known how serious the menace of Hispano-Suiza engines had proved to the Germans. It was found out later that the first of these which was captured in Germany was carefully studied, and plans made for its production.

When the United States entered the war, we had only a few training planes and no fighting ships at all. The Government had not seen the value in aviation and had, therefore, not encouraged its development in this country as had been done abroad. We therefore had very little of an aviation industry, with its need for trained engineers and artisans, and were therefore totally unprepared as a country to supply either planes or engines. In an endeavor to make up for this deficiency with the least possible loss of time, the Aircraft Production Board was organized.

Acting on the advice of the allied representatives, it was determined that the United States' initial program should consist of observation and bombing planes and engines, as that was the area where most assistance was needed at that time. The Board set out with the aid of several well-known engineers from the automobile industry to design the Liberty engine, the idea being that this would be a standardized all-purpose engine which could be produced in great quantities by the automobile manufacturers. The idea originally was to build six, eight, and twelve-cylinder models, many of the parts to be interchangeable. But after building and testing the eights and twelves, it was decided that at least 400 horsepower was needed to power the ships which it had been determined to build in this country. Therefore, production was planned for deHaviland "4" planes powered by twelve-cylinder Liberties to be built in great numbers. France was to produce the pursuit planes and engines.

In 1915 the Wright-Martin Company had decided to go into the production of aviation engines. Henry Crane, their chief engineer, went abroad to investigate the engine situation in Europe. After carefully going over the designs of various engines, he decided that the Hispano-Suiza, which had just come into prominence, was the most efficient type and had the greatest possibilities for further development. Arrangements were then made with the parent company to license the Wright Company for the manufacture of these engines.

The original engine, known as the Model A in this country, was an eight-cylinder, water-cooled, 90 degree "Vee" engine, having an approximate bore and stroke of 4-3/4 inches by 5 inches. This engine developed 150 horsepower at 1450 r.p.m. and weighed 438 pounds. Its design embodied many novelties, the principal ones being the cylinder blocks, method of valve operation, and the connecting rods.

Many problems came up with the manufacture of the first Hispanos. Even though the facilities and experienced personnel of the Simplex Company, which was now part of the Wright Company, were the finest in the country, the difficulties were enormous. All the French drawings were in French metric measure and had to be re-drawn to American standards. Few, if any, limits or tolerances were stated, so that limits had to be established for the fit of the parts. Tools and fixtures had to be designed for these parts. The castings, particularly the cylinder block and upper crankcase, involved intricate foundry problems, as these were made of aluminum, and the best foundries in the country had very little experience with any but the simplest aluminum castings. The French standards of steel had to be developed, as the major parts of a pursuit engine had to be very highly stressed in order to reduce the weight as much as possible.

Suitable accessories, such as magnetos, carburetors and spark plugs, were not at first available in this country. Gradually American sources of supply were developed. By the time all these matters had been straightened out and the first engines actually assembled, the problem of the proper testing equipment came up. The most satisfactory means of test proved to be reaction stands, on which the engine was run with a flat-bladed propeller or club. After preliminary tests, and the setting of proper tolerances, the 50-hour run required by the French government was accomplished without difficulty, and production began on these engines. This was an interesting example of the fact that no matter how good the equipment in machinery and men, satisfactory production of such a highly specialized engine could not be secured without the necessary "know-how."

A constant effort to secure better plane performance led to the "gearing" of the engines, which permitted the engines to turn up to 2000 r.p.m. while leaving the speed of the propeller at 1400 r.p.m. as had been the case in the direct drive engine. These engines developed up to 220 horsepower, but it was found that gearing was difficult to manufacture in quantities with sufficient accuracy to insure satisfactory life. About this time, higher compressions were tried, and it was found that in pursuit planes, the propellers could turn much faster than had originally been believed possible without excessive slip, so that the gearing of engines was dropped, and the compression of the standard engine was boosted, and the propeller speed allowed to run as high as 2000 r.p.m. This made available the same horsepower as with the geared engines without either the complication or the added weight.

Much experience had been gained from the manufacture of the A model engines, and from the experiments on the geared engines, but these were not really satisfactory, and the development of the high compression engines known as the E model was undertaken in earnest.

Hardly had these engines been put into service when the demand came for greater power. Both the French and American companies began the development, almost independently, of a larger edition of the original engine, which would develop about 300 horsepower. The French and American experimental engines were completed about the same time. The French engine proved to be almost an exact enlarged copy of their high compression small engine, whereas the larger engine developed in the United States called the Model H was considerably different from the Model E which was then being produced.

To begin with, the American engine used a 140 millimeter bore, and stroke of 150 millimeter, while the French made both stroke and bore 140 millimeter. The American engine had the marine type connecting rods, and the rods were considerably longer than the French type in order that the piston should not travel down into the crankcase, thus collecting oil. The design of the cylinder

> block casting was changed in order to carry water completely around the exhaust valves. This was accomplished by a slight increase in height, and by making the exhaust ports elliptical in shape. A much higher lift was used on the cams, and the cam contours were considerably changed. The compression ratio was the same as in the Model E. The result of these changes enabled the American engine to develop 325 horsepower at 1800 r.p.m. with a fuel consumption of 0.50 pounds per horsepower hour. The weight worked out to be 1.92 pounds per horsepower. This showed this engine to be the lightest of any thus far produced.

This was the first H model developed by the Wright Company with which Jack had been especially identified, and in which his clear creative thinking began to manifest itself even more forcibly.

He made a careful study of all the different types of engines developed during the war in an effort to determine which type was the most efficient and embodied the greatest possibilities for future development. The study covered such engines as six-cylinder verticals, eight and twelve-cylinder Vees, radials and rotaries. Each type was measured by the requirements of pursuit aviation, such as weight per horsepower, compactness (which involved not only length, but head resistance), ease of overhaul, durability, and manufacturing possibilities. The result of the study was a decision to continue, for the time being, the development of a 90-degree, water-cooled Vee engine. This type had no rival in pursuit work. Jack was not satisfied with a purely academic investigation. Therefore, designs were made of several of the types which most nearly competed with the Vee-8.

Jack's next task—the development of the H-3—grew out of this study. Among the many changes and improvements were a better timing device and a complete water piping system as a part of its own equipment, which made necessary only three water connections in the plane. A change in the carburetor permitted better fuel economy. The oil strainer was reinforced to prevent its bursting in cold weather. All exposed steel parts of the engine were rust-proofed.

The compression ratio was increased to 5.5:1, which gave better performance at altitude. These engines averaged 340 horsepower at 1800 r.p.m. at sea level. They weighed 620 pounds, which gave a weight factor of 1.82 pounds per horsepower.

This engine was further developed into what was called the superfighter. It developed 400 horsepower at 2000 r.p.m. and weighed only 610 pounds—or 1.5 pounds per horsepower. The engine had at that time the lightest weight per horsepower and was the most compact pursuit engine in the world. It had a fuel consumption of 0.46 pounds per horsepower hour, and oil consumption of 0.015 pounds per horsepower hour. Because particular attention had been given to altitude performance, this engine at 15,000 feet or over was far superior to earlier models.

To get the maximum horsepower, with minimum weight, was and is a very difficult problem. Since weight becomes a tremendous factor when gravity has to be overcome, each pound saved is of vast importance when a plane is climbing. We would all do well to remember this when we object to the weight limitations which have been placed on our baggage in commercial travel.

Chapter III

The First Three Wright Aeronautical Years—1920, 1921, 1922

In 1919 Jack returned to the Wright Aeronautical Corporation as its chief engineer. This company was the successor to the Wright-Martin Company, which had undergone a rather thorough reorganization after the close of the war. Henry Crane had resigned as chief engineer and Jack was asked to succeed him. Excerpts from Mr. Crane's letter to Jack of April 13, 1920, are interesting.

> I was certainly sorry not to see you again before leaving and was correspondingly glad to get your letter of March 15th which reached me in Bermuda. . . . You ought to be able to go a long way in engineering lines as your mind seems to go at things in a direct and definite and, what is more important, an absolutely honest way. I have greatly appreciated the able and strenuous work that you did under my direction during the war, and it is a great pleasure to me that you also enjoyed our association. . . . With best wishes for your continued success.

The reorganization of this company had been directed by George Harrison Houston, who had been asked to become its president and who, incidentally, was my brother-in-law. This remarkable man was an industrialist whose business was the reorganization of corporations.

When the United States entered World War I in April 1917, George had helped immeasurably to get the country's industrial resources mobilized so that much needed war materiel would be available in the necessary volume, in time. When the war was over, many corporations which had expanded far beyond their natural potential did not know exactly how to go about re-establishing themselves on a peacetime basis. George's incisive, creative thinking helped them to go forward usefully and profitably. He would go into such companies as their president, work out with their officers the best peacetime products for them to manufacture, cut down planned output where necessary, select men of assured ability for the key positions, and try to make sure that the board of directors included men of sound business standards. When things were running smoothly, he would be ready to go on to another job.

George would often be engaged in several of these "presidencies" at once. It was as if he had a perfect filing system in his mind. There used to be a saying at Wright Aeronautical when the men needed to fix something fast or if they had been dragging their feet: "Let's get George over to G.H. them." And when he came on the scene, it was best for everyone to watch his step.*

At Wright, George was president for a time while Frederick B. Rentschler, a brilliant young executive who was destined to be its president, was learning the ropes and getting the feel of the job that was to prepare him for the wider field that lay in the future. The Long Island plant was closed, and all operations were concentrated in Paterson, New Jersey. Some of the men besides Jack and Fred who contributed most significantly to the work of the

*In 1919 George Houston went to Europe on an aeronautical mission, headed by Benedict Crowell, Assistant Secretary of War, to study developments there in the aeronautical field. One of the plants visited was the Bristol Company in Bristol, England, and while there George bought the blueprints of their air-cooled engine, as Jack Mead had been working on such an engine. When he returned home and showed the plans to Jack, he said, "But G.H. we have already gone further than that,"—and they had!

Wright Aeronautical Company during this period were Andrew Willgoos, who was Jack's assistant and head of the drafting department; Harold Pope, factory manager; Don Brown, head of experimental shop; Jack Borrup, head of machine shop; Danny Jack, assistant to Borrup; Leslie Pierce, assistant in engineering department; Bill Willgoos, foreman of assembly; Harding Woodall, in charge of sales; and Thomas Carlisle, head of testing. Later Hugh Chatfield came in as head of research.

It was at Chevy Chase in the spring of 1918 that Jack's life first touched mine, and this is how our meeting came about. The previous fall my parents had persuaded me to go to Chevy Chase Junior College in Washington, D.C., not so much for the courses the school offered, as for the opportunity for me to see history in the making. I loathed the whole idea of boarding school, and besides I was twenty years old, but I agreed to go if they would consent to my doing war work the following year.

John Cautley, the son of an old friend of my father's, was the sales representative for the Wright Company in Washington. Sometimes, on a Sunday afternoon, he would suggest that I invite two other girls and a teacher, and he would bring any of his associates who happened to be in town and take us all out in the Simplex car that the company provided for his use. You can imagine how that made my stock go up! One Sunday, Jack was in the party, and we went out to Bolling Field to see the first "Bellanca" plane fly. I was thrilled at the performance of this beautiful plane, which was far ahead of its time. I can still see it in my mind's eye as it soared and looped and out-maneuvered anything I had previously watched. (Incidentally, a later model of this plane was the first one to make a loop from level flight. The others had to dive in order to get up enough speed for this feat.)

It was a glorious afternoon in the late spring, and we stayed watching all the flights until the last plane had landed safely. Then we all had dinner together at one of the hotels in Washington. Jack made himself very delightful to us all, but I thought he was rather taken with one of the other girls—especially when he sent her flowers when he couldn't attend a dance she invited him to the next week. In our book, that meant he was hers. He, in his turn, thought that, since John Cautley had arranged the Sunday party through me, I was John's girl.

In the fall of 1920, my sister Mary—Mrs. George Houston—

took her nine-year old son to the Automobile Salon in New York. There she met Harding Woodall, whom I had met years earlier in Cincinnati. With Harding was Jack. After introductions, she said to Harding, "Cary is coming for a visit next week. Don't you want to come to see her while she is here?" Jack said, "Is Cary's other name Hoge?" "Yes," my sister said, "do you know her?" "Yes, and, please, may I come too?"

He did, and we went on from there. The weeks that followed were filled with a happiness that was a promise of the greater joy that was to come with our marriage.

On Christmas the Houstons invited several of the men at the plant, whose homes were not close by, to spend the day with them. Harding Woodall, Bob Dabney and Jack were there. The Houstons' little daughter, Mary Stuart, aged 2, was considered too young to come to the table and had been fed ahead of the family and guests and put down for her nap. This did not coincide with her ideas, however, and while we were at the table, she appeared, and not seeing any place for her, she climbed up into Jack's lap. The delight he showed at being singled out, and the chivalry and tenderness with which he held her in his arms and fed her from his plate, were a revelation to me, showing me a side of him that I had previously had no opportunity of seeing. I had admired everything I knew or heard about him before. But here was a new Jack. That day will always stand out in my mind as one of my most significant milestones.

One day early in January Jack took me on a tour of the plant and introduced me to pistons, cylinders, camshafts and valves, crankshafts and connecting rods, crankcases, and all the other parts that made up the intricate power plants. That day I learned why piston rings had to fit tight and the meaning of such terms as "venturi." The functions of such things as "cams" were explained to me; I saw how they "bumped" the valves in and out for exhaust and intake and witnessed the careful machining of the connecting rods and other parts. With pardonable pride, Jack showed me the engines in various stages of assembly, all the parts laid out, readily available in their little boxes, so that the assembly crew could reach for them almost without looking. I learned the functions of the parts in relation to each other, and to the whole engine. Each moving part had been machined to plus or minus one thousandth of an inch, and in some instances a ten thousandth. On this day I learned of the existence of a special measuring device called a "micrometer," with which these accuracies were achieved. Each part shone with its careful polishing, demonstrating by its perfection the meticulous care that had gone into its manufacture. Faces lit up as we visited the different sections of the plant in the consciousness of jobs well done, and the assurance of his appreciation of their careful work.

That day also gave me an added insight into Jack's character: his joy in his work; his pride in its high quality; his humility; and deep sense of responsibility for the human lives that depended on the integrity and accuracy of his thinking; his longing to share his hopes and dreams with someone who could understand his feeling about his work and share his happiness in doing it well.

On January 16, he asked me to marry him. I had known since Christmas Day that he was and always would be the only one in the world for me, and I felt sure he cared for me; yet it seemed almost unbelievable that there could be such complete fulfillment to all my dreams. It turned out that he had planned to ask me two weeks before, when he had made quite a point of a date we had but was afraid I'd say "no." I was too happy to reproach him for keeping me in suspense all that extra time. Soon after this, I went to meet my parents in Florida, according to plan. The separation was made bearable by the thought that it would be our last long one, as we were to be married on May 18.

Jack, Harding Woodall, Leslie Pierce, and Jack Rogers had rented a house in Ridgewood, New Jersey. This was presided over by a housekeeper who had neither skill nor imagination in the meals she planned and prepared; and the whole atmosphere of the house lacked everything that would make it homelike and attractive.

In the course of that winter Jack had a severe case of flu, which went into pneumonia. When letters came, day after day, indicating that he had not been able to go to the plant, I grew increasingly anxious. I had not met his parents and felt some hesitation about seeming to tell them what they should do; yet I thought it quite probable that he had not told them of his illness. This proved to be the case, and when I wired them that I thought he was more seriously ill than they realized, his father went to Ridgewood immediately and took him home to Winchester, where he could be nursed back to health.

That winter was finally over, and my parents agreed that I could go back to New York for a couple of weeks, reassure myself about Jack, and go to Winchester to meet his mother and father. After that, he and I would return to Kentucky so that he could meet my mother and father. The weekend in Winchester was a precious one, the beginning of a warm, close relationship with the senior Meads that grew with the years. Jack had warned me that his mother was somewhat reserved; and realizing that he was their one and only, I prayed they would like me. But she was never reserved with me, and showed from our first greeting that she was as ready to receive me as her daughter as I was to be that daughter. She invited many of their closest friends to meet me, and in their desire to do honor to the daughter-in-law-to-be of their beloved physician and his wife, they completely cleaned out the florist, so that the whole house was a mass of flowers. I did my homework carefully, memorizing the names of the different ones and identifying them with the flowers they had sent so that I could thank them personally when I met them that afternoon, before writing my notes.

It was on this day that I first met Mr. and Mrs. Frank Jealous, and two of their sons, Alwyn and Bill; Mr. and Mrs. Alfred Higgins and their sons, John and Richard; Mr. and Mrs. Charles T. Main and their sons, Charlie and Ted, and Alice, who had already written me a sweet note when our engagement was announced, and whom I have always regarded as my first New England friend. There were many others who have been cherished friends through all the years that have followed. We loved Mr. and Mrs. Jealous so dearly that we always called them "Mother and Father Jealous." Their son, Arthur, had been one of Jack's earliest boyhood friends. He and his wife, Helen, and their little daughter, Barbara, lived in Newark, New Jersey, and were our dearest friends.

Our visit to Kentucky was quite a workout for Jack, as he had to run the gamut of my whole big family. I had grown up in a suburb of Louisville, Kentucky. My father had for many years been the minister of a large Presbyterian Church in Louisville, but after a grave illness he had accepted a call to a smaller, less demanding parish in the suburbs. There my two brothers and two of my sisters and their families gathered to meet and welcome

Jack. My other sister, Mary Houston, and her family already knew and loved him.

May 18 came at last and was one of those perfect days whose matchless beauty stays with you forever. Strangely enough, in all the forty-nine years since our wedding day, there has been only one rainy May 18. Dr. and Mrs. Mead and the Rev. Mr. Greenleaf, who had loved Jack during his school days, and our family, and most of the bridal party had lunch out under the trees, just quietly enjoying the day and one another.

My father's church was packed when we took our vows late that afternoon, and the shadows laid cool fingers across the lawn when we returned to the house to receive the good wishes of all our family and friends. To our horror, the house, which had been delightfully cool and lovely with its flower-decked rooms, was like an oven. We found that our dear old gardener had thought "the ladies would catch cold in their thin dresses" and had built a huge fire in the furnace! (The temperature outside was at least 75°!) One of my brothers banked the fire with wet ashes; and with every door and window open, the house soon became bearable again.

Then followed the long line of guests streaming into the house to bring us their heartfelt congratulations, and to receive our personal thanks for all their beautiful gifts—again I had done my homework assiduously. Then came the bridal table, with all the poems, telegrams and letters which always mean so much.

Finally, after almost everyone had gone, except those members of the bridal party who were staying at the house, Jack and I changed into our traveling clothes, and we all sat on the veranda in the delicious May night, watching the stars come out one by one, and talking over the events of the day, until it was time to drive into Louisville to take the train which would start us on our way to the Adirondacks. It was great to have this quiet time to visit with our families whom we would not be seeing again for several weeks.

I say "*almost* everyone" advisedly because Alice Huff, one of the bridesmaids from Roanoke, Virginia, and Clem Johnston, a Louisville friend of many years, came to what was known in those days as "an understanding" that evening. Alice was a bit stern with me when she wrote me of their engagement some weeks later, because she and Clem hadn't met on her previous visits to me. The fact that he had been off in the armed services at the times of those other visits mollified her slightly, but not entirely.

We had rented a little house in Ridgewood, and to this we came ten days later after a brief sojourn at Lake Honandaga in the Adirondacks. I had hoped that we could go to Jack's beloved White Mountains for our wedding trip, but there was no place open at that time of year. Lake Honandaga was beautiful, and as I had never been in the north woods before, Jack delighted in pointing out to me the trillium and bunchberry which were in full bloom and the different evergreens. The fragrance of the pine and balsam with the sun on them was delicious. We walked miles over soft mossy woodland paths, soaking up health and sunshine and well-being.

Of course, no one was to know that we were bride and groom, and we tried all the time-worn methods of seeming like an old married couple. There was one lady in particular, whose table was near ours in the dining room, who was determined to satisfy her curiosity on this point, and our efforts were aimed mostly at her, but they didn't work very well. I would say, for instance, "Wasn't it awful last summer when the children put sand in the pump at camp?" (this having been a camp I went to on the Kentucky River, and the children being those of the chaperones). Jack would answer, "What children?" Or she would bustle brightly into the dining room of the lodge, where we were already at breakfast, with a "Good morning, Mrs. Mead," to which I would not immediately respond, as I was not yet accustomed to my new name, until a gentle kick under the table made me come to, with an extra hearty "Good morning, Mrs. Fulljoy." (We called her Mrs. Killjoy in private!)

One day she said, "How can a young man like your husband get away from his work at this time of year?" I answered, "He was ill with pneumonia last winter." "Well," said she, "it seems very strange that he would dive into that icy lake every morning;" and I answered, a trifle flustered, and, I fear, not altogether truthfully, "That is the new treatment!"

The payoff came, however, when a batch of mail originally addressed to Miss E. Cary Hoge was forwarded by my father to Mrs. George Jackson Mead. That was the only unkind thing he ever did to me, and I'll never forget the quizzical expression on the manager's face as he handed me all those proofs of our recent marriage.

In Ridgewood, a wonderful life began for me, sharing the hopes and dreams of one who, in spite of his great attainments, was infinitely modest and unassuming about all he accomplished. Housekeeping was pure happiness—it was a joy to create a home, and to try to make up in some measure for the drabness of the previous winter. Cooking was no problem, as I had always done a lot at home and had taken some courses in home economics at Columbia. Only parts of the days were needed for housework and note-writing, and I spent hours reading all Jack's engineering magazines, so that I could listen more intelligently when he told me about the problems in connection with the engines and could also rejoice with him intelligently when they fulfilled his plans for their performance.

That summer of 1921, the Houstons decided to move to the country. They wanted their two young sons and daughter to live in a place that was really home, where they could put down some roots, instead of becoming citified apartment dwellers who saw no flowers except in vases and few trees except in Central Park. George felt that the peace and refreshment of the country would more than make up for the added fatigue of commuting. Sometimes on Saturday afternoons, they would invite us to accompany them on these house-hunting expeditions. Once, when we had stayed for dinner at the country club, a storm came up with a tremendous downpour. When we went out in the rain to go home, our car almost started, then sputtered and died. Jack knew what the trouble was. The driving rain had come in through the louvers of the engine hood and wet the plugs. When the engine tried to turn over, it drew the water inside through the valves. There was nothing to do but take out the spark plugs, one by one, dry them thoroughly, and dry down inside the holes. It was a slow, painstaking process, which completely fascinated all the chauffeurs who were waiting in the parking lot. One of them solicitously held an umbrella over Jack but became so intrigued that he held it so that the rain which was still falling quite heavily was channeled down Jack's back.

All gave copious advice, which simply convulsed George, as he thought how taken aback they would be if they realized that the man they were talking to knew more about engines than anyone else in the country. Jack went quietly ahead, drying the plugs and the insides of the cylinders, answering courteously, and never showing the amusement he must have felt at some of the suggestions. The climax, which almost finished us all, came when the manager of the club, a fussy little man, came bustling out and said, "Now, young man, the question is, have you any gas?" Fortunately, the job was done, and the motor started, and away we went.

That trip was epoch-making for another reason. Jack had put on our car a gadget which was earth-shaking at that time. It was a windshield wiper that worked off the intake manifold of the engine. Yes, believe it or not, up to that time we had worked the windshield wiper (in front of the driver only) by hand, and even that had only been in existence for three or four years. Before that you either hung out of the window in bad weather, or opened the windshield, or stayed at home. George was so intrigued with this device that Jack lost no time in sending for one to put on the Houstons' car.

The Houstons finally found the place of their dreams. The house nestled among trees which cast the coolest shadows on the lovely lawn. They named it Glen Oaks, and it became the meeting place for all the family and friends and was the spot we always thought of as the scene of some of our happiest times, the gracious hospitality of the family being somehow reflected in the whole atmosphere both inside and out-of-doors.

We could have our first little furnished house only until August 15, but we had finally found a very nice one which we could rent for a year. Jack and I moved to our second home the second week of August. Jack's father had deposited $100 in a savings account for him when he was born and had added to it from time to time, but he never told him about it until we were married. Compound interest over a period of twenty-nine years had brought it up to over $2,000—a sum which staggered us. We dipped into this to get a little furniture. My parents had given me my bedroom furniture, and his parents had given him his, which included a chest of drawers which his grandfather Mead had made, and which we always loved and still have. We bought a comfortable sofa and two wicker chairs because the sofa had really been all the upholstered furniture we felt we could afford. And we bought a sideboard, six dining room chairs, and a dining table. Those were to me quite the most beautiful pieces of furniture in the world, and all but the wicker chairs are with us to this day. We had received some end tables as a wedding gift, and somebody gave us a lamp. I bought material and made curtains. There were no rugs, but the floors were nice, and we didn't mind hearing our own footsteps. The sun shone in the kitchen window, making the glasses and silver pieces sparkle as I washed and dried them. All was bright and charming inside, if somewhat bare; but outside—well, that was another story.

Every Eden has its serpent, and ours reared its ugly head in the form of hayfever, coupled with severe asthma, when ragweed season came. The embryonic lawn had looked nice enough when we signed the lease, but that was in July. Now, small plants *that were not grass* began to appear and grow fast. When I realized that these were ragweed, the thing above all others that meant misery for Jack, I set to work with a paring knife to uproot them. I worked most of the day and I put them in a carton as I pulled them up and covered it with newspaper and put it out behind the garage. I bathed and changed, putting the clothes I had worn in the basement and felt very happy at the thought that I had done something that would help Jack. But in my zeal I had forgotten about my hair. Much of the pollen had caught in it, so he was more miserable than ever when he got home. Luckily, dinner was a casserole, so I washed my hair while the casserole was baking, brushed it dry, and happiness reigned once more.

By August 20, however, the hayfever season was in full swing, and we went up to New Hampshire to visit his parents in the bungalow that had been the scene of his happiest boyhood days. We went by way of Williamstown, Massachusetts, so that he could show me that lovely country and take me over Peru Mountain and through parts of Vermont. We spent the night at Williamstown, and I woke when the sun was just rising, and the early morning mists were curling around the foot of "Greylock." I was in ecstasies and exclaimed, "We just must have a son, and he just must go to Williams!" Jack laughed at my enthusiasm and remarked drily that of course all a college needed to make it a great institution of learning was a beautiful sunrise over mountains! As it turned out, Williams later gave him an honorary degree, and two of our boys did go to Williams, and it is very dear to all our hearts. We had a marvelous two weeks with the family, and Jack taught me the names of many of the mountains. His love for them was contagious, and I found even that first summer that each one had a special quality and personality that made it a well-loved friend.

Jack's cousin, Heather James, Aunt Neva's daughter, was visiting her Aunt Jennie that summer. She and I formed a warm and lasting friendship, though we never managed to see each other after that summer until 1959. She was a beautiful girl, with dark curly hair like Jack's—it ran in the family as did the heavily lashed eyes, though hers were blue and his were brown—and a tiny dainty figure like Mrs. Mead's. Her mother's death, and all the sadnesses that the war had brought, had hurt her cruelly, but she met all her troubles with a gay and undaunted spirit.

That summer we also met Sidney Lovett and his fiancee, Esther Parker, who have been very close and special friends ever since. At that time he was the well-loved young minister of the Mt. Vernon Street Congregational Church in Boston. A few years later, he was to become the eminent and adored chaplain at Yale, where he remained until his retirement in June of 1958.

The ragweed was rampant that summer on all the roadsides, so we did not do any climbing, but Jack did take me on our long-anticipated camping trip. Dr. Mead and Bill Jealous decided they would come too, and we set off with all the paraphernalia to go and camp at a certain waterfall in Sandwich Notch. Unfortunately, some careless campers had been there first, so the campsite was pretty well ruined. We tried several other places but found nothing near water. We finally settled at one beautiful spot, not too far from water, and cut quantities of small hemlock boughs for our beds, cooked our supper, and eventually settled down for the night. We didn't sleep too much, though. All through the night, every time a twig would snap, Dr. Mead would start up and shout at the bears he imagined were attacking him. The next morning storm clouds gathered, so it seemed wise to go back to the bungalow. But I had had the joy of camping out, if only for one night.

We returned to New Jersey after the first of September on a clear, cool, sparkling day which seemed to clear the air of pollen and sent Jack back to work renewed, refreshed, and ready to overcome any "bugs" which any engine might produce. It was a good thing he was refreshed, for there were plenty of "bugs" to lick. Several engines were in the works, including the first big radials. Air-cooled radial engines, as their name implies, were so designed that their cylinders "radiated" in a circle from the center. By this means, the flow of air could reach each cylinder. Development of air-cooled engines had been started in earnest in 1920 when the company won the design competition of the Army for a radial engine with a 250 horsepower rating. This was the R-1 and was the first large radial in this country to run satisfactorily and was followed by the development of the "P" series which were progressively 400 and 450 horsepower. Of these, more later.

One of the most interesting of the miscellaneous engines developed during this period was a large, six-cylinder dirigible engine built for the Navy and intended primarily for the Shenandoah. The cylinders in this engine were huge, 7 × 8 inches. Jack had his team test one cylinder all by itself before they built the whole engine. It was surprising to see that great big cylinder chugging away on the stand all alone. These engines were wonderful, going through their tests perfectly and delivering the required horsepower, and giving no trouble at all. However, because of the accident to the English dirigible, R-36, which was ascribed to too much power, the five experimental engines were never used.

This was a thrilling period in aviation. It had passed from the experimental period when men succeeded in flying in machines heavier than air through the grim period of military development, when safety, durability and dependability had to be subservient to speed, maneuverability and a certain amount of stunting. Now, though the Army and Navy were still the best customers for planes and engines, there was a chance for the engineers to pause and consider what was good and what was not. They could take time to refine the designs: evaluate, test and experiment with the various materials.

Those with vision—and my husband was one of them—knew that commercial aviation could be one of the great industries of America if good, dependable, safe engines could be produced and mounted in steady and reasonably comfortable planes. Just as in boyhood, he had tried to assure the efficient and quiet shifting of gears by reducing the possibility of clashing them, so in this wider, more serious field, he tried to reduce the opportunities for failure by straight-forward, clean design. In a paper which he delivered at a meeting of the S.A.E. (Society of Automotive Engineers) in November 1925, there is this paragraph which is apropos just here, for it expresses his code.

> Dependability is the most important of all the requirements, for the whole success of flying depends on it. Any improvement is valueless if it detracts from this prime requisite. Unfortunately, it is often overlooked in an endeavor to catch up with the "weight per horsepower" bogey. Dependability involves experience in design, intelligent engine rating, conscientious manufacturing, and proper service care.

In the annual meeting paper of the S.A.E., March 1924, there appeared the following paragraph:

> Some of the parts which had caused the most trouble during World War I were exhaust valves, connecting-rod big-end bearings, and spark plugs. In cylinder construction three difficulties presented themselves—(a) the valves warped and burned; (b) the valve seats did not remain true; (c) in long runs, the valves hammered into the seats, so that the tappet clearance was lost, and the valves were held open. The steel cylinders would allow approximately only 110 pounds M.E.P. (mean effective pressure) without serious detonation when operating on aviation gasoline. It was, therefore, obvious that a different valve as well as seat material had to be obtained, and a more efficiently cooled combustion chamber had to be provided.

Jack and his assistants set about overcoming these troubles. The evolution of the cylinders in the "E" engines was epochmaking, for materials as well as design underwent great changes. In the E-2, which was the first post-war engine—an eight-cylinder, Vee-type, 90-degree, water-cooled engine—the cylinder construction consisted of flanged, closed-in, steel sleeves, threaded into an aluminum block. It could not be operated at full throttle for more than twenty or thirty hours before the valves had to be ground. The threaded sleeves of the cylinders were a source of trouble both in machining and assembling. The least inaccuracy in machining, or slip in assembling, would cause cross-threading, and so spoil them.

On the E-3 engine the sleeves of the cylinders were plain instead of threaded and were shrunk into position at assembly and were held in position on the block by two studs per cylinder that passed through the block. The plain sleeves, however, were not so good as the threaded sleeves because there was less surface for heat dissipation. More thought was needed, and was given to this problem.

The E-4 cylinder design which finally evolved provided an aluminum combustion chamber. The cylinder sleeves were open-ended and threaded on for only a short portion at the top. The new cylinders cooled more efficiently as shown by the fact that it was possible to develop 130 pounds M.E.P. (mean effective pressure) without serious detonation. In addition, the improved cylinders reduced the weight of the engine plus water by five percent.

Valve material and design were the next consideration. The engineers substituted a mushroom-shaped valve of silichrome, instead of chromium steel which had been used previously. This helped but did not solve the problem. Then Jack designed a tulip-shaped valve to replace the mushroom type. These were a real innovation, and Jack was thrilled with their performance. After a 310-hour test with the tulip-shaped valves made of silichrome, there was no measurable difference in tappet clearance, and the power developed was slightly greater than at the start of the test.

Connecting rods were the engineers' next concern. The connecting rod design originally consisted of a steel forked rod, bearing on the babbitt-coated bronze shell of the blade rod. This in turn was babbitt-lined and bore on the crankpin. The principal difficulty with this construction was caused by the flexing of the bronze shell which, in turn, disintegrated the babbitt lining. Jack and his assistants experimented with many combinations of materials and finally decided that the babbitt used with bronze was the cause of the trouble. The most satisfactory material proved to be a copper-lead-tin alloy which would operate for short periods without oil. This alloy was, therefore, chosen for the final bearings. These bearings ran for 572 hours without adjustment, and no appreciable wear could be measured at the end of this time.

Further development of the 90-degree Vee, eight-cylinder, water-cooled engine resulted in a study of the 90-degree crankshaft, which was first used in a Wright engine. This solved the grave problem of vibration which had been a serious cause of "fatigue" failures of parts. This was, according to Leonard Hobbs, who is probably America's greatest living aeronautical engineer, one of the strokes of sheer brilliance which Jack and his associates achieved at that time. These 90-degree shafts later became standard equipment for automobiles which were powered by this type of engine. In this period, three years after the close of World War I, the E-4 engine set a new standard for endurance and reliability. It ran for over 300 hours at rated power without overhaul.[1]

This test was conducted by the Bureau of Aeronautics under the United States Navy. The E-4 developed 122 pounds M.E.P. on a dynamometer at 1800 r.p.m. During this test, there were only external repairs and adjustments, none of which would have caused a plane to come down in ordinary flight. Practically everything about the engine, except the cylinders, had run a total of 572 hours at full power with no attention of any kind. The cylinders had run for 310 hours. In other words, the cylinders had been operated long enough to have carried an airplane 31,000 miles at 100 miles per hour, and the other parts had been in operation long enough to have carried a plane 57,200 miles at the same speed, without any attention. In this day of jets and rockets breaking the sound barrier, the performance of the E-4 may seem almost negligible, but it was truly remarkable for that period forty-nine years ago. This little engine, with its 200 horsepower rating, with a displacement of only 718 cubic inches, was the real forerunner of commercial aviation, for it proved that flying could be a steady, dependable means of transportation and was not just a military necessity or a hobby for unusually daring individuals. It was really a link between military and commercial aviation, and that is why I have gone into such detail about its evolution. It came into prominence later as The Gold Cup Engine.

As has been said, the development of radial engines began in earnest early in 1920 with the R-1, followed by the "P" series. Air-cooled engines are as logical for airplanes as water-cooled engines are for marine purposes, for several reasons.[2] The first and most important is the weight saving. The air-cooled engines save directly the weight of the radiator, piping, water, pumps, shutters, and radiator supports. Besides this, there is saved in the plane structure itself the weight necessary to carry this water radiation equipment. This is very important, as it saves 50% of the total saving. I say "is" rather than "was" for it is as true in 1970 as it was in the 1920's. At that time it increased the speed 15% and the cruising radius 51%.

Other vital factors were:

1. Freedom from radiation troubles, which at that time caused many forced landings.
2. Better than water-cooled for flying in extremely hot or cold weather. Tests under actual service conditions proved this to be true.
3. Decreased cost and weight of spare parts.
4. Good cooling at high altitudes.
5. Decreased first cost.
6. Decreased upkeep and handling expenses.

Next, why are air-cooled aviation engines generally radial in form? One reason is that more uniform cooling can be secured for each cylinder than with any other type. There is also greater accessibility of parts, making it possible to change a cylinder or piston without removing the engine from the plane, thus increasing flying time, and reducing labor costs. It also makes possible an aerodynamically superior and more symmetrical fuselage, and gives a high center of thrust that allows ample propeller diameter.

The R-1, mentioned earlier, the design for which won the Army competition for the Wright Company in 1920, was a nine-cylinder, fixed radial type with 5-5/8 × 6-1/2 inch cylinders, having a displacement of 1454 cubic inches and weighing 880 pounds. When built and developed, it delivered 350 horsepower at 1800 r.p.m. instead of the 250 horsepower which had been specified for the competition.

In radial engines, the crankshaft has one large throw on which the master rod turns. The master rod is a beautifully designed part, at one end of which is a large hole surrounded by a cluster of smaller holes. The large hole revolves on the crankpin of the large throw of the crankshaft. The rod extends into one of the nine pistons. The eight link rods are mounted in the small holes in the cluster and extend into the other eight pistons. To equalize the compression ratio of the various cylinders, it was necessary to vary the knuckle pin centers with respect to the crankpin or to use different heights of cylinder pads. The mechanical balance of a radial engine involved the use of counter weights. These were calculated to balance almost the entire weight of the master rod and the link rods which were attached to it. The counter weights were large, thick pieces of steel shaped like segments of a circle, and mounted opposite the throw of the crankshaft, and, of course, the accuracy of their design made the difference between the satisfactory and unsatisfactory running of the engine.

An air-cooled cylinder is simply a good water-cooled cylinder, with the water jacket replaced by suitable fins, properly disposed. A mistake that had been made in connection with air-cooled cylinder design was lack of metal in the cylinder head. It was just as essential to have ample metal here as in the piston head. One factor that had most effectually retarded the development of air-cooled engines was the effort to reduce the weight. This resulted in insufficient metal for proper heat distribution and dissipation. It was also true that many designs were lightened to a point at which fatigue failures in highly stressed parts occurred long before the engine as a whole had outlived its usefulness. The ratio of weight per horsepower of an air-cooled engine should not be compared with that of a water-cooled engine, but should be compared with the weight of the water-cooled engine plus its cooling system.

In 1921 Commander B. G. (Bruce) Leighton, then in charge of engine development for the Navy in the Bureau of Aeronautics, gave the Lawrence Company a contract for a small, nine-cylinder radial engine. He felt that it was of vital importance to develop radials in different sizes as well as the water-cooled power plants. This was to be a 200-horsepower fixed radial and was known as the J-1.

B. G., as Jack called him, came to our house for dinner one night during the late fall of that year. I had pictured a "Commander" as being someone very high and mighty, and was in some trepidation lest our simple hospitality might fall short in some way. What was my delight and relief to find in him a young man as quiet and unassuming as my husband, and as full of charm, warmth and friendliness. He made our house seem like a palace and our simple dinner like a feast. With him, we didn't even ignore the dishes and pretend they weren't there, as we usually did with guests, and I remember how he helped us clear the table and watched Jack "wash" while I "dried." He was always one of our cherished friends.

Another eagerly welcomed guest that fall was Fred Rentschler. He really was our first dinner guest in the Glen Rock house. In those days I thought that no company meal could have less than four courses. I laugh when I think that it took me all day to prepare that dinner, which really wasn't very difficult or remarkable. Of course, the house had to be completely cleaned from attic to cellar and all the wedding silver polished. There was enough of that to make up for the lack of furniture. I was rewarded for my efforts, because Fred really enjoyed our home-cooked meal—he was living at a club then, preceding his own marriage—and his steps reverberated on the rugless floors as he investigated every nook and cranny. It was a red-letter evening in every way. Jack's radiant happiness at having him in his home, and having him so obviously enjoy being there, was something to remember.

My parents visited us for a couple of weeks before going to Florida. They brought my dog, Lvoff, with them, and their arrival was dramatic, to say the least. After greetings, Father went to get Lvoff from the baggage car. As they were walking sedately across the expanse of the Penn Station in New York, Lvoff suddenly caught sight of me, jerked the leash from Father's hand and dashed across the intervening space. The bystanders stepped back as they saw that white streak speeding across the floor. They were terrified and then amused to see him plant a paw on each of my shoulders and start licking my face and hair and neck, whining in ecstasy all the while at finding his long lost "missy."

He complicated our lives to some extent, as he was a Russian wolf hound and simply enormous. I learned about putting things up high from him. One wag of his long plumy tail, and anything in a radius of six feet seemed to be swept to the winds. He was probably the stupidest dog that ever lived, but he was lovable and adored us. One day Mother, Father and I planned to go into New York for the day. The laundress was supposed to come but phoned she couldn't. That meant Lvoff would be alone. The family wouldn't go without me; we couldn't leave him out of doors to get into all sorts of mischief, so we finally decided to leave him in the cellar. When we got home, not too long before Jack did, we found to our dismay that in his despair at being alone all that time he had tried to gnaw down the cellar door. As we were surveying the damage, Jack got home. He looked and was horrified. The family decided to absent themselves from the conference.

Jack examined the great gouges and, seeing the misery written in my face, told me he was sure he could mend it with plastic wood, stain and varnish so it would be as good as new. We had a lot of fun kidding the family over their strategic retirement. While they were there, my sister Mary gave us a rug for the living room which had previously been in the "Glen Oaks" house—they had their own rugs—and that inspired us to get a little one for the tiny front hall, and a slightly larger one for the dining room, so that we felt very complete.

In the early weeks of 1922, Henry Crane came out to have lunch with us and go over to the Paterson plant to see all Jack's treasures. Jack had been wanting him to come for a long time, but there always seemed to be something to interfere. However, Mr. Crane finally agreed, and the day was set. He was probably as terrified of me as I was of him, for he was a very shy bachelor. He was also uneasy about what he might be expected to eat, because he told Jack he never had anything but a sandwich for lunch. However, Jack could not bear to treat him to such uninspired fare, when for so long he had been hoping to have him in his home. We conferred long and thoughtfully about the menu and came up with something delicious, though I don't remember what. This time we did ignore the dishes, and to my horror I heard the spoons sort of clinking on the dessert plates as Lvoff did a little preliminary rinsing for me. I could see by Mr. Crane's expression that he also heard it and was remembering cartoons he had seen of dogs being a "help in the kitchen." I hastily excused myself and audibly washed the dishes while Jack and Mr. Crane continued their conversation. In spite of my chagrin, I couldn't be too severe with Lvoff. He looked so innocent and I had left an irresistible temptation in his way.

Toward the end of February Jack had a cold which he couldn't seem to throw off. We had made no contact with a doctor in New Jersey—we hadn't needed one. We wrote his Dad, and he suggested a week in the north woods to avoid a repetition of the previous year's experience. So we drove to Winchester—it took us nearly a whole day, the roads were so icy and full of frozen ruts. Then after spending the night with the family, we took the train to Mt. Whittier to stay with the Waldens of "Chinook Kennel" fame at Wonalancet, New Hampshire. I had been told that the snow was several feet deep on the level, but when we got started on the twelve-mile ride in a horse-drawn sled, the piles at the side didn't look so high. I then learned that they used a big roller about six feet in diameter to roll the snow down to a hard surface, so there were two or three feet of hard snow under us. Some people had a "snow mobile," which was a model "T" Ford with a shortened rear axle so that the wheels would fit in the sled tracks, and runners on the front. This was quite a contraption but never won universal popularity, as a few years later the state started plowing some of the main roads.

We had a glorious week at that beautiful intervale. We walked miles on snowshoes, though we didn't attempt any real mountains, as Jack was weak from his cold (though it disappeared almost immediately when we got into that clear cold wonderful air). Chinook was not only the lead dog of Mr. Walden's dog team, but a delightful pet as well, and when Chinook wasn't "working," he went everywhere with us. One day Mr. Walden took me for a ride on the dogsled. He mounted the rear runner behind the body of the sled where I was cosily wrapped in blankets, gave the command "Mush," cracked his whip, and away we flew. It seemed awful to let those six dogs pull us both, but they were used to it and loved it—and did I ever love it, too!

We had left Lvoff in a boarding kennel. He caught distemper, which proved fatal, and about three weeks later he died. He had caused us many complications and much embarrassment with our neighbors, digging up their lawns as he used the houses as centers around which to run figure eights, or licked the cream off the tops of their bottles of frozen milk when they didn't take them in promptly, but we both grieved at his death as sincerely as if he had been an admirable dog in behavior as well as in looks.

About this time we knew that the next Thanksgiving our first baby would be coming to rejoice our hearts.

Fred Rentschler had done a splendid job of managing Wright Aeronautical. Jack and his assistant, Andrew Willgoos, had, with their engineering team, built engines of superb quality which were far ahead of their time. Their production under Harold Pope, the factory manager, had been achieved with a minimum of waste. Sales equaled capacity production. All who participated in making this possible shared in the extra profits which resulted; therefore, we all had a fine bonus.

Jack had been concerned because the water at my parents'

house was pumped by a cantankerous gas engine that had to be cranked, and often kicked back, nearly breaking my father's arm on one occasion. So, an electric automatic pump for Father was the first item which the bonus made possible. Our car needed replacing, and we also bought a lot on which to build a house, for we could only have the one we were in until August, and we had not found anything for rent that we could move to. We asked Jack Ingles, an architect friend, to draw up some plans for us along lines we had thought out. We called it our "cloverleaf" house, with a central hall, living room on the right, kitchen on the left, and the dining room behind the front hall, with access both from living room and kitchen. There were to be three bedrooms and two baths upstairs. The garage, with another bedroom over it, was to connect at the side, in case we ever had a maid. Mr. Ingles drew up a charming set of plans for us, but alas, the building and loan company would not finance it unless the whole business, lot and all, was financed through them, so we had to give up that dream. Both families offered to help, but we knew it would cut into their savings more than was right at their respective ages, so we did not accept their offers. Jack's mother was mightily troubled for us, as she thought of us with our baby coming, and no home for him to come to. However, we eventually found a little house which we made into a home. We were so happy that its shortcomings did not trouble us greatly.

The T-2 engine was in the works at this time. It was a twelve-cylinder, 60-degree, Vee-type, water-cooled engine, originally designed for Navy bombing service and had a rating of 500 horsepower at 1800 r.p.m. The T-2 engines ultimately developed 600 horsepower at 2000 r.p.m. and were standard power plants for bombers for several years. While it was in the design and building stages, Jack and I used to have a lot of fun kidding each other about whose baby would get born first—his or mine. But under the fun and the kidding, there was a deeper impulse—the urge to put even greater care and thought into all his work, in order that his son might always be proud and happy about what his father had done. Jack could certainly feel a deep and abiding satisfaction in the design and later in the performance of this engine, for it embodied the best features in all that he had previously done.

Our first son, George Nathaniel Jackson, was born on Tuesday, November 28, around six in the morning. He was a fine little baby, with dark eyes which promised to be brown like his father's, a shock of dark hair, and a strong, well-muscled little body. He probably was no beauty at that point, as his journey into the world had not been easy, but we thought he was the most glorious child that had ever been born. Thanksgiving Day that year had for us both a deeper, richer significance than ever before, as we thought of this crowning blessing that had come into our lives, and of all the potential goodness and fineness and ability that was wrapped in that small bundle of love held close in our hearts. I wanted him to be named for his father, but Jack insisted on including the "Nathaniel" so that he would be named more decidedly for his grandfather and great-grandfather.

Chapter IV

The Wright Aeronautical Years from 1923–1925

The T-2 (Typhoon) engine was completed and tests were begun. Again Jack and I had fun—though sometimes it wasn't so funny—this time deciding which baby caused us to lose the most sleep. The test crew reported readings at stated intervals through the night, and sometimes it seemed that we would no sooner get settled after the ten o'clock feeding, than the phone would ring, and there would be a discussion about the engine's "temperature" or what-have-you. The standard Navy tests consisted of ten five-hour periods, nine of which were run with the first 4-1/2 hours at nine-tenths the rated power and speed, and the last half hour of each period at full throttle. The whole five hours of the tenth and last period were run with the throttles wide open, and at the rated power and speed.

On this engine, the test was completed in sixty hours elapsed time. There were only two stops—one at the end of twenty hours, to replace a defective oil line, and the other toward the end of the run to replace defective spark plugs.[1] Considering that this was a high compression engine with 6.5:1 ratio, running at 2000 r.p.m., this was a remarkable test, particularly when one considered that during the last five hours the engine developed 138-1/2 pounds M.E.P. These engines were flown principally in the C.S., the S.D.W. and the P.N.7 types of ship and were manufactured by the hundreds (this was a large number for those days). Two of these power plants, in a P.N.7 airplane, which was a heavy-duty scouting plane, accompanied the fleet to South America[2] and back in the winter of 1923 without overhaul, covering the entire distance under their own power, and being away from their home station for over four months.

Jackie throve mightily, and in the spring of 1923 I took him to Kentucky to show him off to all my family and friends there. By this time, he was a handsome baby with brilliant brown eyes, a fine head covered with golden hair, and a gay and engaging disposition. He was strong and plump and healthy, always ready to smile, provided his food was produced promptly. Jack Senior soon joined us there where two years before we had been married, and Father baptized our first son.

Early summer found Jack especially hard at work. The Lawrence Engine Company had recently become a part of the Wright Company. It was on a blistering evening, when Jack was leaving for Washington on the night train, that I first met Charles Lawrence, who had become vice president of Wright's when the two companies had merged.

It had been a hot steamy day, and I realized as I was preparing dinner that though my dress had been fresh around five, it was now wilted and rumpled. I couldn't bear for Jack to come home to such a hot and disheveled-looking wife, and even though I knew I'd soon be just as bedraggled again, I thought I'd at least try to look nice to welcome him home. I gave Jackie another bath, and fed him, and put him down to sleep out in his carriage, clad in little besides his skin. Then, after doing the last especially heating things about dinner, I ran upstairs and got freshened up again. Ten minutes later, in walked not only my husband, but with him a complete stranger. Mr. Lawrence had missed his train and was stranded in Paterson. Jack couldn't phone me, because the switchboard was closed. Cold chills ran down my back in spite of the heat, as I thought how nearly I had let him down. By a merciful providence, his faith in me had been justified, and a prayer that this might always be true went up, along with my little prayer of thanks.

August came with its ragweed and goldenrod, and, therefore, hayfever. There was no sightseeing this third summer of our marriage en route to New Hampshire. We went as directly as possible and had three grand weeks there. There was no plumbing in the bungalow, and it was a dry summer, so we had to be sparing with the water from the spring. "Grammy," as we now called Jack's mother, thought it bad for me to stand in the lake and wash Jackie's clothes, so we devised a complicated system so as to use every drop of water to the fullest. We would boil the bottles in a large kettle at breakfast time. Then I would pour that water, when it had cooled, into the little tub to bathe Jackie in, and subsequently to wash his clothes. Meantime, the formula was pasteurizing in some more water, and when this was done, I used the pasteurizing water for the first rinse, and then took the clothes to the lake for the second rinse. How does that sound in this day of automatic washers and dryers!

Arthur Jealous was at the bungalow briefly, and he and Jack went off for an overnight climb up Passaconaway and over the Beeline Trail to Whiteface. They came back all enthused and insisted I must climb a mountain too. Grammy suggested Chocorua as being not too hard or long, but very sporting and rewarding, because it was like a miniature Matterhorn. She would be happy to take care of Jackie for the day; and so we set off on a radiant "mountain" day when the sky was clear and blue, and only toward midday did beautiful white puffy clouds come in to lay their lovely shadows on the shoulders of the mountains. It was the first real mountain I had ever climbed, and as we reached each lookout point on the Liberty Trail, and the view widened, my feeling of ecstasy increased. It was a happy day for Jack, too, because he knew that my love for the country—which was the very breath of life to him—was real and not synthetic. We drank in enough beauty that day to last us through many cold, foggy, miserable spells of weather. I was feeling pretty smug and pleased with myself, as we gained the summit after the last scramble on all fours, but was promptly whittled down to size when I saw on the summit a man on crutches and a little boy of six who had come up from the other side, which was even steeper.

All too swiftly, the vacation weeks sped by, and before we knew it, Jack was once more hard at work in New Jersey. Engineering, like woman's work, is never done. When the R-1[3] had completed its tests satisfactorily for the 350 horsepower rating, the next step was, of course, to see how much Jack and his associates could improve on this first large radial engine. Work, therefore, began on the P-1. The Navy required that this engine should be capable of replacing the Liberty, and that it should have a maximum diameter of 45 inches. In order to meet this requirement, it was necessary to make great sacrifices in the design of the cylinders. Accordingly, the cylinders were drawn in toward the crankshaft by scalloping the barrels and the pistons as well. The ports and valve guides were necessarily cramped. After several months' endeavoring to make the P-1 function properly, the Navy agreed that the engineers could increase the diameter three or four inches, so as to eliminate the cut-outs on the cylinders, provide for somewhat longer cylinders, and obtain proper cylinder ports. The operation of this modified engine showed that these changes were justified. This engine was later superseded by the P-2 which delivered 450 horsepower.

Here it might be well to speak of one method of developing a design for a new engine, provided it included a new type of cylinder construction. Jack evolved this while with the Wright Company and used it on the dirigible engine. This method saved a great deal of time and money. A single cylinder would be constructed and tested thoroughly, using the proposed piston as well as the entire cylinder and valve operating mechanism. From this test it was usually possible to decide on the value of these items of design, although, of course, all parts connected with the crankcase assembly had to be tested in a complete engine.

The T-2 had also been going through a period of evolution. It had been designed primarily for reliability and long life, but every effort was made to make it compact as well. The result was an engine approximately five inches shorter than the Liberty. Block cylinders with three cylinders in a block were used, each bank of two blocks being tied together with a cam box that was carried across the top of both. The crankshaft with three-inch diameter journals was supported in the upper half of the crankcase, and cast aluminum bearing caps of generous proportion were used for the central forward main bearings. Duration running showed that this cast material, although heat treated, failed from fatigue. Therefore, these castings were replaced with forged aluminum, and that overcame the trouble.

In a like manner, forged aluminum rocker arms were used to reduce weight. Since they were subject to severe reversals of stress, they also proved to be unreliable. To make them sufficiently strong, it appeared that they had to be approximately as heavy as the steel forgings they were to supersede. The original T-2 engine had been intended to develop 500 horsepower at 1800 r.p.m. It was soon obvious that there was a demand for a more powerful engine. Consequently, the power was raised to 650 horsepower at 2000 r.p.m. for certain special work. In 1924 this engine developed 750 horsepower, and the plane attained a speed of 240 miles an hour.

Based on the results of these tests, Jack and his crew developed a new model with modifications designed to overcome certain defects which they felt would be sure to cause trouble in longtime operation of the original model at higher power and speed. The crankshaft main bearings were increased from 3 to 3-1/4 inches in diameter. To lighten the engine, the shaft was shortened approximately one inch in the center main bearing, and the connecting rods were also shortened. This drew the cylinders in toward the crankshaft, making the crankcase shallower from the center of the shaft to the cylinder pads. Bearing surfaces were increased at some points, and certain parts were made stronger to guard against fatigue failures. This engine was used at speeds greater than 2200 r.p.m. developing 750 horsepower with a mean effective pressure of 140 pounds. Its running was exceptionally smooth, and none of the troubles previously ascribed to lack of rigidity developed. Despite the increased size of several of its parts, the engine which evolved—the T-3—weighed approximately 20% less per guaranteed horsepower than the original engine.

When the first experimental engine in any series was assembled, it was usually given a 50-hour test, followed by a 300-hour duration run, after which tests were conducted at higher compression and speeds. Jack and his associates thought that all engines should be designed to stand 10% to 15% overload.

The tests on the T-3 are noteworthy. The Wright model T-3 high compression engine completed the standard Navy 50-hour test, developing the highest M.E.P. that had ever been recorded on such a run. Moreover, this was the lightest big engine for the power developed in the world, weighing 1.7 pounds per developed horsepower on test. Not only did this engine finish the run, developing 680 horsepower at 2000 r.p.m. for the last five hours, but it showed remarkably low fuel and oil consumption, the fuel consumption on the nine-tenths run being .47 pounds per horsepower hour, and the average oil consumption for the entire run being .0065 pounds per horsepower hour.

The engine was taken from a *production* run of T-3 engines going through the plant for the Navy, and after its regular test runs covering a period of sixteen hours, power curve runs were made to determine the characteristics of the engine. It was then put on a 50-hour test with a rated power of 675 horsepower at 2000 r.p.m.

	Results of 50-Hour Test Condensed Corrected H.P. 2000 R.P.M.	Fuel Consumption Pound per H.P. Hour
9/10 power running	602	.470
Rated power running	670	.528
Last 5 hours running	680	.548

M.E.P. last 5 hours	138-1/2 lbs.
Oil consumption 50 hours	.0065 lbs. H.P. hour
Weight of engine dry	1155 lbs.
Weight of engine per H.P.	1.70 lbs.

(Disassembly inspection showed all major parts to be in excellent condition.)

Mr. Lawrence's J-1 engine was ready to put into service in 1923. It had given a good deal of trouble and was never really satisfactory or reliable until the engineers at Wright's carefully and thoroughly redesigned it. The J-1 was superseded by the J-3, predecessor of the "Whirlwind" of Lindbergh fame, and the J-4 and J-4A. These were used in large quantities by commercial operators, as well as in training planes.

It is interesting to note that the E-4 water-cooled and J-4 air-cooled, both rated at 200 horsepower, were flown in practically identical Navy planes. The plane with the air-cooled engine went fifteen miles an hour faster than the one powered by the water-cooled motor. The facts were stated fairly and accurately, as Jack compared the two engines in a paper, "Aspects of Aircraft Engine Development,"[4] but the E-4 was very close to his heart, and he could not resist reminding those who heard or read the paper that the E-4 had made aviation history, having made a duration record of 325 hours at full throttle, which to date had not been equaled.

Though air-cooled engines in the 200-horsepower class were beginning to supersede the water-cooled ones, the E-4 was not ready to be retired by any means. It still had ahead of it one of its greatest moments. Adapted for marine purposes as the E-4M, it was in 1924 to become still more famous and cover itself with glory as the Gold Cup Engine.[5]

Its general design was much the same as the aviation E-4 engine, with the two cylinder blocks of four cylinders each, Vee-type, 90-degree construction. This construction provided the maximum rigidity, which was of course most desirable for high speeds. Each cylinder block in the marine engine was made of aluminum, with steel liners on which the pistons traveled. The cooling water was carried entirely in aluminum jackets so that it did not come in contact with the steel sleeves (cylinders) at any point. It had been demonstrated by service use on salt water that this type of cylinder construction was absolutely satisfactory. There were two large valves per cylinder seating in aluminum bronze rings which were "shrunk" into the aluminum combustion chambers. The tulip-shaped silichrome steel valves used prevented warping and burning. Pressure oiling, cooling, carburetion, ignition and starting, clutch and gear, and accessibility—all these factors had been given the utmost care and consideration.

Two of these engines were mounted in two boats designed by George F. Crouch. These were both built by The Henry B. Nevins Corporation of City Island. The "Baby Bootlegger" was owned by a Caleb S. Bragg of New York. "Miss Columbia" was owned by a syndicate of members of the Columbia Yacht Club of New York. The two boats formed a team to represent the Columbia Yacht Club at Detroit. The boats, of approximately the same length, were of different designs, but both were superb examples of their designer's and builder's skill. In each the power plant was installed amidships with direct drive to the propeller. The installation in both boats could, therefore, be practically identical and was done according to the Wright Company's recommendations.

Jack's experience those two summers in Michigan during his college years, building and racing hydroplanes, proved their worth now, for he had actual experience—not just theoretical knowledge—to guide him as to the most effective installations. All the controls were brought back to the pilot's seat so that one man had complete control of the engine, which could be started, reversed, sent forward, or stopped, all from this point without raising the hatches. A ride in one of these boats left one with a distinct impression of tremendous speed, coupled with absolute smoothness. The ease with which these boats were maneuvered was another subject of commendation. Heretofore, high speed had been considered synonymous with poor maneuverability and roughness. The story of the Gold Cup race in Detroit in 1924 is well known. The two boats received first and second prize and brought the Gold Cup back to the East for the first time in twenty years. The "Miss Columbia" made the fastest time ever made up to that time—46.8 miles per hour. No power plant troubles developed in the three "heats," in fact, in two days of racing. The boats were driven for 240 miles at speeds of 45 to 50 miles per hour, with no power plant troubles whatever. They continued to give a good account of themselves throughout the racing season.

The adaptation of the E-4 as the E-4M for racing boats suggested an even more ambitious use of an aviation engine as a marine motor. Richard F. Hoyt, chairman of the board of the Wright Aeronautical Corporation, desired a seaworthy, but extremely fast runabout for trips to and about New York in Long Island Sound. After the highly satisfactory performance of the T-3, he decided to use one of these engines, adapted for marine purposes, in a boat designed by George Crouch and built at City Island in the Nevins Boat Yard.

The "Teaser" was a beautiful boat, 39 feet 10 inches long, with a 7 foot 1-1/2 inch beam.* Her hull was of the most beautifully grained and matched mahogany, and her lines were of such

*The Motorboat Magazine said of "Teaser"—"Her power plant, one of the most beautifully made pieces of machinery ever carried in any motor boat, is a new 600 horsepower marine motor built by the Wright Aeronautical Corporation. This motor is installed under the hatches a little abaft amidship, with all controls and switches carried forward to the helmsman in the forward cockpit. So smoothly does the motor run, and so securely is it bedded that at all speeds it is completely free of any slightest vibration or tremor of the hull." May 1925.

beauty and symmetry that even a landlubber had to catch his breath. Everything about the "Teaser's" streamlined bow and gleaming sides spoke of swift, sure, near-flight, and she was indeed one of the fastest displacement boats afloat. Jack had permission to take me and Jackie on one of the test runs, when he was working on the installation of the motor. Never before or since have I experienced anything even remotely like it. There was absolutely no noise except the rush of air. On that clear, still summer day in 1924, the graceful prow cleaving the shining water and the wake fanning out astern made it a day to remember always with gratitude and joy.

The "Teaser" was as reliable and as comfortable as a motor car. She had all the features of the Gold Cup boats, that is, complete control from the pilot's seat, which was at that time a real triumph in a boat. The engine was as easily started as that of an automobile. As soon as the boat was under way, the operation of the engine was entirely automatic, there being no need for hand-oiling or other attention. Owing to the design and workmanship of the reverse gear, the boat could be easily handled in making a landing. This, of course, was an essential requirement for the service she was to render.

The installation of this particular engine in this particular boat was for Jack a real climax in joining together two of his great interests. He had always loved boats and had always loved engines, and to install the engine, which represented the finest in design and workmanship that he had at that time produced, in a boat of equally superb design and craftsmanship, was more of a joy than a job.

During the late fall of 1923 we had been passing a house on Elston Road, Upper Montclair, more and more frequently in our walks. It was a charming Dutch Colonial house of grey shingles on a hundred-foot lot, and we loved it. One day we succumbed to the invitation on the sign which invited us to go in and look at it. We came, we saw, and it conquered. It was admirably and ingeniously planned, embodying all that we would need for some time to come. The sign said "easy terms" and we thought we would at least find out what they were. We had sold the lot we had bought, which gave us something for a first payment, and had been saving steadily though slowly from Jack's salary. The lease on the house we were in would soon expire. This meant we had to find a place to live. So we inquired about the terms for the Dutch Colonial and found that we had enough for a first payment and could arrange for a first and second mortgage for the rest.

It was a happy day when we moved into that dream house! It was like having Christmas all over again. And how our parents did rejoice. I think that both sets had been convinced that we would some day land on the street with no place to go.

We soon had the house looking like a home, and it seemed that every joy that life could hold was ours—except, of course, that we hoped there would be a little sister for Jackie before too long, but right now we had to pay for the house, and Jackie did seem to keep me pretty well occupied. He was a delicious little boy, imitating everything we did, and carrying on long conversations which seemed to mean a lot to him but were completely unintelligible to us. One day he picked up his father's sunglasses and a letter and sat down in his little rocker to read the letter aloud. He used to know when dusk fell that it was time for his Daddy to come home, and he would go over to the front window to watch for the car, with a happy "Daddy, come, Daddy come." Once when Jack returned in the late afternoon from one of his trips to Washington or Dayton, Jackie, who was not yet walking, heard his key in the door. He looked up and, seeing Jack there, started calling him delightedly. Then he walked across the room, staggering and chuckling as his love for his father overcame his hesitation about stepping out on his own. What dearer welcome could anyone ever receive than that!

February passed into March, and then April, and we knew that the following Christmas should bring us the little sister that we needed to make our family perfect.

That spring of 1924 was a delight in many ways. It was thrilling to work in our yard—to make a little flower garden, plant some shrubs, and generally beautify it. With our other three houses, we had known we would soon be moving and, therefore, would not see the results of our labors. Each week that we lived in the Elston Road house we found new reasons to be glad we had bought it. It was easy to keep clean, and its many windows gave it a sort of shining expression.

New Hampshire that summer was even more fun than in previous years, because Jackie was old enough to love toddling into the lake and playing in the sand. He waded in after us the first day and was completely fearless, even though he lost his balance and fell down. We were right with him, so he was not frightened—just learned what not to do.

Thanksgiving Day came, and with it Jackie's second birthday. He was talking a lot now and was, of course, into everything. But he was learning more all the time. My mother was coming on to be with him while I was out of commission, but we thought we should have someone to do the housework so she wouldn't have the care of a lively little boy *and* the house. We finally engaged a dear old woman named Nellie. She was big (size 56) and fat and kind, and we all loved her. Jackie adored her. He called her Lollie, and so we did too. She used to go about her work singing a sort of chant that didn't seem to have any beginning or ending, but Mamma said it summed up all her rebellion against life. The main theme of it went something like this: "I got a mind to ramble, I got another mind to leave your hard luck town. I gonna leave here walkin' and talkin' to myself." She did not live at our house but came over from Newark each day. It was a hard life for her, as the street car service was poor between Newark and Montclair, but she didn't seem to mind and was always cheerful and did pretty well in spite of her size.

About the middle of December, it developed that Commander Wilson, who was head of the Bureau of Standards, and his wife would like to stop over on December 23 on their way to spend Christmas in New York. Jack wanted to have them for luncheon. I was a bit dismayed at the prospect, because that was the day our baby was due. But it was a wonderful opportunity to meet these two people who later were to mean much to us. The commander wanted to see all that was being done at the plant, and, of course, Jack wanted very much to show it to him. So we decided to invite them and hope, if they accepted, that the baby would not decide to be born that day. They came, and it was the beginning of a wonderful friendship.

Jackie was old enough to really enjoy Christmas that year, and so our enjoyment was multiplied. During Christmas week both my mother and Jack came down with wretched colds, so I got hold of a practical nurse to look after Jackie in case they were not well by the time the baby came. It was lucky she was there, because both were very sick.

New Year's Day was beautifully clear and not very cold. That should have warned us. The next morning we awoke to a real blizzard. The snow was already over a foot deep. Jack had some work that had to be done, and he got Mr. Bardes, his secretary, to come over to take some letters. The nurse decided she had to go send some money to her daughter, and Lollie hadn't managed to get there because the trolley couldn't get through the drifts.

While Jack was busy with Bardes, I realized that the moment we had been waiting for had come. I bathed Jackie, fed him, and put him down for his nap. Then I phoned for a taxi. None dared to come. Then I called Dr. Scudder and asked him if he could possibly bring a nurse and take care of me at home. He couldn't, because he didn't dare leave his patients at the hospital. Bardes finally left, and I brought Jack his lunch and told him the situation while he ate it. Somehow, sick as he was, he managed to shovel the car out and get me to the hospital. It was a frightful trip, because Jack had to stop from time to time to shovel us out of a drift. Mamma, also sick, managed to look after Jackie and to give him his supper. The nurse finally got back after everything was done.

Our beautiful daughter was born at a little after six that evening, just a couple of hours after we reached the hospital. It seemed too miraculous that we had made it and that she was safe and sound. She was a lovely baby with a fine head covered with just enough hair to show she had her father's hairline. Her eyes were dark like his. She had a cunning nose and a precious cupid's-bow mouth in her heart-shaped face. She was more slenderly built than Jackie but didn't look frail because her face was rounder. We named her Mary Randolph.

Soon after Mary and I returned home, my mother had to leave. We gradually worked out a sort of routine, and it was a happy little family that lived at 22 Elston Road. It was a very snowy year, but Mary slept in the carriage nearly every day. She didn't have a good appetite, so she was never a very robust little girl, and this concerned me deeply because I didn't feel that she had any reserve in case of a severe illness. Other than that, she seemed healthy enough, and no doctor would ever concern himself about it. "She'll eat when she gets hungry" was their summing up of the situation, and "them's fightin' words" to me to this day.

Early in the fall of 1924, Jack had had a wonderful idea

designed to bring the accomplishments of the Wright Company more forcibly before the public. The speed of Mr. Hoyt's boat, "Teaser," was greater than that of the Twentieth Century Limited—the crack train of that day. Jack's plan was to run "Teaser" up the Hudson River to Albany and back, exceeding the speed of the train. Mr. Hoyt was delighted with the idea, but unfortunately it was late in October before he was ready to relinquish "Teaser" to Jack for the necessary tuning up after the summer's use. As a result, the day set for the run was bitter cold. But Jack, Tom Carlisle, and a mechanic decided to go anyway. They made a fine run as far as Kingston. Then they found ice in the river. It would, of course, have been disastrous to proceed farther. They were disappointed but they determined to beat the Century the following spring as soon as the ice was out.

When spring came, there was a big story in the paper one morning about a plan of Gar Wood's to race the Twentieth Century Limited up the Hudson to Albany. Jack's attempt the previous fall had been well publicized, and it was clear now that Gar Wood was out to steal Jack's thunder. I was outraged, but Jack said not to worry. The ice was out, and he would do it first, with no fanfare or trumpets. So he took "Teaser" out of her winter storage and put her in condition for the run.

The day set for the big event dawned clear and warm, with almost no wind. As I went out to the car with Jack to say goodbye and wish him all the luck in the world, I looked down at my feet, and there was a cluster of four-leaf clovers. I picked them for him, and he pressed them in his wallet and said he knew now there would be nothing to worry about. Needless to say, that day was a long one for me. Besides the suspense, I had no idea when I would hear anything. Then suddenly the phone rang. It was Jack phoning me from Albany to tell me they had made it there in two hours and forty minutes—twenty minutes better than the train, though it was against the current.

Apparently news of the intended trip had leaked out; so the bridge at Albany was lined with people and reporters, and a special edition of the paper was published. Jack and the crew were treated like royalty, and they had a hard time breaking away to make the trip back. By now, the wind had come up—against them—and the tide also was coming in. But in spite of these obstacles and rough water, they made the trip back in three hours and five minutes. When they tied up at the New York Yacht Club, there was again a big gathering, with reporters and all manner of personages to welcome and acclaim the performance. All this took a good while, but finally everybody left, and Jack and the crew started up the motor again, preparatory to taking "Teaser" to her mooring. When he slipped into gear, *nothing happened!!* Examination showed the propeller was gone. In all that pounding in the rough water, the pin that held it had worked loose. While they went forward, the thrust of the prop kept it on the shaft, but when he put her into reverse for the landing, it fell off. We got cold chills for years, at the thought of the ignominy of that moment if he had attempted to start her up while the people were all there. His natural courtesy, which forbade his leaving, tired as he was, until they had all left, had saved him. *He* maintained it was the four-leaf clovers.

Chapter V

Hartford—1925
A Company and an Engine Are Born

By the beginning of 1924, the Wright Company had become the outstanding producer of aeronautical engines in America. Curtiss was a worthy competitor, and Packard was emerging—probably because of the part it had played in the development of the Liberty motor. But it was the Wright Company which, because of good management, devoted and well-trained personnel, and above all, Jack's creative engineering genius, stood at the top. Fred Rentschler used to quote from Kipling's "Mary Gloucester" concerning Jack: "They copied all they could copy, but they couldn't copy my (his) mind, and we left them cursing and swearing, a year and a half behind."

There had been many thrilling and rewarding experiences during the years that Jack was chief engineer at the Wright Company. Here he had really found himself as an aeronautical engineer. The time he had spent at McCook Field toward the

George Mead, 18 months old, with his mother Jennie LeMann Mead, 1893.

George Mead, aged 9 years, February 1901.

George N. P. Mead, father of George J. Mead.

The Transmission

It is a perfect mechanical transmision. Of the selective type, three foward speeds and one reverse. The gears are composed of but seven pinions. That is counting the beval gear. As ~~they~~ are very compact, taking about half the space nessary for the ordinary, they are carried in the beval gear housing on the rear axil. And run in oil on four very liberal Hess Bright ball-bearings. The housing in which they are carried is of aluminum. No dog clutch is employed on the main saft. No pinions are in mesh when not in the act of transmiting power. In any speed the drive is direct. Reverse included. When a chang of gears is made nessary one pinion is all that is ~~need~~ moved. The number of pinions in an ordinary transmition of three speeds foward and one reverse is from ten to twelve against the sevan of this one. Being small and compact it weighs very little ~~compared in~~ comparison. And as it is small the the cost is greatly redused. The gears can be shifted quickly and without noise or labor. Combined with the quadrant is a small piece of mechanism by which it is imposible to make the gear shifts whith-out first releasing the clutch. The change speed lever is absolutly locked in position when the clutch is in. The release of the clutch causes the instant release of the lever.

George J. Mead
Feb. 1907

A description of the transmission for the Mead Touring Car.

A drawing of a White Steamer done around 1905.

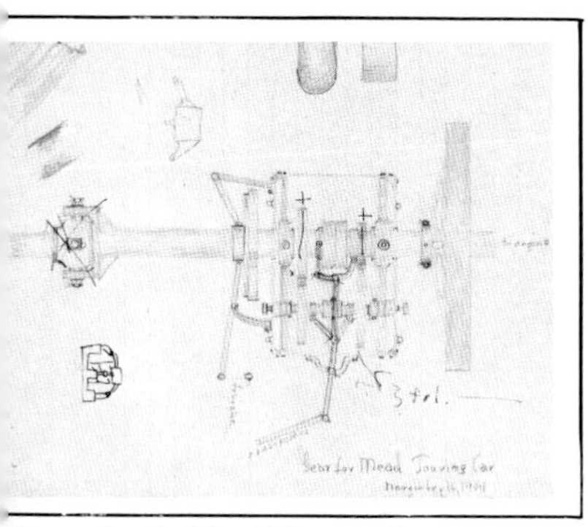

Gears for the Mead Touring Car, 1904.

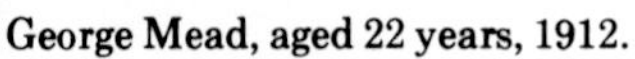

George Mead, aged 22 years, 1912.

George Mead, lumberman, 1914.

A snowmobile made by George Mead in 1920.

Aboard TEASER after her first attempt at a record run up the Hudson in November 1924.

MISS COLUMBIA and BABY BOOTLEGGER, 1924.

WOOD CHALLENGES BOAT THAT BEAT TRAIN

Gar Wood, world's champion speed boat racer (left), has wagered $25,000 that his fliers can beat the "Teaser" which G. H. Mead (right) piloted between New York and Albany when she beat the 20th Century Limited.

Vol. 12, No. 62 | Published Mondays, Wednesdays and Fridays, by Elliott Service Co., Inc., 244-250 West 49th Street, New York. Subscription, $20.80 annually. Entered as second-class matter, December 30th, 1914, at the Post Office at New York, N. Y., under the Act of March 3rd, 1879. | May 25, 1925

The Associated News Release of the Gar Wood challenge to TEASER. The release gave Mead the wrong middle initial.

20TH CENTURY LTD. BEATEN

Motor Boat Races Crack Train—WINS

On Wednesday morning, May 20th, the "TEASER" a 40-footer left New York on the Hudson for Albany at 7:55 A.M., and racing against the time of the crack 20th Century Limited, arrived at Albany at 10:35 A.M., a distance of 150 miles in 2 hours and 40 minutes—an average of over 50 miles per hour.

The return trip was almost immediately started at 1:33 P.M., at the Albany Yacht Club, and the Columbia Yacht Club at New York, reached at 4:40 P.M. Approximately 300 miles had been covered in five and three-quarter hours and the record of the 20th Century beaten by almost 25 minutes.

The "TEASER" was designed by Geo. F. Crouch and built by Henry Nevins, Inc., Mr. R. F. Hoyt is owner. Strangely enough, Mr. Hoyt did not build the "TEASER" for racing. It was built for commuting purposes and for week-end trips to his coun home. It is equipped with a 500 h.p. Wright Typhoon motor.

According to Mr. Geo. J. Mead, Chief Engineer of the Wright Aeronautical Corporatic this has shown the possibilities of the modern high-speed, light-weight marine mot and has set a mark worthy of anyone's effort to better.

It was the first boat to make the round trip to Albany and return in one day.

Occupants of the boat during the record-breaking, history-making trip were—Geo. Mead, Chief Engineer of the Wright Aeronautical Corp., Pilot, Captain Christians Theodore Carlisle and a representative of the American Power Boat Association, Official Timer.

STROMBERG CARBURETOR EQUIPMENT
GREATLY AIDED IN THIS HISTORY MAKING EVENT

THERE IS A SPECIAL

Stromberg Carburetor
For YOUR Car, Boat or Airplane

Form A-299 5M 7-25

A Stromberg Carburetor advertisement from the summer of 1925 following the TEASER'S run up the Hudson to Albany.

The frame garage in Montclair, New Jersey, where George Mead and Andy Willgoos began designing the Wasp engine.

ıdy Willgoos at work on one of the two drafting
ɔles in the garage.

George J. Mead in 1925 when the Wasp engine was designed.

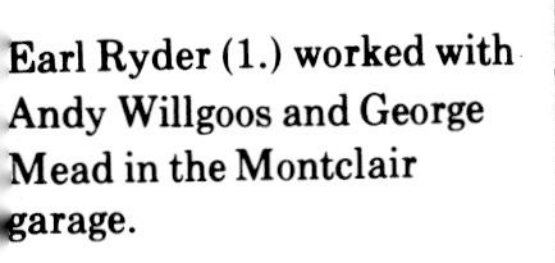

Earl Ryder (1.) worked with Andy Willgoos and George Mead in the Montclair garage.

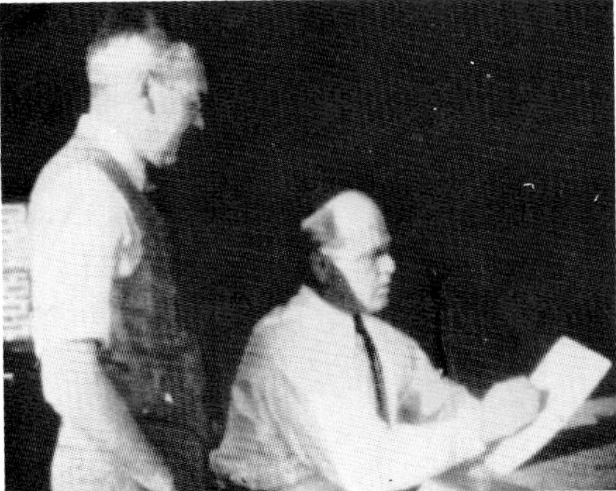

The first Wasp roars to life on the test stand.

Engine #1.

Early Hornet and Wasp engines at the Hartford plant.

The Wright Apache in which the Wasp engine was installed for its first flight.

Pratt and Whitney Aircraft in 1925. l. to r. rear: C. W. Deeds, G. J. Mead, F. B. Rentschler, H. Gunberg, J. J. Borrup, D. Robinson, H. Cudworth, F. Irmischer, W. P. Jones, A. M. Reardon, M. Wilkinson. l. to r. front: A. V. D. Willgoos, E. A. Ryder, L. Castonguay, R. M. Campbell, D. Jack, W. J. Levack, C. Peterson, A. Hokanson, D. L. Brown, N. King, P. Treffert.

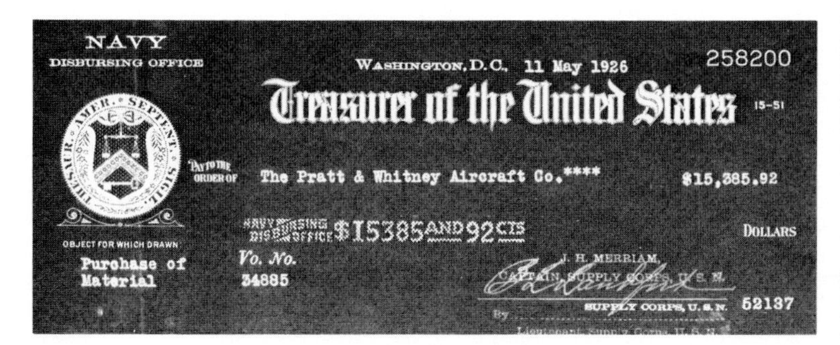

NAVY
DISBURSING OFFICE
WASHINGTON, D.C. 11 May 1926
258200
Treasurer of the United States
15-51
THESAUR. AMER. SEPTENT. SIGIL.
PAY TO THE ORDER OF The Pratt & Whitney Aircraft Co.****
$15,385.92
NAVY DISBURSING OFFICE $15385 AND 92 CTS
DOLLARS
OBJECT FOR WHICH DRAWN
Purchase of Material
Vo. No. 34885
J. H. MERRIAM, CAPTAIN, SUPPLY CORPS, U.S.N.
SUPPLY CORPS, U.S.N.
52137

The Navy's check for the first Wasp engine.

Pratt and Whitney Aircraft's first home on Capitol Ave. in Hartford. The first Wasp was built in the first building to the left of the flags on Capitol Ave..

Lt. C. C. Chompion made the first test flight in the Wasp-powered Apache.

The Curtis Hawk and the Boeing F2B, early military applications of the Wasp engine.

The Chance Vought O2U Corsairs were the first military aircraft designed to be powered by the Wasp.

The Wasp broke many records: here a record climb to 43,000 feet begins over Washington D.C

Boeing 40-B mail planes, Wasp powered, pioneered air mail routes over the Rockies.

end of World War I had yielded a rich harvest of varied and specific knowledge about many types of engines. He had studied the characteristics which made them either practicable or not for aeronautical purposes—the qualities in the different types of design which made for dependability and durability. These were naturally "musts" that had to be inherent in engines which were to be used in planes. All this knowledge and experience had been brought to bear on the problems presented by the need for more power, and especially more power per pound of weight, and, of course, greater speed.

But the winter of 1924–1925 brought changes. Some years previously Charles Lawrence, a relative of one of the board members, had experimented with radial engines. His nine-cylinder, 200-horsepower radial had received some notice from the Navy. But since Lawrence was not a trained engineer, the engine had some serious defects. An engine of this horsepower was needed to power the planes which were to be used on the carrier Langley—a converted Collier. Commander Jerome C. Hunsaker had been assigned the task of designing the new planes for the Langley, and amazingly their wing span had to be governed by the size of the Langley's elevator!

Charles Lawrence's plant was really an experimental shop rather than a factory. When the Navy evinced interest in his engine, he made overtures to the Wright Company concerning merger. Fred Rentschler had thought that it would be quicker and cheaper for Wright to design and develop an engine of its own than to undertake to redesign and rebuild the Lawrence engine. However, Admiral Moffett urged the Wright Company to agree to the merger and so insure for the Navy an adequate source of engineering and production. Moffett felt the merger was a necessity if the Lawrence engine was to be used.

Under the circumstances Fred felt he had no choice but to agree. After all the formalities were completed, the whole Lawrence operation was brought over to Wright's Paterson, New Jersey, plant. Jack, with his assistant, Andrew V. D. Willgoos, was assigned the task of "cleaning up" and redesigning the Lawrence engine. Jack was in an awkward position. As vice president of the company, Lawrence was theoretically his superior. Yet if Lawrence's engine was to be used, it was necessary for Jack to do some very basic redesigning. This he did, and the eventual outcome was a virtually new engine which was christened "Whirlwind."

However, things were not happy. Fred had been increasingly at loggerheads with the board. The members of it were undoubtedly able and experienced financiers, but they were interested primarily in the balance sheets. The products which those balance sheets represented were of minor importance to them. These men completely lacked the vision necessary for the task of getting this infant industry off the ground. When I think of the golden opportunity which was theirs, which they threw away—of their blindness in being unwilling to plow back into the company a percentage of earnings to be used in research—of their short-sightedness in allowing nepotism and politics to upset the excellent organization which had put the Wright Company aeronautically in first place in the country—I marvel that they got on as well as they did.

Fred resigned as president of Wright sometime late in 1924. He told Jack of his plans ahead of time, and Jack's reaction was to tender his resignation also. But George Houston urged him to stay on for the time being at least. However, Fred asked Jack if he would be interested in joining forces, if at some date in the not-too-distant future there should be an opportunity to team up again. Indeed he would! Fred went to Andy Willgoos, Don Brown and Jack Borrup and was rewarded with the same reactions—the same hopes for the future.

Fred had to undergo a mean operation that winter, which was theoretically the reason for his resignation, but of course he could have had a leave of absence. During his convalescence, conferences about the future between Fred and Jack became more frequent. Often Colonel Edward A. Deeds, a friend of long standing, would sit in on these conferences. As time went on, he took a more active part. The Colonel was chairman of the board of Niles Bement Pond Company in Hartford, Connecticut. The board members realized that the machine tool industry, though healthy and necessary, had reached its peak. The company's expansion and growth had fixed limits, and James K. Cullen, president of the company, was therefore interested in investing some of its surplus capital in a concern with a greater future potential. It was Colonel Deeds who laid the ground work and enlisted the interest of officers and board members of Niles

Bement Pond in financing the daring new venture that was to become the most spectacularly successful aeronautical company there has ever been.

Gradually plans for the new company began to crystallize. It developed that Cullen and the directors were very much interested in helping to found a company for the manufacture of aeronautical engines with Fred as its president. They would be prepared to provide the necessary capital for the initial costs of building three experimental engines and putting them in production, *provided* Jack would leave Wright and come in as vice president in charge of engineering. They were well aware that it was futile to endeavor to found a new company unless Jack would agree to join them. He had proved time after time that he surpassed all other aeronautical engineers in forward thinking, in meticulous evaluation of all ideas, and in overall ability. The success of any new company would depend on its being able to produce engines far superior to any previously built.

Pratt & Whitney Tool Works had a large factory on Capitol Avenue which was being used for tobacco storage, of all things. This factory could house the infant company for the time being. There would be an initial issue of $1,000,000 worth of preferred stock to build three experimental engines and put them through their tests—and, if all went well, a subsequent issue of $1,000,000 to get them into production. This stock, by the way, paid the Niles Bement Pond Company 7%.

This was, for us, the opportunity of a lifetime. It was also a tremendous chance to take. Jack would be trying to surpass his best work to date. We had two very little children, a partly paid-for home, and a *very* small savings account. To move would mean leaving comparative security, and launching out into the unknown. We talked it over thoughtfully—all the pros and cons. I don't think either of us ever had any real doubt as to what our decision would be. No one but a craven fool would pass up such a golden opportunity to undertake satisfying, rewarding work under a board of directors who were interested in seeing a good product manufactured, and in giving aviation the real shot in the arm it needed, and for which the time was right.

The Hartford Courant for July 24, 1925, carried the following headline: "New $2,000,000 aircraft firm to locate here. Pratt

& Whitney announces organization will make engines. The new company will occupy part of the space which was used during the late war for the manufacture of precision tools. The officers of the new concern are men who have had wide experience in aeronautical engine design."

The company was to be called the Pratt & Whitney Aircraft Corporation. Fred Rentschler was to be president, Jack the vice president in charge of engineering, and co-founder. Andrew Willgoos was to continue in his capacity as assistant to Jack and would have the title of chief engineer. Donald Brown was to be factory manager; Jack Borrup, the head of the experimental shop; Danny Jack, assistant factory superintendent; Earle Ryder, experimental engineer and design assistant to Andy Willgoos; Ed Godfrey, chief designer; Jerry Tallman, chief draftsman; Charlie Marks, chief of tool design; Bill Willgoos, head of assembly; O. C. Christiansen and Ben Gilpin, service department; Ted Carlisle and Dean Ballard, test engineers.

How all those grand people come up before my mind's eye! I wish I could portray the spirit which animated that band of men. There was loyalty, cooperation, mutual affection and respect, admiration for each other's skills—a team spirit which I have never seen equaled. Perhaps the best way to describe them is to say that they worked together as perfectly as the parts of the engine they were building. They were one and all faithful and devoted friends to be cherished always. No one had urged them to leave the Wright Company; but when those they loved and admired were going to start a new company, they with one accord wanted to come and help. There never was a finer group of people; and the wives were equally fine, joining eagerly in encouraging their husbands.

As soon as the decision to found the new company was reached, resignations were sent in to the Wright Company. The executives worked with the board of directors and lawyers, drawing up the papers for the new company. Jack and Andy Willgoos labored endlessly in Andy's garage to design what was to become the first Wasp engine.

We put our home on the market the end of May, and the first couple who looked at it fell in love with it, as we had, and bought it. Somehow their delight in it helped to ease the pang of giving it up. The problem of finding places in Hartford for all of us to live was a tough one. Prices of real estate were higher than in New Jersey. Being a New England city, the winters—theoretically at least—were colder and harder; and the houses were proportionately more expensive. The one house-hunting expedition I could arrange proved fruitless. And most of the other wives had the same discouraging experience. It fell to the lot of the husbands to seek out homes for us, as well as to get their work done and the company underway.

The first home of the Pratt & Whitney Aircraft Company deserves more than a passing glance. It was located in part of the old Pope-Hartford building on Capitol Avenue between Sigourney and Broad Streets. The building belonged to Pratt & Whitney Tool Works, which was one of Hartford's large and flourishing industries. Its buildings were the sound, well-built, dignified structures of an earlier day. The Pope-Hartford building was five stories high and covered the equivalent of a fair-sized city block.

The tobacco people were reluctant to give up their storage space, so Don Brown and his crew had difficulty in getting them to clear out the area of 3,000 square feet which was all the space the aircraft company needed in August 1925. In this area, only slightly larger than a tennis court, the men laid out their modest office requirements, the drafting room, and the experimental machine shop where the first engine would be built. Fred, Jack, and Don each had a small office with partitions made of bare tongue-and-groove boards painted gray. Andy Willgoos presided over the drafting room, which had to be somewhat larger than the offices. Borrup erected a small platform at one side of the experimental shop with his desk within reach of Don's office wall. A tiny window was cut in this wall, and as Jack released drawings to Don, he passed them to Borrup through that window.

As soon as the space was cleared and the partitions in place, Borrup had started tooling up the shop. Trailing a hand-cart behind him, he went through the well-equipped tool company, requisitioning the small tools he would need and ear-marking the machines he would soon require. He and Charlie Marks secured two small lathes, two big milling machines, a Lucas boring mill, an external grinder, an internal grinder, a vertical, a horizontal and a hand milling machine, a radial drill, and two small drills.

He also secured work benches, vises, and some lay-out plates.

We certainly didn't splurge in setting up that small factory. The offices were equipped as meagerly as the shop. To say that we were cramped for space is to put it mildly. As we went along the little corridor which led to our part of one floor of that mammoth building, we could not walk two abreast without brushing against the tobacco stored against and occasionally sticking through the wire partition. Everything was done as simply as possible, and the smell of tobacco persisted for a long time, transcending the odor of machinists' oil, cotton waste, and metal—in other words, the factory smell. No money was spent on lush office furniture. Every available dollar was dedicated to the dream of producing the best aeronautical engine in the world.

One night early in July Jack got home about 1:00 a.m. He bounced into the house full of enthusiasm. He had found a house that we could afford, and that was the right size and most attractive. It wasn't quite finished but would be by fall. I marveled that, after his grueling day, he could still be so buoyant, but it was because he had found a house for us that he knew I would love, and which we could make into a home. After all these forty-five years, I can still see the sparkle in his eyes—the light in his face as he told me about the house. This was wonderful news, for we were within days of having to vacate our Elston Road house. Arrangements were quickly made with Hartford Dispatch to move and store our furniture, and the children and I went to Holderness, New Hampshire, to spend the intervening time at the Mains' farmhouse, which Jack's parents had rented for us for the rest of the summer.

Jack lived at the Elm Tree Inn in Farmington part of that summer; and then finding he needed to be closer to the plant, he moved to the Hartford Club. He would take the night train to Ashland, the nearest railroad station to Holderness, on alternate Fridays, and we'd have Saturday and Sunday together. He maintained that the refreshment of being in the mountains more than compensated for the fatigue of the train journeys. We climbed Whiteface one beautiful Saturday, and it was a rapturous experience. I wanted to climb Sandwich Dome, but he didn't feel I was quite ready for it. We cherished every minute he could be there that summer; they were all too few, as there was, of course, no vacation for him.

Mr. Main's farmhouse was a delight—comfortable, airy, roomy and charming. The porch overlooked the lake, and we had our meals there, unless it was pouring or freezing cold. However, the water pump was a small fly in the ointment. It was a kerosene-fuel affair which lived in a little pump house about a hundred feet from the house. Mr. Main's chauffeur showed me how to start it. First, you took a long pin and cleaned all the holes in the jets. Then you turned on just enough kerosene. Too little wouldn't light—too much would blow up, or so he said. You nursed this flame tenderly for about fifteen minutes. Then you hopefully gave the big wheel a whirl. The "arm" would go up and down, and you'd watch, wondering if it was really being pushed by the hot air, or simply continuing on momentum from that push. Finally you would decide it really was started, go back to the house and start your work, only to look out of the window and see that the big "arm" was no longer moving. So you'd go through the process all over again. The whole business often took an hour. Then, one day when I was especially exasperated with the pump, and was thinking uncomplimentarily that it was a mighty inefficient contraption for an hydraulic engineer to select for his house, my eye fell on what appeared to be a hand pump. It looked easy to attach, and was; and in less than twenty minutes I could pump enough water to run the house for twenty-four hours. Never again did I have any dealings with that miserable hot air pump.

By August 1st, Jack, Fred, and their associates were ready to go full steam ahead in the part of the Capitol Avenue factory that they needed at that time. The office boasted two secretaries and an accountant. The total number of employees, was, by Christmas, thirty-three. We used to say that we started August 1st with about ten men and a few lead pencils, and by Christmas we had an engine on the dynamometer. And this was substantially true. As the work progressed through September and October, the lathes began to turn in earnest; the machinists to exert their skill; parts to take shape; shafts, crankcases, cylinders, fins, pistons, connecting rods, valves—all the minutiae of the engine to evolve from the drafting board stage to steel and aluminum parts. Colonel Deeds said that if one engine could be completely assembled and on the test stand by Christmas, he would give a turkey and all the "fixings" to every family in the company. This gave a sporting incentive to the already enthusiastic workers.

By October our house was at last sufficiently ready for us to move in. The days in New Hampshire had been wonderful, but it was getting pretty nippy for little children in a summer cottage; and anyway Jack needed us, and we needed him. So, we moved into the Hartford house on October 3 on top of painters and carpenters. Soon it was home. Never was there such a glorious autumn. For thirty-seven consecutive mornings I was able to give Mary her breakfast and put her out in her carriage in the sun, there to crow and kick and generally enjoy herself until I brought her in for her bath around 10:00. Then out once more for her morning nap. It was grand that the children could be out, for there were painters doing small finishing touches here and there for several weeks, and there would have been even more "finishing" touches on Jackie than there were, had he had to be in the house much during his waking hours.

As the weeks went by, Jack, Andy, and the others worked tirelessly on the design for parts, scrutinizing every rod, piston, valve, shaft, cylinder sleeve, fin—everything—with the utmost thoroughness. The beauty of those carefully machined parts thrills me to this day, for they were turned and burnished with all the loving care that a silversmith bestows on his choicest hollow ware. Now and then when I could get a baby sitter for a couple of hours, I used to love to go to the plant and actually see the parts being machined. The workmen knew I admired and appreciated their beautiful work, so they never minded my being there. There never was a more wonderful team of people working on a project; nor was there ever a group of workmen who took more pride in a job well done. Their ultimate product demonstrated this fact.

Conferences with the Army and Navy were held frequently, and Fred and Jack told them of some of their hopes and dreams. It became increasingly evident that there was a market, ready and waiting for the kind of engines they would manufacture. The moment in time, which had been slowly approaching, when flying would no longer be a stunt, but would be considered a practical, useful arm of the services, had arrived.

What were some of the attributes which made the Wasp so far

superior to previous engines? How were power and dependability *in*creased, and weight per horsepower *de*creased?

Some of the basic design changes include the following. One of the limitations inherent in radial engines had been the speed of the crankshaft. Most designs had provided for a solid crankshaft and a split master rod. This arrangement was all right if the speed was limited to 1800 r.p.m. (revolutions per minute). But higher speeds were needed in order to increase power without increasing weight, and higher speeds tended to make the master rod pull apart. This, in turn, damaged the bearing, thus causing disintegration of the whole engine. Jack and Andy, working in Andy's garage, decided to reverse this procedure. By splitting the crankshaft, it would be possible to use a solid rod. This provided greater strength for the master rod on which the link rods and all other parts depended. The stronger rod meant that it was permissible to plan on 1900 or more r.p.m. This one change gave increased potential power.

Jack and Andy then decided to change the crankcase from a casting to a forging, and also to split the crankcase. This meant greater ease of assembly and better accessibility of parts. Heretofore, the crankshaft and rods had been assembled through a large opening in front of the crankcase. This arrangement required a large bolted-on cover plate which supported the front bearing. With the split crankcase, the two halves could be slipped over the ends of the crankshaft after the master and link rod assembly was completed, and then bolted together between each two adjacent cylinders. The result was a light, strong construction. The load was divided uniformly between the front and rear main bearings, and this was equally important. The cylinder design employed an all-steel barrel with cooling fins machined from solid metal. Thus the solid master rod and split crankshaft provided higher power through greater rotating speeds and promised sturdiness and dependability in spite of lighter weight.

Earle Ryder, who had joined the group in July, worked with Andy to design a good arrangement of rocker boxes, valves, and push rods, in which the rocker boxes would be an integral part of the cylinder casting. This was a distinct innovation. Ryder also designed a telescoping cover for the push rods.

The handbook for the Wasp shows that Jack's tulip-shaped

valves, which had proved their superiority over the mushroom-type for exhaust valves in the E-4 tests several years before, were used in the Wasp. Jack also devised a rotary induction system which made it possible to use only one carburetor instead of three. An impeller provided forced oxygen feed for the engine. Jack was looking toward the eventual use of an incorporated impeller in order to achieve more than nominal supercharging. By means of the use of gears, the engine could ultimately be fully supercharged.

For better cooling Jack and Andy worked out a system for finning the cylinders that would result in thinner, more numerous fins. The tri-section feature of the engine which they developed, with accessories in the rear, made it possible to service the engine without dismantling it.

One can easily see even from these few simple examples that the basic design of the Wasp incorporated features so advanced that its immediate success was inevitable, and its almost legendary popularity among the pilots was understandable.

November slipped into December. Excitement mounted at the plant and in our homes. Time dragged—yet it flew. But finally, on December 22, the first engine was complete. Carefully it was placed on the test stand and cranked over a few times, just to show that the rods and pistons moved in their proper firing order, as the master rod turned on the single throw of the crankshaft.

A few years ago a plastic model of a Wasp motor was put on the market in kit form, and one of our engineer sons received one for Christmas. He worked for days assembling it, and what a thrill it was to see the different parts working together—something I had always wanted to see and understand better, and which the clear plastic made possible.

True to his promise, the Colonel provided Christmas baskets for all. Faye Rentschler and I had the pleasure of doing the shopping, fixing them up attractively, and passing them out to everyone at noon on Christmas Eve. That was one of the times of perfect happiness which come occasionally to many people and stay with them all their lives. This generous, hospitable idea of the Colonel's was just what was needed to give that first Christmas in Hartford the warm, personal touch that made it a supremely happy one. It also pointed up what was to be the attitude of the board toward those who worked in the company, whether management or labor. Each man's job had a sort of dignity to it, and however small it was, if done well, this fact was recognized.

Always before, it had been almost an axiom that an engine took eighteen months from drafting board to dynamometer; yet this beautiful engine with perfect symmetry and power written all over it had taken but six. The sense of accomplishment was so rewarding we could hardly come down to earth.

We went to our homes to celebrate Christmas with joy and gratitude and deep humility. We had been given a great opportunity to do creative work, and the work spoke for itself. If any of us had felt like strangers, we were strangers no longer. Hartford was our home and always would be. As I look back after forty-five years, I don't believe that any of the original thirty-three who shared the joy of producing the first Wasp engine ever left the company to go into any other.

Chapter VI

The Wasp Becomes a Fact and a Factor

Soon after we got home from the plant, having distributed the Colonel's gift baskets, Jack's parents arrived for Christmas. Now at last Grammy could feel her children were housed and happy. She came armed with home-made bread, a gorgeous plum pudding, and her famous oxtail soup which she made by the gallon and gave to various special friends. With our turkey, Christmas dinner would be tops, and very little trouble.

That night after the children were in bed, we all trimmed the tree together. It was a truly happy time, for Jack's parents as well as for us, for now they could feel we were fairly permanently settled. They were charmed with the house and with Hartford and, of course, thrilled and proud about Jack's accomplishment. True, we were only a few steps along the way to success, but in their minds we had arrived.

Both children were at ages when the joys of Christmas filled them with wonder and delight. Their reactions to the tree and their gifts were such as to fill parents and grandparents with enjoyment and happiness.

Tests and all the problems of production—should all go well—were still ahead of us; but the first big milestone had been passed, and so it was a marvelously happy Christmas.

Do joys *seem* more joyful in retrospect because of sorrow that follows hard on their heels, or are we given these poignant happinesses to help us bear the sorrows? I wonder.

The Rentschlers went to their former home in Hamilton, Ohio, for New Year's to show their beautiful little daughter Jean to both families and to see old friends. On the night of January 4, about two in the morning, the phone rang, and it was Helen Rentschler, Fred's sister, saying that little Jean had died. She had had a slight cold; had waked around midnight asking for a drink of water; and as they were giving it to her, she had suddenly had a slight convulsion and was gone. I shall never forget the pain, sorrow and overwhelming sympathy which flooded our hearts that night, and through the days, weeks and months that followed. No matter how deep and sincere your Christian faith is, no matter how sure you are that you will see your loved ones again after they have passed from this life, there is stark tragedy when death comes to a precious, dearly loved, little child. All through the rest of that night Jack and I whispered to each other, trying to comfort each other, and trying to think of ways we could help our dear friends through this heartbreaking loss.

The next day we had the task of going over to their home and telling their good "Haiah"—Jean's way of saying "Sarah"—about it, putting Jean's toys in her room, and leaving the door only partly open, taking down the tree, replacing faded flowers with fresh ones—trying to make the house look homelike, with the poignant reminders put where they would not be really visible, yet not shut away.

I had often heard of people staying in bed after a death and had thought they were pretty babyish, but that morning I understood. My knees trembled so that I could scarcely drive to the Rentschlers' house. Then Haiah's grief was such that I felt I must not leave her until the sharpest edge of her pain was eased a little. Faye and Fred would be coming home next day, and we racked our brains trying to work out some way to make that homecoming less shattering. Jack and I worked and wept over our letters to them, which we left near one of the vases of flowers; we asked them to let us know when they would like to see us. It was our first experience with a sorrow of this sort, and we felt woefully incompetent to deal with it, or help them. But the genuineness of our love and the depth of our sympathy must have meant something, for they wanted us right away, and again that evening, after we had gone back home and put our children to bed. We all seemed to become fully mature during those days. Never again would we feel really young.

The Rentschlers had told us that they were hoping for another little one in July, and so we tried to focus our thoughts and interest on this hope. I spent a part of nearly every afternoon with Faye, except when she and Fred were out of town, at first without Jackie and Mary, but later, when she asked for them, included them in our visits. She and Fred were both wonderfully brave, but sometimes the tragic truth would hit her again. Generally, though, no matter how her heart was aching, she was gallant and outwardly cheerful.

Life and work had to go on. And this, in a way, was a blessing. Fred, of course, had to be deeply absorbed in the progress of the infant company, and he threw himself whole-heartedly into the business end of it. That helped him, for he was an unusually tender and devoted father.

Tests of the engine were still ahead of us. Jack and Andy, Bill Willgoos, and others went over every beautifully machined part with a critical eye. No debutante, getting ready for her first ball, was ever more meticulously groomed, more carefully scrutinized for perfection. And, in a way, it was not only the Wasp engine that was preparing to make its debut, it was the Pratt & Whitney Aircraft Company. On these tests hung its whole future—and ours, too.

Tests of an aircraft engine were always an ordeal, but it was worse in Hartford. In Paterson we could get the fifty-hour tests over in less than three days. (You always had to tear the engine down after twenty-five hours, look at the parts to make sure there was not undue wear, and then resume.) But in Hartford, as we were fairly near residential areas, the roar would be disturbing at night, so we could run the test for only ten hours the first day, ten hours the second, then five the third, and tear down; then ten the fourth, ten the fifth, and five the sixth, and then tear down—so it meant a whole week of suspense. Even so, we received some unkind comments after the tests started, such as, "Oh yes, you are the people who have come to disturb the peace of Hartford," and other rather acid observations of like nature.

The Wasp had in an unbelievably few months come from ideas and drafting board to test stand. It had met the Navy's weight requirement of just under 650 pounds. As the formal Navy test would take a long time, Jack finally agreed to run an informal test at 380 horsepower. This rating, you will note, was well beyond the "2 pounds per horsepower" which had formerly been considered a sort of rule of thumb.

The Wasp met every demand so confidently and smoothly that Jack agreed to try for 400 horsepower. Again she was rigged for informal testing, and again she responded well. She delivered 410 horsepower in her stride. After further consideration, Jack agreed to a third informal test in which the goal would be 425 horsepower. She delivered the horsepower running strong and true.

In February 1926, there was a tremendous blizzard. It came completely unannounced, in the night, and by morning not a wheel was turning anywhere. There were some abortive attempts later in the day to clear the main arteries, but with snow nearly two feet deep on the level, and drifting, and no plowing having been done before the snow got so deep, the city's efforts were pretty ineffectual. Jack felt sure that Hartford would release itself from this snow-locked paralysis before evening, and he felt he must get to the plant and make sure everything was O.K. We both shoveled manfully to get the drive cleared. We finally did, but the road to the corner of Albany Avenue, about 500 feet or more away, was untouched, and even Albany Avenue was still hopelessly clogged. Not even the street car tracks were clear. There was no hope of going anywhere at all!

Wearily we went into the house, showered and changed, and had some hot tea. Jack was, of course, worried about the engine that was undergoing tests. Was anyone able to get to the plant? No one was in the office to answer the phone, for the same reason he wasn't there.

Next morning he woke with a hard cold and some fever. We had not needed a doctor, except a pediatrician, so we didn't know one; but someone had mentioned to me that Dr. Orin Witter was a kind and wonderful doctor. Rather diffidently I phoned his office to get suggestions about what I should do with the limited materials at hand. I never dreamed of his coming to see Jack. Albany Avenue was barely passable, and Westerly Terrace was still untouched. Dr. Witter certainly knew nothing about us, but his voice was deep and kind and reassuring. Instead of giving me instructions, he said he'd be there in an hour. "But you can't *get* here," I objected, "the snow has drifted and is hip high from Albany Avenue to our house." "That's all right, I'll walk." And he did. There began a close friendship. The minute he got in the house, things seemed less desperate. He had brought everything needed, including an "electric finger" so I could get some steam in the room to help Jack's mean case of grippe. During the nearly thirty years until Dr. Witter died, he was our "beloved physician"—our comfort and help in many emergencies. Scarcely five feet tall, and a bit roly-poly, he took care of his patients in fair weather or foul. And always, as on that first visit, as soon as he entered the house, the anxieties and burdens seemed to fall away, and the sick ones seemed better almost immediately. Jack was finally well and able to go and see for himself that all was well on Capitol Avenue.

During the weeks that followed, the first Wasp was put through continual informal runs. Meantime, a second Wasp was almost assembled, and four more Wasps were being manufactured. Jack and Andy were well along with the design of a larger engine, the "Hornet," which would have a displacement of 1690 cubic inches and would deliver 525 horsepower.

The Hornet was similar in many respects to the Wasp—many parts were interchangeable. Jack and Andy had come up with two new engines within nine months, which was an extraordinary achievement. The team confidence which ran all through the organization had contributed immeasurably to the success of the entire enterprise.

The official Navy test of the Wasp began on March 4, 1926. Ted Carlisle, the company's first service man, and Bill Willgoos were named official observers. Andy Willgoos was the company's representative. H. G. Seik represented the government. In those days, the tests on experimental engines were fifty hours running time and could be interrupted and the engine examined at any time. However, the only changes which could be made during a test were very minor, such as replacement of spark plugs. Later, the time required was 150 hours of intensive running, though only a tenth of the test time was at full throttle.

This test for the Navy was an anxious time for us all. Everything about the Wasp had been designed for 350 horsepower. Spurred by the enthusiasm of all concerned, Jack had allowed the horsepower to be pushed up 75 points beyond the original plan. Always a strong believer in a very large safety factor, he was troubled at the extra load—almost 18% higher than had been planned. The tests seemed to go on interminably.

Jack came home for lunch on the day that the tests would be completed. He looked simply awful. I thought something catastrophic must have happened, but said nothing, knowing that he would tell me when he felt he could. As he was leaving for the plant, he said something about four more hours to go. I asked if I might bring Jackie and Mary to see the last half hour or so. He brightened a little and thought that would be great. I longed to be able to say just the right word to ease his anxiety.

We went and watched. There was a tense and solemn hush as the hands of the clock crept toward 5:00 p.m. How slowly they crept! There was a big lump in my throat that I couldn't swallow, and I guess this was true of others. Finally 5:00 o'clock came. The engine was shut off. The silence was intense. We all looked numbly at each other. Then Carlisle came out of the test chamber, beaming, but deaf for a while from the roar which had assailed his ears for hours. The expression on his face told us that all was well. Suddenly the flood gates opened. The pent-up anxieties which had haunted us since Christmas broke loose in a flood of joyous mutual congratulation.

But I looked over at my husband—I could see him visibly disintegrating before my eyes. I knew the trouble and could explain it to others. If the tests had failed, it would have been a bitter disappointment to all concerned—would have meant that they had given up good jobs and an assured future to embark on a highly speculative venture that had failed—but for him it would be worse, because he would be the one at whose door the blame for the failure should be laid. He would be responsible for having wasted nearly a year of all those men's time, and over half a million dollars of Niles Bement Pond's money. To a man with such a deep sense of responsibility, this was a dreadful, soul-shattering thought. Somehow, he could not throw off the worry of it all. His nerves had been strung to the breaking point for weeks, and now the let-down was complete.

So in our home that evening, there was none of the rejoicing which was present in the other Pratt & Whitney homes. I am sure I failed Jack badly that time, for I felt he should have been full of tremendous gratitude for this success, instead of giving in to nerves. I tried to buck him up but only succeeded in hurting him. Months later when I saw my mother and told her about this incident, she looked at me in disgust and said, "I didn't think I *could* have a daughter who was so utterly stupid and lacking in understanding. Surely you could see that what he needed was a chance to pull himself together, and the quiet assurance of your love and appreciation of what he had been through." I knew she was right, and I hoped I had learned a valuable lesson which would help me be a more understanding wife to this man, who held so much of aviation's future locked in that marvelous mind of his.

The Wasp had swept through its official fifty-hour test, registering between 410 and 420 horsepower at full throttle. The Navy sent its congratulations and asked that this particular Wasp be earmarked for an earthbound existence. This seemed sad to us. She had gone through test after test. She had delivered more horsepower than she had been designed for. She had fulfilled all that had been asked of her and had come through everything gloriously. It seemed unfair that she couldn't be allowed to experience the joy—the freedom—the surge of her own power, as she lifted a plane proudly, swiftly, exultingly into the wide blue yonder—for to me, and I am sure to Jack, she was a living thing. However, we naturally acceded to the Navy's request, and this first Wasp was retired to a permanent place of honor in the Franklin Institute in Philadelphia. She is there today. She has never flown.

Test-stand success was all very well, but long experience warned us to hold our jubilation. Everyone concerned knew that it is one thing to build a perfect test engine, and quite another to build one that will function properly in an airplane.

The second experimental Wasp was scheduled to fly on May 1. My mother had sent me $100 as a gift to enable me to engage a nurse for the children, so that I would be free to go to Washington with Jack and the others, and see the Wasp on her "maiden flight" so to speak. (Since the company was operating on borrowed money, we kept our salaries to the minimum, and we could not have afforded the extra expense without this gift.)

The Rentschlers had invited us to ride with them in their car. Ina Vought, wife of Chance Vought who designed and built the Vought Corsair, was also a passenger on this joyful ride. Our hearts were light and full of hope as the miles slipped by, probably at the stupendous average of thirty miles an hour. We were on the road two days!

The Wright "Apache" had been designed as the plane which would be powered by the Wright "Simoon," but the Navy decided that the Wasp should make its initial flight in this plane. The Chance Vought Company was assigned the task of making the necessary adjustments of the nacelle of the airframe. I was looking forward with eager expectation to seeing this plane, about which I had heard so much.

We had gone down two days ahead of the date set for the flight, which was to mean so much to so many. Our hearts were full of confidence, and we sang most of the way. When we arrived, we found that some minor adjustments to the plane had delayed its arrival, and this meant that I would have to return home before the flight, because the nurse could not stay past the original date set. This was a bitter disappointment, of course, and to add to the feeling of frustration, the other women decided to go to a vaudeville show on the one free afternoon. I hate vaudeville anyway, and to waste a spring day in Washington, listening to rather vulgar jokes in a stuffy theatre, when all the world was bursting into blossom, gorgeous memorial buildings waiting to be visited, and history on almost every street and square, took all the self-control I could summon.

Sadly I left, before the great day—the climax of the past year of dreams, suspense, anticipation and work.

The Wasp took to the air May 5, 1926. Lieutenant C. C. Champion, a young Navy test pilot on duty at the Bureau of Aeronautics engine section, was the man assigned to this momentous flight. He was a daring, skillful, wonderful young pilot, and when we knew it was he who would be at the controls, most of our worries vanished. A phone call from Washington told me that the engine roared, the plane rolled along the runway a hundred feet or so, and then almost leaped into the air—soaring at a steeper angle than the jets do now on take-off. Afterwards Jack told me about this in more detail.

Champion had wasted little time feeling out the plane and its engine. Long before he landed, observers on the ground knew the verdict. The confident manner in which the young lieutenant "wrung out" the new combination expressed his verdict more eloquently than any formal report.

As a result of this initial success, the Navy ordered the Wasp into additional experimental installations in Boeing and Curtiss fighters which had been originally designed and built for water-cooled engines. The following paragraphs are taken largely from the Pratt & Whitney Aircraft Story, since I do not have other printed material describing the events listed below.[1]

> Within six months, flying in planes never meant to take its bulk and power, the Wasp demonstrated speed, rate of climb, performance at altitude that revolutionized American aviation. Within the year, the Wasp shattered its own first world record and went on to smash existing standards for both land planes and sea planes, carrying airframes and pilots higher, farther, and faster than they had ever gone before.
>
> Through countless exhibitions of durability in military testing, its swiftly growing reputation as "the faithful Wasp" set the stage for the rapid growth of American airlines which soon entwined the world. With her sister engine, the Hornet, the Wasp was a fundamental factor in lifting American airpower to a position where, for the first time in history, it was the leader of the world. These two engines, opening new vistas of altitude, load carrying, and endurance, played an integral part in crystallizing American air strategy by providing the first public proof that the offensive roles, so long sought by airmen, were technically feasible. Out of this confidence grew the Army Air Corps concentration on the long-range, high-altitude bomber, and the forging of the Navy's fast carrier task force—two of the most revolutionary and devastating weapons the world had yet seen.
>
> During these early test flights, the Wasp was flying into a new era in aviation. In a way she created this new era. During the year preceding the appearance of the Wasp, there was turmoil and near desperation among military airmen over the lack of American progress in aviation. The handful of Army and Navy flyers were convinced they could never over-take their foreign competitors unless they got more financial support and a free hand for developing new equipment and tactics.

The few survivors in the aircraft industry were caught in a cross fire between direct government competition for the meager military market and procurement policies that auctioned off their best designs to the lowest bidder for production contracts and handed their technical skills freely to competitors. In this ruinous economic atmosphere the industry faced early extinction.

France still led the world in military aviation. The United States stood *third* in the international scale. Most of the world records were held by foreign countries—16 were held by France, 18 by the rising Italian air force, while the United States held but 7. American jubilation over Jimmy Doolittle's victory in winning the Schneider Trophy in 1925 was short-lived. The next year Major Mario de Bernardi flashed around Hampton Roads, Virginia, speed course in a scarlet Macchi (M-39) sea plane to win the trophy and smash Doolittle's records.

It was in this atmosphere, sparked by the fiery public crusade of Brigadier General William Mitchell of the Army air service, and the quieter and equally effective campaign of Admiral Moffett, that two groups of government investigators reported their diagnosis of aviation's ailments. The investigators were a Congressional committee headed by Florian Lampert of Wisconsin, and a board appointed by President Coolidge which took its name from the chairman, Dwight W. Morrow, a New York banker. Their primary conclusions were:

1. Adequate national defense required a more prominent role for air power with a sustained aircraft procurement program to provide for regular replacement of obsolescent types.
2. Military air power should be built on the foundation of a privately operated, economically healthy, and technically competitive aircraft industry of sufficient size to support peacetime military requirements and capable of swift expansion in time of war.

These groups concluded that the task of supplying technically superior aircraft on the scale required for defense was far too big for the Army and Navy. These findings were published in mid-December of 1925, about when the early employees of Pratt & Whitney were assembling the first Wasp.

Thus the Wasp began to prove herself at exactly the historic moment in time when the military skies, so murky the year before, had suddenly cleared. The Wasp quickly proved the advantages of a high-powered, air-cooled engine for military aircraft. The Wasp saved between 250 and 300 pounds of total weight. This weight saving meant swifter rate of climb, higher ceiling, shorter turning radius, and slower landing speed—all with equal top speed. This was flying in planes which were not designed for her—"cobbled up" jobs, Chance Vought called them.

Navy pilots knew that as soon as the airframe designers had an opportunity to build "around" the Wasp—from the start—they could expect superior speed. Before the summer of 1926 was over, Commander Eugene E. Wilson, chief of the engine section of the Bureau of Aeronautics, wrote in Aviation magazine, "The Wasp incorporates some of the finest engineering yet seen in aircraft engines, plus workmanship for which Pratt & Whitney is known. There seems no doubt now that this new engine is, even at this early point of development, considerably advanced over any other air-cooled engine of its class that we know of. . ."

In the fall of 1926 there was a 7,000-mile transcontinental round trip for the Wasp, without a hitch. Service men had been sent on ahead to all the fueling stops with full supply of tools and spare parts, but none of them worked a moment on the engine. Boeing and Curtiss had designed planes around the Wasp, and when Lieutenant Ralph Oftsie (later Rear Admiral) took her to San Diego for tests in "dog-fighting, carrier landings—everything in the books"—she came through with flying colors. Ted Carlisle, Pratt & Whitney's own service man, reported the scene at San Diego when Admiral Reeves' pilots got their first experience with the Wasp.

> "At San Diego I found two Wasp engines in combat at 8,000 feet in the air—the Curtiss Hawk flown west by Lieutenant Oftsie and the new Boeing. I checked the Hawk engine and found everything O.K.
>
> "The Boeing was then taken over by the Test Board for three weeks' test of speed at different r.p.m. to determine gas and oil consumption climbing to different heights in a stated time. Lieutenant Compo also made some deck landings on the Langley and he said it was the finest ship and engine he had ever taken off and landed on the Langley. The engine was so quick on the throttle.
>
> "Then came the last and hardest test on the engine and ship. Orders came that every pilot on the station could have fifteen minutes flight time in the Boeing ship. That fifteen minutes was always extended to about thirty minutes, and every flight was a dogfight between a Curtiss water-cooled Hawk and the Wasp-equipped Boeing. Every stunt that is known was brought into the show. Every pilot would go up to 12,000 feet and then dive to within 2,000 feet of the ground. The Wasp would turn up to 2500 r.p.m., the highest figure on the tachometer, before it was halfway down. The radiators on the Hawk could not stand that work and would leak.

> "After three days of this work with 100 hours flying time, the engine was just as good as when the ship started from Seattle four weeks before. Every pilot in VF-2 squadron commented on the fine performance of the engine. . . ."

By October the Navy was ready to give its initial production order—for 200 Wasp engines. Fred and Jack had been so confident of receiving this kind of approval that the plant was tooled up and ready to go full steam ahead when the initial contract was signed. The first five production engines were delivered to the Navy in December of 1926, one year after the first experimental engine had been assembled. By February, Wasps were being delivered at the rate of fifteen a month. Think of it—instead of eighteen months from drafting board to test stand, it was eighteen months from drafting board to full production!

That wasn't all! The Hornet, the design for which had begun before the first experimental Wasp was assembled, was complete and ready for the test stand in June of 1926; and after six months of testing on both direct and geared engines, she began a fifty-hour qualification test. When she passed this test in March of 1927, with a rating of 525 horsepower and weight of 750 pounds, the Pratt & Whitney team had performed an unprecedented miracle. They had designed, built, and qualified two of the most advanced and successful power plants of that time in well under two years. More than half the Hornet parts were interchangeable with Wasp parts—a big factor in field maintenance, especially aboard Navy carriers. The Hornet gave promise of her future greatness in her first test, delivering 570 horsepower during the last five hours. Her weight was 1.3 pound per horsepower compared to 2-1/4 pounds per horsepower for the liquid-cooled engines she was scheduled to replace.

I have gone into a good deal of detail about the Wasp, because it was on the foundation of her magnificent performance that the superb reputation of Pratt & Whitney Aircraft Company was built. I will later add some details about the Hornet, which had all the matchless qualities which the Wasp had shown, but was bigger, more powerful, and destined for heavier duty.

And as I watched the man to whose creative genius these engines owed their excellence, my heart swelled with pride in his accomplishments—and equally in his modesty about them. The two engines were designed and built by a team, it is true; but it was that indefinable "plus" in him—call it genius, if you will—which put Pratt & Whitney Aircraft, after less than two years of existence, in the forefront of the aviation industry.

Chapter VII

A Highway in the Sky

The summer of 1926 not only brought unbelievable success to the Pratt & Whitney Aircraft Company, through the amazing performance of the Wasp in all tests she underwent, but it also brought joy to the hearts of the Rentschlers, for in July a daughter was born, named Helen for Fred's sister, and Faye for her own mother. I think we were almost as happy about her coming, and her perfection, as if we had been her kinsfolk. With all the rapid march of events in recent months, our hearts had ached constantly at the lack of a child in their home, and though no child can ever quite take the place of one that has been lost, the empty places in their hearts were filled with this new love. The baby's room was alive and full of activity once more, and the whole house had that warm happy "feel" that pervades a home when there is a much wanted child.

Once more there was no vacation for Jack. There was too much that needed his attention. I am sure we couldn't have borne being away from it all anyway. The Wasps were being proved in military tests. Some of the early airlines were already in business with the newly won contracts. None of them were making adequate profits, however.

The government made a start in establishing law and order in air transport. The air commerce act, pushed hard by Herbert Hoover, then Secretary of Commerce, did three things which were of great help in building the airlines:

> *First,* the government assumed responsibility for establishing and maintaining airways, as it did waterways, and later, highways. The maintenance of the expensive beacons for night flying and radio facilities and weather service, which were "musts" for the airways, were too costly for privately owned and operated airline companies. Without these facilities, we would still be back in the barnstorming days of the aviation industry.
>
> *Second,* the government established the first unified code of air traffic law and took the responsibility for enforcing it.
>
> *Third,* it gave the public the much needed assurance that adequate safety standards would be maintained by federal licensing of planes, pilots, and mechanics.

Barnstorming in America had just begun to give way to tentative efforts toward commercial aviation, when the Wasp took to the air. We had a limited transcontinental airmail service flown by gallant post office employed pilots. There was nothing in 1926 that could honestly be called an airline. The few charter services were rendered highly dangerous by out-worn, out-moded war surplus equipment.

In the spring of 1925, the United States Government had announced its intentions, through the air mail act of that year, of getting out of the air mail business, and throwing open the field to private operation. Sponsors of this act contended that, not until such time as air mail was removed from government monopoly and opened to sound private competition, would it add significantly to American air transport. With the new rate of 10-1/2¢ an ounce, and government authorization to pay operators up to 80% of the revenues collected therefrom, the prospects of commercial aviation suddenly brightened.

While Jack and Andy Willgoos were working in Andy's garage in Montclair over the details of the first Wasp, newly formed airlines all over the country were vying with each other to win the air mail contracts. The first air mail contracts were for comparatively short haul feeder routes.

The 2,800-mile transcontinental Columbia route was not let out for bids until November of 1926—the month before Pratt & Whitney moved into production of the Wasp. The entire route was deemed too tough for any one operator. The post office split it into two parts—the first, from New York to Chicago; the second, 2,000 miles, stretched from Chicago to San Francisco. This had to span the highest mountains, and the greatest unpopulated expanses of territory, and the greatest divergences in temperature.

The summer of 1926 had melted into fall. Almost imperceptibly the days had grown shorter, the nights cool. Then fields began to seem greener than ever; the maples turned to a tapestry of red and gold; the sky reminded us of that poem "October's bright blue weather;" the air was crisp and sparkling.

Things were going well at the plant. The big hurdles of the moment were past. There was a little respite, and Jack and I decided we could take a few days in the mountains. We had learned of a farm in the town of Chocorua where we could board. To this haven we repaired the last weekend in October. The owners made us welcome, fed us too well, and gave us the equivalent of a month's vacation in less than a week.

Sunday was rainy, but we went for a walk in the afternoon anyway, to—appropriately—"Sabbaday Falls." We had to wade across a couple of streams—I'll never forget trying to walk on the pebbly bottom of that swift, icy, running stream, carrying my shoes and stockings, and holding my skirt out of the way of the ripples. It ran so fast, it made me dizzy, but it was fun. Fortunately my feet were so numb with cold that I didn't mind the rocks too much. Laughing, we wiped our feet on our handkerchiefs, redonned shoes and socks, and finally reached the falls, which were worth all the effort.

We woke next morning to a glorious, cloudless day, the air tingling and delicious. Jack said, "Let's climb Chocorua," so we did—up via the Hammond Trail which goes up over the eastern spur and is long, but has more gorgeous look-outs than any of the others. Having climbed only in summer when it was hot and buggy, I felt the sparkling air lent wings to my feet. First we went through fallen red and gold leaves, wet from yesterday's rain, so extra brilliant, then pine needles and moss, all packed and cushiony, then *snow* as we hit the higher part of the shoulder—then *ice.* The cone was all coated in ice. I am sure my husband, who could always read my mind, could see me thinking, "I can go *up* this icy rock all right, but I'll never get down."

We saw big footprints of a bear and noted that he had feasted on all the blueberries. I felt I was becoming almost too well acquainted with nature. When we reached the summit and looked north, there they all were—the Franconias, Mooselauke, Carter Dome, and the Presidentials—Madison, Adams, Jefferson, Clay, and, towering above them all, Mt. Washington, its summit crowned with snow, and one big white cumulus cloud just kissing the very top whose whiteness matched its own. I have carried that picture in my mind's eye all these forty-four years. Nothing ever seemed quite so beautiful.

Thanksgiving came, and with it Jack's parents. It was a real Thanksgiving in every way. There was happiness in Fred's and Faye's home. Grace Willgoos had been ill but was better. So many of the question marks of the previous Thanksgiving were now questions no longer. The company was doing so well—orders for both Wasps and Hornets coming in—that the future of the company seemed assured, and the board raised our salaries.

Jack had been concerned about his father's car—a ten-year old Chalmers. It was high and stiff, and it rode very badly, and it *was worn out.* This raise meant we could give him a new car. We almost burst with the joy of this secret. As we saw Jack's parents start off in the Chalmers the Monday following Thanksgiving, we thought that when we next watched them leave us, after Christmas, Dad would be driving the sleek new Buick coupé which was promised for December 15.

We were so excited about this that we could hardly attend to our other Christmas preparations, but I am sure that no one was neglected that year. Christmas Eve came—a chill, threatening, cloudy day. Dr. and Mrs. Mead had planned to have an early lunch and leave Winchester by one, at the latest. In those days, it took about four hours to drive from Winchester to Hartford—thus they would easily reach us by suppertime—but about noon, the murky atmosphere condensed into a freezing rain. Cars proceeded sideways, if at all.

We had had some difficulty in delivering our gifts, even before noon. Our lunch didn't seem to appeal. What if instead of making them happy with the new car, we should cause them a serious accident because of having urged them to come by car (Jack wanted to make sure his Dad never drove the old Chalmers again). The afternoon dragged on interminably—we knew it would be a long, long wait—and there was no way for them to let us know where or how they were. Around seven they phoned us from Worcester. Six hours for forty miles! They had had the chains put on, the roads were awful, and there were many accidents, but at last some sanding was being done. They would be careful, they would come slowly, we were not to worry!

That was easier said than done. We wouldn't draw a good long breath until our dear ones were safely in the house. After the children were in bed, we made ourselves trim the tree and put their presents under it. We knew Grammy and Grampy would be too weary when they finally did get there to do anything but have some good hot supper and go to their well-earned rest. When two headlights actually turned in the drive soon after midnight, we could hardly believe it. Few explorers ever coming from the Pole, or even from outer space, ever received a more ecstatic welcome. Hot tea, a glowing fire, and a hot meal restored them somewhat after the eleven grueling, anxious, horrible hours. Everyone had always kidded Dad about his driving, but I maintained that anyone who could make that trip on that day, and arrive with car, passenger, and himself in one piece, was tops!

Christmas morning dawned clear, cold, beautiful. At breakfast, there were some keys tied with red ribbon at Dad's place. "What are these?" he asked, mystified. "Look out of the window," Jack said. And there, in the exact spot where he had left the old Chalmers the night before was the Buick coupé, complete with a Christmas wreath on the hood (well padded underneath, lest the finish get scratched) and tied with a huge red bow. Tears welled up in his eyes and spilled over as he tried to tell Jack what the car would mean to him. The old one was so tiring to drive, but he hadn't thought he could afford a new one. With characteristic thoughtfulness, he insisted that we have the tree and the children's presents before he tried the car, though of course he was just itching to get behind that wheel, get the feel of the car, savor the delicious new smell. Later on, he and Jack had a blissful time with it. Nothing would do in the afternoon, but that we should go calling on all our friends, so Dad could show them his treasure. He and Grammy drove the Buick, and we drove ours, as his car couldn't take us all. That night we went to sleep in a glow of happiness.

The morning of the 26th brought us back to earth with a dull, dull thud. Snow had fallen in the night—was already deep, and still falling. This was a real blow. We were pretty sure the ice from Christmas Eve had been worn down on Christmas, but this snow was deep. The excellent snow removal equipment we have today had not been developed. Jack's parents had had an awful trip down, and we didn't want them to go through another, but Dad felt he had to get back to some of his patients. Though not desperately ill, they needed the reassurance of having their doctor near at hand. We argued that it wouldn't do them any good for him to get all worn out, if not hurt in an accident, but all to no avail. Nothing would do, but he must go.

We all shoveled. Our garage was under the house because the lot sloped steeply to the backyard. So, he had to get up that hill, first of all. The plows were at work on Albany Avenue, and once we managed to reach the upper level, it would not be too hard, as Westerly Terrace sloped down hill to Albany Avenue. By noon we were well enough dug out for them to set forth, but it was a far different departure than the one we had dreamed of. They reached home safely, however, and in spite of our anxiety, we felt it was the finest Christmas ever.

That winter marked another tremendous step forward for aviation in general, and for Pratt & Whitney Aircraft in particular. When the Columbia route bids were opened in January of 1927, the infant airline industry discovered that William Boeing, a Seattle aeroplane manufacturer, had exploded an economic bombshell. His bid for the western segment was incredibly low—just HALF of what the government advertised that it was willing to pay. In contrast to his bid of $2.89 to carry a pound of mail 2,000 miles, his nearest competitor's bid of $5.09 looked like "sky-way robbery." Nobody believed he could carry the mail for that price. His critics thought he planned to take losses to insure a market for his aircraft. Others thought he was trying to freeze out competition and would raise the price later. Amid all the frustrated fury of his competitors, he signed the air mail contract and, ironically, took the train for Hartford.

Boeing knew as well as his fulminating competitors that he couldn't fly the mail successfully or profitably for that price, in the equipment then available. Before the post office gave up on the air mail, it had tried to stimulate better design of planes by instigating a competition. But the designers were hamstrung by having to plan on using the Liberty engine. Boeing had built a new "night" mail plane for the competition, the 40-A, but he knew it wasn't good enough. In the summer of 1926 he had gotten his first inkling of what Wasp performance could be, even when it was installed in planes that were not designed specifically for it. The Wasp could boost the payload to 1,500 pounds instead of 1,000. This meant that Boeing's mail plane, the 40-B, could carry two passengers in addition to 1,000 pounds of mail and so could add $400 revenue to each one-way trip. Boeing stated bluntly that his company would rather carry more mail than a radiator and water for cooling. Navy experience had indicated that maintenance on the Wasp was minimal. These engines could go far beyond the 100-hour overhaul period required by the Liberty motor.

The Navy agreed that Boeing could buy five Wasps a month for priority delivery, even though its own orders were not yet filled. So, five of the fifteen Wasps which were manufactured each month were earmarked for Seattle, beginning February 1, 1927. This meant that, to meet this schedule, production would have to overflow onto the top floor of the Capitol Avenue plant.

The company paper was rightly named "The Bee Hive," for the plant was surely a hive of activity. Everyone poured out all the energy, ability and creativity he or she could muster to get the plant reshaped, the tools installed, the parts manufactured and machined, and the beginnings of mass production achieved without loss of individual perfection.

With the increased need for skilled labor, those taking responsibility for securing personnel had to scrutinize applicants with the utmost care. There could be no diminution of quality. Perfection of each part—care in assembly—thoroughness in testing—all must be tops.

One would have thought that, having produced this brain-child which had more than fulfilled all dreams for its performance, Jack's work would have eased somewhat, but this was not the case. Just as when a child is born—and we often spoke of all the engines as "Jack's babies"—the real work of the parents has just begun, so it was with the Wasp and Hornet. Jack and Andy were always thinking of refinements to make the engines better. Real development on an engine seems to begin when it has passed its qualification tests.

So the winter and spring of 1927 were almost as demanding as the previous year had been. But each month brought new evidence of the dependable worth of the Wasp. In March, the Hornet roared through its qualification test, delivering 525 horsepower during the last five hours. All this added up to a thrillingly happy and deeply satisfying winter.

We had something to be especially happy about too, because we were looking forward to the coming of our third baby at the end of August. I took Jackie and Mary to Kentucky for a visit in April so that my family and friends could see them at the delightful ages they were going through. We didn't mention our happy hopes to my parents for two reasons: Mamma always worried about us when our children were coming, and our house could not quite accommodate a grandmother and a new baby at the same time, so her inability to be with us would also increase her concern.

A unique and remarkable achievement which stimulated the growing interest in aviation was Lindbergh's solo flight to Paris in May 1927. Not only did this amazing performance give added impetus to the budding industry, but Lindbergh himself, with his modesty about his triumph and his friendliness to all, was a real ambassador of good will for America. We could have wished that the Wasp had powered the "Spirit of St. Louis," but it was Jack's work on the Whirlwind that had enabled it to keep turning up those revolutions per minute which carried the ship and Lindbergh safely across the ocean.

Another aeronautical event which took place in Hartford in the early summer of 1927 was the dedication of Brainard Field. All the planes which could get off the ground were flying, and, as they had no brakes, they slowed themselves down by zigzagging slightly as they came in to land. Jackie, watching these maneuvers, remarked, "Look at those planes coming in wagging their tails." It was on this day that we met H. Mansfield (Jack) Horner and his bride Lela. Horner had just come to work for Pratt & Whitney. Our friendship with them was to mean more and more with the passing years. Toward the end of the afternoon, the dramatic arrival of Lindbergh roaring low over the field, and then pointing the nose of the "Spirit of St. Louis" at the sky and zooming straight up, put the perfect climax on the afternoon.

Coupled with our happiness as we looked forward to the coming of the new baby were the added pressures in connection with the new venture—for us—of the air mail. The time was fast approaching when the Boeing 40-B, powered by our Wasps, would start carrying the mail daily, summer and winter, through the cold, rarified air above the 15,000-foot Rockies and the terrible heat above the Great Plains. As usual, Jack carried an extra burden of responsibility, and this time there would be no letup of the strain. This would be an ongoing, daily, grueling experience for the pilots who pioneered the mail service; and, as always, the fact that human lives depended on the integrity of Jack's engineering increased the tension—the load of care. There were times when, witnessing the strain he was undergoing, I almost wished, in spite of my pride in his work, that he was engaged in making some uninspired thing like safety pins.

The Wasp had proved the advantage of high-powered, air-cooled engines for military use in both Boeing and Curtiss fighter planes. Now came the opportunity for it to show its value for commercial use. Boeing's redesigned mail plane was a biplane with the conventional struts and wire cross-bracing of that era. Its wings were of spruce framework covered with "doped" fabric. The frame of the body was steel tubing covered with aluminum forward and doped fabric in the rear. Just behind the engine was a 100-gallon gas tank. Behind this was an aluminum-lined mail compartment.

The passenger cabin, with *cushioned seats,* was located in the fuselage between the wings, just behind the mail compartment, and forward of the pilot's cockpit. Passengers had to squeeze past struts and wire bracing to crawl into their tiny compartment.

The basic design for this early mail plane had been completed before the Columbia Route bids, but the Boeing Company was faced with producing 24 planes and test flying them in less than five months, because operation of the mail route was scheduled to begin July 1, 1927. As fast as a plane was completed, it was trucked fifteen miles to Sands Point, where a cleared pasture served as a test flying area. It was given a short whirl in the air, then flown off to one of the ten route division points. As we look at our huge, sleek, multi-engined air transports today, it is hard to realize that such a relatively short time ago people and mail were entrusted to those tiny, frail, single-engined aircraft.

By midnight on June 30, all 24 Boeing 40-B's were in their places at all points along the route, while a host of aviation "experts" sat back waiting hopefully for Bill Boeing to lose his shirt. (Ironically, seven years later when the airlines were being flayed by the Senate investigating committee, the substantial sums netted by this operation were cited as a prime example of "exorbitant profits" allegedly mulcted from the government on the air mail contracts.)

On the first of July, Wasps started droning over the Columbia Route, to set a new standard of air transport. Never before had such large payloads been carried over such a long, rugged route with such safety and regularity. Every 24 hours, the Wasps logged 4,000 miles of flying time on a round trip between Lake Michigan and the Pacific. The schedule called for 20-hour mail service from Chicago to San Francisco, as against 63 hours by train. The Wasps pulled the Boeing 40-B at 110 miles an hour, carrying with each horsepower 3.9 pounds of payload.*

During the early weeks, some difficulties developed because of over-heating when flying over the Great Plains. This was due to the fact that there was a sort of fat pillow of extremely hot air, about a mile thick, which rose up and hovered above the plains. It was not safe to fly below it, but to fly above it meant that the planes lost contacts with their beacons, so they had to fly through it. Since the Wasp was air-cooled, this inferno-like air was no help. Jack and Andy had the task of developing small oil radiators which would circulate the oil in order to cool the motors. The worst problems seemed to be between Omaha and Cheyenne.

One day late in July, Jack came home early, telling me he had

*It is interesting to note here that by the end of two years, Boeing air transport had flown 5,500,000 miles and had delivered 1,300 tons of mail and carried 6,000 passengers. By 1931, after four years of operation, seven of the original Wasps were past the 2,000-hour mark. Some of the more powerful Hornets that had, in 1930, begun replacing the Wasps, to carry more payload faster, had reached 1,800 hours. Boeing's original estimate had placed the total life of an airmail engine at 1,000 hours. In 1937, just ten years after the first Wasp went into commercial service, the American flag became the first to span both the Atlantic and Pacific Oceans.

to leave for Omaha that night. He would supervise the installation of the radiators and would be one of the passengers to test their effectiveness. These tests would go on for several days. I had never been anywhere near Omaha, but somehow the very name seemed to be synonymous with heat, dust, ragweed—everything that was bad for him, and it was with a heavy heart that I saw him off.

He flew with the mail, often at night, squeezed into that tiny compartment, once with a very fat man as his fellow passenger. There was no sleep at the proper times or any comfort at all. At the landing points they produced their own meals on a little gasoline stove, such as we used for camping. There were no airports then, with snack bars or coffee shops. Can't you picture Jack and the pilots huddled around that little stove in the chill dawn air, eagerly sniffing the comforting aroma of bubbling coffee or sizzling bacon and eggs? Then, after refueling both man and engine, up and away once more to the next landing point.

The first attempts at cooling were helpful but, as he traveled, Jack had some better ideas. Here I must mention that contrary to some tales and a cartoon or two, he did *not* travel perched on the wing listening to the engine, and taking its temperature at intervals, so to speak. In those planes there was no problem about hearing the engines. Their song was abundantly audible.

An article which Jack wrote in the summer of 1927 was first published in "Aviation" magazine, then reprinted in the October issue of "The Bee-Hive." It gives such a vivid account of the early days of Pratt & Whitney's association with transporting air mail, that I will quote a few paragraphs from it, so that he can tell the story in his own words.

Journeyings with the Boeing Air Mail

Plane coming! Thus came the cry as I sat in the superintendent's office at Omaha at one o'clock one night in July. Walking through the brilliantly lighted hangar by the silent ships, I saw several hundred people collected around the westbound plane on the ramp in front. Above the steady throb of its idling engine was heard the cheerful hum of the homing plane just finishing its 500-mile run from Chicago. Overhead the big 500,000 candlepower revolving beacon light was throwing its beam for miles around as if reaching out for the invisible sound that was rapidly approaching.

For an instant we distinctly saw the plane as it was picked up by the finger of light from the beacon. Finally a pair of wide-set eyes was seen, one red and one green, then a white light from the plane blinked out its signal and the field was flooded with light from a 500,000,000 candlepower lantern.

Then the welcome sound of the plane rolling along the ground came to us as the floodlight was turned off. On came the plane right up to the hangar door where its brakes stopped it as exactly as a motor car. Quickly then the night crew transferred the mail to the outgoing ship. Three trips of the hand truck were necessary to carry the 900 pounds of mail.

While it was being securely stowed away, Frank Caldwell, the superintendent of the eastern division, was introducing me to Jack Knight, the pilot of the westbound plane. After he climbed in and ran up his engine, I entered the passenger compartment and we started. Taking off in the middle of the night with the aid of the floodlight seemed simple, but the moment we were in the air we plunged into darkness and heat.

On the ground it seemed comparatively cool after a day when the mercury stayed around 100°. Once in the air, instead of enjoying a cool ride through the night air, it was necessary to close the windows to prevent the scorching blast from penetrating the cabin. At first everything seemed inky black, but gradually it was possible to make out objects on the ground. To take advantage of a tail wind, we flew at a very low altitude. Relatively few lights were visible on the ground except as we passed over an occasional town. A few revolving beacons could be seen along the way as well as emergency landing fields neatly outlined by border lights. We soon came to the North Platte River which was followed more or less all the way to North Platte, Nebraska. This point was reached in about two hours and forty minutes.

I had been so interested in watching the country beneath us that it first seemed as though there must be something wrong when Jack Knight throttled down and started to turn the ship. Almost immediately, however, the boundary lights of the field were visible, and then the big floodlight came on, illuminating the field and buildings, as well as the river. This was one of the prettiest sights I have ever seen, coming out, as we did, from inky blackness onto a brightly illuminated field, bordered on one side by an emerald green river.

As soon as the plane came to rest, the night crew serviced it with gasoline and oil and took off the mail for North Platte. . . . This field has an altitude of 3,200 feet. As a result, the air temperature was considerably cooler than Omaha.

After a fifteen-minute stop, we were on our way again, headed for Cheyenne, Wyoming. The moon came up during this part of the journey, so that some more detailed idea of the country could be secured. It seemed as though we were flying over a huge checkerboard. Each little square represented a 160-acre homestead, which was one-quarter of a government section of 640 acres. The fences of these farms run absolutely east and west, and north and south, which is of great assistance to the pilots. . . .

As the moon went out of sight, it was just possible to see light in the east. To look directly behind the plane, which was then traveling due west, it was necessary to put my head out of the cabin window. So smoothly was everything going that I had almost forgotten we were traveling at over 100 miles an hour. My inquisitiveness about the day rapidly enlightened me on this subject, however.

As we approached Cheyenne, some of the Rocky Mountains could be seen to the south, in the direction of Denver, Colorado. At the same time the neatly laid out farms gave way to prairies, on which were seen herds of cattle, and occasional ranches. I can truthfully say that I never had had such a smooth ride in the air as Jack Knight gave me from Omaha to Cheyenne. Hour after hour the plane flew on without a bump and, when it became light enough to see, without the wings ever changing their relation with the horizon. . . .

Cheyenne, with an altitude of 6,400 feet, was reached about five o'clock. This city is 500 miles west of Omaha. . . . The mail was transferred here to another plane which was waiting with the engine idling. . . . Pilot Barker was scheduled for the trip to Salt Lake City, and when all was ready, I climbed in and we took off at six o'clock.

The country changed rapidly from prairies to hills and then mountains, as we left Cheyenne. Perhaps half an hour out we passed over Sherman Hill, which has the highest airway beacon in the world at 8,600 feet. During three of the winter months its keeper is out of communication with the world.

After leaving the "hump," which is the local name for Sherman Hill, behind us, we flew alternately over prairies and mountainous country. . . . Occasionally the Union Pacific Railroad was in sight, and, as the day wore on, automobiles could be seen on the Lincoln Highway. Both means of transportation certainly seemed slow to us in the air, traveling, as we were, more than twice as fast as they.

We finally climbed another ridge and swooped down on Rock Springs, Wyoming, which has a field at 6,400 feet. . . . Across the field to the westward runs a serrated cliff, the summit of which is perhaps 2,000 feet above the field. It was on these cliffs in the winter that a mail plane landed within a few feet of the top in a snowstorm. In the spring, horses were able to draw the plane to the plateau at the top of the cliff, from which it was flown away. On account of the altitude, the planes land very fast, but due to the good brakes with which they are equipped, they are able to stop in a remarkably short distance.

As we taxied down the field to take off, I wondered how quickly the "Wasp" could lift the eight or nine hundred pounds of mail, together with the ship and its occupants. Barker turned the plane around and headed directly for the hangar, and up we went, without any apparent effort. These sagebrush landing fields demonstrate the remarkable qualities of the Boeing Oleo landing gear with which the mail planes are equipped.

On a prairie like this each clump of sagebrush collects a mound of sand around it, making a field of innumerable bumps, with the result that it takes a really remarkable gear to stand the landing and taking off of such a big ship. . . .

From Rock Springs to Salt Lake City the country is almost continuously mountainous, particularly if a compass course is followed. . . . The coloring on this part of the trip is most remarkable, especially under the bright sun of the morning. The greens of the river bottoms shade off into browns and reds of the rocks, changing into gray at the tops of the mountains, the whole being set off by the blue of the sky.

After we had been out about an hour, and had been more or less steadily rising, we came to the summit of the Wasatch Range. This range reaches an elevation of ten or eleven thousand feet. It certainly is a sight to be remembered when the plane starts downward after crossing the ridge, and you see below you a tremendous plain with mountains in the background, at the foot of which is Salt Lake, and directly below, the city of Salt Lake, with its green trees and lawns strongly contrasted against the brown of the desert. . . .

Upon our arrival at the field, I was met by Wilbur Thomas and was certainly glad to see him, after nine hours in the air, without any sleep for two nights, and no breakfast. Mr. Hubbard, the vice president in charge of operations at the Boeing Air Transport, flew over from San Francisco and met me at dinner that night. A mere 625-mile journey in the air over the Sierra Nevada mountains for a dinner engagement is nothing to the officials of the Air Mail. . . .

On the way to Cheyenne after turning eastward, I suddenly noticed out of the window, on the opposite side from which I had been looking, the wall of the canyon. It seemed as though we were

> going to fly right into it. As the canyon narrowed, pilot Boonstra maneuvered until he took advantage of the up-currents which seemed to set the plane up in a series of steps, each perhaps 100 feet high. This was a most interesting operation, in view of the nearness of the end of the canyon. However, the faithful Wasp kept right on with its work and we cleared the ridge by a good margin.
>
> As we started to coast down toward Cheyenne, forty-one miles away, we could see to our right or southward the lights of the city of Denver, which was 100 miles away, nestling among the Rocky Mountains which surround it. To our left we could see by their lights occasional little towns along the Union Pacific Railroad. Finally the city of Cheyenne loomed up ahead and below us. The big beacon light at the hangar was searching in every direction for us as it swung around the horizon. These big beacons certainly beckon in a hospitable manner to the wayfarers along the airway. . . .
>
> The weight saving due to the air-cooled engine and the efficient plane design are both responsible for the 50 percent increase in the payload handled. The take-off is remarkably quick, and the planes when fully loaded climb rapidly to 10 or 12,000 feet in negotiating the various mountain ranges. Regulation port and starboard lights are carried, as well as a white tail light. Under each wing is a 250,000 candlepower landing light. Two parachute flares are provided to facilitate forced landings at night. Each of these will light up nearly a square mile of ground for a few minutes. . . .
>
> We reached Omaha about half past two in the afternoon. . . . It seemed like home-coming to me to see Frank Caldwell on the ground, with Hobbs of Stromberg, Eric Stohlstrom, and Bill Wheatley. . . . This fleet of 24 Boeing mail planes, all equipped with Wasp engines, had covered approximately 300,000 miles in the past two months.

Jack told me later that there were some highly amusing, as well as hair-raising experiences on this trip. When they would see a train coming along, the pilot would lose altitude and fly along beside the diners to see what people were eating. As mentioned in Jack's article, near Laramie, Wyoming, there was a canyon where there was a good up-draft all the time, so the pilots depended on that draft to boost the plane the 200 feet needed to go over the top. "But suppose it didn't blow that day?" "It always does." I have it on good authority that the pilots of small planes are "still riding the draft."

My relief that these experiences were over and our joy at having Jack safely home again were short-lived, for after a week or so he had to go back and put those "better ideas" into effect. This time the problem was really solved, but he stayed on a while longer to make absolutely sure.

One night the Rentschlers invited me for dinner rather suddenly. We had a delightful time, but Fred seemed nervous and on a strain. Around eight, he excused himself, saying there were a few things he had to see about at the plant. This was puzzling, as he had nothing to do with the engineering end. Andy would see about that if there was any problem, and Fred, being the meticulous executive he was, always had his work well in hand. But I thought nothing of it really—maybe he had to meet someone whom they were considering for some job. Faye and I had a good visit, discussed our happy hopes, for they were hoping for another little child in October. Soon after nine, Fred came back all smiles, his face relaxed. He then told me that there had been a forced landing due to fog and that they had wanted me with them so as to be sure I wouldn't hear about it until we knew Jack was safe.

It must be remembered that in 1927 there was no radar to lead a pilot to his destination or show him where there were mountains or other dangers. There was not even the kind of radio that could "talk" them down. In a fog, a plane was more helpless than a ship at sea, for the pilot could not tell whether or not he was right side up until he started to fall out of the plane. As the pilot saw the fog rolling toward them, he headed for a ranch and landed there. A cowboy, hearing the plane come down, came galloping up to make sure all was well and to ask if he could help. "Indeed you can," said the pilot, "could you get hold of a truck so we can get the mail to the next point?" He surely could and would. While his buddy, who had joined him, went to see about the truck, he looked at the plane with loving interest and told Jack all about the engine—all the details of stroke and bore, horsepower, etc., to which Jack listened with rapt interest, asking a question now and then to draw him out more and, of course, never letting on who he was. It was great to find this lad, way off here, so interested and so knowledgeable about the engine. He had read everything he could lay his hands on relative to this engine. He was so eager and so accurate, we always hoped he would never know he was talking to the man in whose mind that engine had been born.

The trip in the truck through the mountain pass had one amusing episode. Since they were carrying the mail, the driver was armed. When they were far from their destination, they noticed a car following them; it could have passed them, but it didn't. The driver was troubled, and when he went around one curve where he could pull the truck off the road a little, he did so, and jumped out with his gun, and when the car came round the curve, he held up his gun and challenged it. A lady opened her window, told them that she was driving alone along this remote road, and seeing that it was a mail truck she was following, she thought by staying close to them she would be safe. His face red with embarrassment, the driver apologized profusely and explained their concern for the mail. He also assured her that they were happy to have her stay close to the protection of the mail truck. And so they proceeded to whichever point they were heading for, and Jack phoned the plant to let them know that all was well.

This time when he got home, I could really rest my mind. The problems about over-heating were solved, the mail was being flown regularly and on schedule. By mid-August the Wasps had buzzed through 200 hours of service without any need for overhaul. For the moment, we were over the hump.

In a recent paper which Leonard Hobbs wrote describing Jack's engineering ability, he made the following statement which is appropriate here, as it pertains to the problems discussed in this chapter.

> His foresightedness was evident in many engineering things. Originally with the Boeing 40-Bs, which were designed around the Wasp engine, there had been a tacit assumption that the engines should go 300 hours between overhauls. This was a considerable advancement as it had taken extensive development work at this time to bring the famous Liberty engine of World War I up to a 100-hour period between overhauls. Before the 300-hour period was reached, the Boeing Air Transport operation got into serious difficulty because of the failure of the integrally cast rocker boxes on the cylinder heads. Utilizing only a single-cylinder engine, George (Jack) devised a gross overload test which duplicated in a matter of only 50 or 60 hours of operation the failures being encountered in service. The part was redesigned, new castings obtained, and very quickly proof of the correctness of the redesign was obtained.
>
> As a result of this single situation, George (Jack) devised a broad

service policy for the company which is a standard world-wide procedure today. He worked out a pro rata cost formula under which Boeing would pay only for the operation they had actually gotten from the engines and new parts would be furnished to them. Foreseeing that this one part was only an example, the agreement was put into general form to cover the entire engine. Boeing, who had apparently expected to have to pay the entire charge, was most agreeably surprised. Although many others had a hand in the eventual program, it was George's (Jack's) original conception of overload testing which probably had the most to do with the development of reliable engines, and this alone was what made possible air transport as we know it.

Chapter VIII

Aviation—A Force and Not a Farce

The productive years of Jack's life and the development of aviation are so inextricably intertwined that it is impossible to keep them separate. The events of the year 1927 are written in strong, bold type as the time when flying became a real factor in American transportation.

It was also a year of very special significance to us, for on September 7 our third child, and second son, was born. He was a fine bouncing baby, weighing 9.1, with a beautiful head covered with enough silky red-gold fuzz to show what his hairline would be, fine features, and—amazingly—blue eyes. He was born at home, since it was necessary to have a mother's hand at the helm, even though temporarily limited as to activity. When he was about an hour old, the nurse brought him in to dress him on my bed so I could see how beautiful he was. He grasped my finger tightly, and even then, his little biceps stood out as he pulled that finger. He was so delicious, I could hardly bear for her to take him back to the little attic over the sunroom which we had made into a room for him. The weeks when I had been worried about Jack's adventurous flights over the mountains had been made more bearable by the need for putting the finishing touches on this delightful project.

We sent a wire to my parents, announcing his birth, which went like this: "Arrived safely, after short and pleasant journey. Mommy and Daddy very happy," and signed it, "Peyton Hoge Mead." My mother answered the phone when the wire came and said firmly after the message was delivered, "There is no such person." The telephone operator and I had gone to school together, and she said, "Mrs. Hoge, don't you think Cary's got another little boy and named him for Doctor?" "Oh no," said my mother, "we aren't expecting any grandchildren from Hartford just now." But Ida called her back again, insisting that this must be what it was, since the wire came from Hartford. Mamma needed a good deal of convincing, but finally she and Father thought it must be so. They sent a warm and loving night letter of congratulation and love and many admonitions to take care of myself.

The children were enthralled. They could enjoy this baby from the very first, and they did. And he was the best baby—ate and slept and flourished, right from the start. Jack was simply ecstatic about him. He would come home, tired from a day at the plant, and a few minutes with Peyton would erase the lines of strain and fill his face with light. Having spent most of his early life as an only child, and since he was the son of a busy doctor who never had a chance to enjoy regular hours and family life, our children were a source of unending wonder and joy to him. He always managed to have a little time with them before they went to bed, and those times came to be known as "love time."

The day Peyton was three weeks old, Leonard and Idamae Hobbs came to Hartford to live. He was to work closely with Jack. We had met him some time before when he was with Scintilla Magneto, and the two men had realized an instant affinity. They had the same approach to all engineering problems: meticulous attention to detail and complete integrity in their thinking. Between the two there was the close understanding and congeniality which made them the best of friends. The Hobbses came for luncheon the first Sunday they were in Hartford, and there began for me one of the most wonderful friendships of my whole life. In the years that have passed, whenever there was a crisis of any kind, the Hobbses were there to help us meet it. No one was ever blessed with such loving, loyal, helpful, and devoted friends.

It developed that Idamae's birthday and our Jackie's were on the same day. Leonard had to go away just before the 28th of November, so we had a joint birthday party for her and Jackie to keep the day from being so desolate. It worked fine. I invited four little boys to make up the five for his fifth birthday, and as many adult friends as I could corral on short notice, to meet Idamae. It was a horrible, dreary afternoon, with rain coming down in dismal November fashion, so I was glad that she was not cooped up in her hotel room. The Bond was Hartford's only respectable hotel at that time, and that was about the only complimentary thing you could say about it. This sharing of birthdays became a habit, and when on occasion the Hobbses went to visit their families in Chicago or New Mexico at Thanksgiving time, we always felt we had been swindled.

Soon the Hobbses found an apartment at the corner of Quaker Lane and Farmington Avenue; thus they could bid goodbye to the Bond Hotel, and I think we were almost as happy as they were. It didn't take Idamae long to turn that apartment into a home.

In the spring of 1928, steady hard work with little time off finally caught up with Jack. He was dragged down by severe, stubborn colds; and a tooth extraction, which had broken into the underside of his antrum, releasing and distributing a great deal of infected drainage, necessitated an operation. Dr. Pinckney W. Snelling—Pink, we called him—had come into our lives when the children's tonsils needed to come out. He was an ear, nose and throat specialist. He went over the problem and explained to Jack what he thought should be done. It sounded awful to me, but it made sense to Jack, and we decided to go ahead when the present infection cleared up.

My mother came on to be with the children. Even though we had a wonderful little nursemaid named "Dell," they would need extra loving with their Daddy in the hospital and me with him most of the time. Dad Mead came down to watch the operation. Since I am the kind of person who can work best when not being watched, this troubled me some. I wanted Dr. Snelling's full and complete attention on what he was doing—not partly on an older visiting surgeon, who was also the patient's father. I should have realized that it is part of a surgeon's training to teach others as he operates, but I wasn't thinking about anything except that my dear one was undergoing a dangerous operation.

The night before the operation, Mamma and Dr. Mead tried to make the evening meal a pleasant and enjoyable occasion. Jack responded gaily to their conversation, but this time I was the one who had trouble holding up my end. As the meal went on interminably, with Mamma and Dad—who were both great talkers—trying to out-do each other in the matter of anecdotes, Jack would twinkle across the table at me, as much as to say, "Cheer up, Honey, this time tomorrow night, you'll be feeling cheery, too!" But all I wanted was for that everlasting supper to end, so I could take Jack to the hospital and come home and say my prayers in the quiet of our own room.

The next morning everything went beautifully. Dad was most admiring of Pink's skill, and Jack came along far better than we had dared to hope. Each day I'd bring one of the children down for a little visit. How he did enjoy those visits! However, after he had been home a couple of weeks, Dr. Snelling thought it would be a good idea if the house could be quieter and suggested that I take Mary and Jackie, with Dell, up to Grammy Mead for a couple of weeks, so that Peyton would be the only one there. The trained nurse, Miss Ruth Geer, whom we all loved dearly, and who was still needed for Jack, could look after Peyton the parts of two days when I would be gone. Having Dell and the children put a fairly heavy load on Grammy, but she was all for it, and so that was what we did. By the time I went up to bring them back, Jack was in really good shape.

Margaret Todd and T. E. Tillinghast, a former Army pilot, had been married in late June, and they were spending a few weeks at Weekapaug, Rhode Island. They came up to lunch one day, and we enjoyed them greatly. I had met Tilly several times, but this time with his bride was different, and we were crazy about Margaret. It was tantalizing to meet two people in whose friendship we delighted but who lived as far away as Dayton, Ohio. Peyton was his most delectable self that day. Clad only in a sunsuit which fitted his plump little person like the paper on the wall, he was pulling up and trying to walk but was not quite ready. He was full of unintelligible conversation and as gay as could be. It was a delightful day.

In August we went to a lobster dinner on the Connecticut shore. Colonel Horner, Jack Horner's father, who was also chairman of the Pratt & Whitney board, was our host; and we had a delicious dinner and a delightful evening, smelling the good salt air and feeling made over new. When we got home, Jack asked if I would mind opening the garage door. This puzzled me, because I had broken my wrist several days before, and he had been concerned about my even going to this party. When we got in the house, he told me his side hurt so much that he could hardly walk. It could not, of course, be his appendix. What could it be? He had me feel a strange lump near the old appendix scar.

I got him an ice pack and managed to screw on the top with my one useful hand. It helped some, but Jack was in great pain all that night. As soon as it was decent to do so in the morning, I called Dr. Witter. He came quickly and said it was a hernia. The only way for Jack to get really well was to have an operation and repair job. This was a blow: two operations within two months! Dr. Witter called in Dr. H. Gildersleeve Jarvis, one of Hartford's leading surgeons, who came that afternoon, and Jack went into Hartford Hospital.

The aftermath of the operation was long, painful, and slow, but the illness was the beginning of a wonderful friendship between "Gilder" Jarvis and the "V.P.," as he always called Jack. This was one of the deepest, most rewarding friendships of Jack's life. It was entirely different from his friendships with other people. "David and Jonathan" is the only way to describe it. Through all the crises that came to us in the years that followed, Gilder was the sturdy oak on whom we leaned for courage, for help, (he operated on most of us at one time or another), and for comfort in anxiety or grief.

A miserable bug had attacked my interior while Jack was in the hospital. I ignored it as long as I could, but one day when Dr. Witter was visiting Jack, he looked at me and said, "You look awful," and took my temperature and sent me home. This was humiliation with a capital H. To succumb to some stupid illness when Jack needed me was the bitter bottom. The day he came home from the hospital, his side still hurt so he could hardly lean over to kiss me, and I was so weak I could hardly rise up enough to reach him. Sick as we were, the humor of it struck us both, and we laughed and began to improve. It surely helped for us both to be under the same roof once more.

When we were better, we had a celebration. One day, back in August, when Jack had been especially discouraged, Gilder had bet him a steak dinner that he would feel better the next day. If he didn't, Gilder would be host; if he did, Jack would be. Well, Jack *was* better the next day, so eventually the day came when we would have that dinner. The Witters and the Jarvises came, and in the course of discussion, Dorothy Jarvis mentioned "a little island in a lake in New Hampshire" where her family had spent the summers for three generations.

"Which island—in which lake?" Jack wanted to know.

"Oh you probably never heard of it: Kent Island in Squam Lake."

"Of course, I know it well," Jack answered.

What a bond that created! The rest of the evening was devoted to rapturous reminiscing between those two. The rest of us just listened.

So the summer of 1928 passed, filled with problems and pleasures—illnesses and troubles—but on the plus side, new and wonderful friendships to compensate for all the minuses.

Meantime, the amazing success of the Boeing air mail operation in 1927 and early 1928 had set the basic pattern for subsequent airline development, which before many years gave the United States the finest air transport in the world. There had been a variety of ideas about the possibilities of making money in civil aviation. Lindbergh's flight from New York to Paris in the spring of 1927 had triggered a surge of emphasis on personal airplanes. Enthusiasts thought it would be great to hop in your plane, as you would hop in your car, and go places in the "wide blue yonder." Pratt & Whitney was not impressed. They brought out no small engines to power these imaginary planes. In their wisdom, they realized that nothing would give aviation such a black eye as having a group of irresponsible, ill-trained pilots zooming around, getting lost in fog, bumping into mountains or each other, and generally impeding the steady growth, development, and design which could mean that the airplane could be a practical, viable means of getting from here to there, fast. Some airline operators believed that financial salvation lay in passenger service, not the mail. Others believed that passenger service would never pay, and that only airmail would yield any profits.

Pratt & Whitney and Boeing officials had many conferences to evaluate the situation. They talked to others about their ideas. They were convinced that by building larger, more comfortable planes they could pile increasing passenger revenues on top of the solid mail-pay foundation. Their objective was to work out a merger whereby they could produce under single management all the equipment needed for a complete operation. Thus they would be able to coordinate the production and assembly of engines, planes, and propellers, and operate them over their own airline.

The original group included Pratt & Whitney to supply the engines; Boeing Airline Company and Chance Vought Aircraft Corporation to build the different types of planes; Hamilton Standard Propellers (this was the result of a merger of two propeller companies) to supply the propellers; and later, Sikorsky Aircraft Corporation to build flying boats. Stearman Aircraft came in still later to build small planes if desired. The merger of these companies was finally completed late in 1928. The name of the new company was the United Aircraft & Transport Corporation.

Pratt & Whitney's importance in this merger is attested by the fact that it was the only engine company in the group. We were, of course, proud and delighted that Wasps and Hornets had proved their universal worth so quickly. The fact that other companies had wanted to merge with Pratt & Whitney was a tribute to the sound engineering and good management which characterized our company. Yet there was a pang, too. We would no longer be a little family company. Our original thirty-three employees had already expanded to over 800 in 1927. Now, with all the other companies, the Capitol Avenue plant was completely out-grown. After much thoughtful discussion, a site which could accommodate a complex of buildings, hangar, flying field, etc., was secured in East Hartford.

By careful planning and coordination, the first real transcontinental airline was inaugurated. Pratt & Whitney officials and Boeing felt that the time was right for a real emphasis on passenger traffic to add to the airmail service. Various other short-haul airlines were brought into the transport group, which bore the name "United Airlines."

By the time Pratt & Whitney celebrated its third birthday in August of 1928, commercial orders had pushed production to more than 100 Wasps a month, with the demand still outrunning the supply. All over the country, airplane builders, in an effort to expand the transport market, were designing planes around the Wasp. Ford's aviation division was one of the first to switch to Wasps. The Ford trimotor design was converted from 200-horsepower Whirlwinds to Wasps and became the standard airline work-horse until the mid-thirties. With its distinctive corrugated metal skin, the "old tin goose" became the most familiar sight along the nation's airways as passenger business expanded.

Anthony Fokker, the Flying Dutchman who was doing business in the United States under the sponsorship of General Motors Corporation at Hasbrouck Heights, New Jersey, switched both his single and trimotor transport designs to Wasps. Fokker also designed a tremendous thirty-two-passenger, four-engine monoplane transport powered by four Hornets. This was far ahead of its time. The four Hornets were mounted in tandem pairs, and Wright A. Parkins, later engineering manager of Pratt & Whitney Aircraft, designed a special cowling in order that the "pusher engines" could be properly cooled in each underslung nacelle. Fokker's wooden spars and plywood veneer wing covering came in for heavy criticism in 1931 after the crash of a tri-motor, so that wooden planes gradually gave way to all-metal designs.

In California the Loughead brothers, Allen and Malcolm, set up shop to begin the Lockheed line of high-speed transports. One of their first efforts was the sleek five-passenger Vega monoplane powered by a Wasp that was soon breaking transcontinental speed records which had formerly been held only by military racing planes. Also in California Donald Douglas converted an observation plane design into a commercial transport by substituting a Wasp for a Liberty and sold it in Canada, where there was an urgent need for a load-carrying aircraft that could get in and out of short, rough fields. In Buffalo, New York, Major Reuben Fleet converted the design of his Wasp-powered Navy flying boat into a thirty-two-passenger air transport, equipped with two Hornets, that pioneered passenger service to South America with the New York, Rio, and Buenos Aires Airline.

In 1930 Boeing and Pratt & Whitney had a new type of transport in the design stage, which was to give new efficiency for combined air mail and passenger service. This was the 247. The new concept marked a completely new era in plane design, and around this basic formula transports have been largely designed ever since. The plane was a low-wing, streamlined, twin-engine, all-metal monoplane with retractable landing gear. The original design called for a gross weight of 16,000 pounds and powered by two Hornets. United Airlines pilots, however, had become so accustomed to the "faithful Wasp" that they were reluctant to fly behind any other engine, and they didn't think it safe to operate a plane of 16,000 pounds gross weight from the airports of that day. In the face of this pressure, Pratt & Whitney and Boeing yielded. The 247 was scaled down to 12,000 pounds, with two Wasps and twelve passengers.

An early 247 became the company plane. She was loved by all of us, and so was Benny, her pilot. He would sit there in his seat, straw hat on head, his hand sure at the controls, and set her down in small fields as gently as the modern planes come in on their two-mile amesite landing strips, complete with radio beam.

Igor Sikorsky, even before joining United Aircraft & Transport Corporation, had built a famous line of amphibians and flying boats designed to be powered by Pratt & Whitney motors. "In 1929, Captain J. K. Montgomery, piloting the Hornet-powered Sikorsky, 'Southern Star,' was the first to fly a transport through the 18,500-foot Andean Pass between Chile and Argentina. When regular airline service followed across these frozen, gale-lashed peaks, it was in the Wasp-powered Fords and Fairchilds of Panagra and NYRBAA. In Mexico, Sweden, Peru, Czechoslovakia, Brazil, Finland, and Central America, dependable and now world-famous engines from Hartford were carrying mail, passengers, and freight."[1]

During this era Noel Wien and Calvin Cripes made the first commercial flight from North America to Asia—a 2,300-mile trip above the Arctic Circle—to deliver a $150,000 cargo of furs. They flew from Fairbanks, Alaska, to Cape North in Siberia. In steaming New Guinea, Wasps flew heavy machinery, men, and supplies to open up a fabulous vein of gold buried in the tropical wilderness. The Wasp made some of Canada's mineral treasures accessible. The Canadian bush flyers took to the Wasp so quickly that a Pratt & Whitney branch was opened in Longueuil, Quebec, near Montreal, to service and overhaul engines. James Young was president of "Canadian Pratt & Whitney Limited" from its founding until 1948 when he became chairman of its board.

Part of the history above was written as I was flying at 37,000 feet on October 18, 1968, from Los Angeles to Hartford on a United Airlines non-stop flight—scheduled flying time four hours and thirty-two minutes. It had, of course, been forty years since United Airlines became a fact, but that was quite a change even for forty years.

I never cease to marvel at the miracle of flight each time I board one of these great leviathans of the air. They often carry 150 or more passengers who are comfortably seated, who will be served a delicious hot meal, who will be entertained by a movie or music if they prefer, who can plan on going ahead with their desk work because it is so smooth. Then I think back to the time when I was a girl, when, for instance, Ruth Law did stunt flying at country fairs—looping the loop and what-have-you in a small fragile plane; or, a few years later, in 1919 when I took my own first flight—a twenty-minute hop in a Curtiss flying boat; and still later an earth-shaking experience in Bill Stout's famous Ford tri-motor which carried twelve passengers behind three Wasps, and *we flew all the way from Hartford to New York, non-stop!*

Chapter IX

The Wasp Goes International and We Go Rural

Ever since we had moved to Hartford, we had liked to drive three miles west on Albany Avenue and then to walk four miles around Reservoir #6. Everyone kidded us about our "country estate," but kidding or no, we loved it. Perhaps it made Jack feel less removed from his beloved lake and mountains, though the Avon hills were certainly a far cry from the White Mountains, and the two-mile-long reservoir was not very much like nine-mile-long Squam Lake with its islands, bays, beauty, and infinite variety. But it was country and there was no traffic: we could have been many miles from a bustling city.

One gorgeous Saturday in February, when in spite of deep snow the air held a promise of spring, we went to "our reservoir" and as we were walking on the high ground east of it, we noticed still further to the east a stand of pine on a hill, and south of that an open field. We took off cross-country, through or over fences and scrub cedar, and came at last to a more or less flat hilltop east of the pines. There were several fences, but no buildings, and only a very rough, almost unused farm road. No one had been up there since the snow. We could see cars going along a road less than a half mile away, a weathered house on the near side, and some farm buildings on the far side. The field we had seen south of the pine woods did not seem to be part of the place. That particular fence looked like a boundary, and not simply a fence for a pasture. To the north, we could see Mount Tom and some lesser, nearer hills; to the south, the "hanging hills of Meriden"; to the east, Hartford, the windows of its buildings aflame in the late afternoon sunshine; and beyond it, the hills which form the eastern rampart of the Connecticut River Valley.

It was a case of love at first sight for us both. "Oh, if only"—could it be possible that the owners wanted to sell? How could we find out? We crawled back through all the fences and went home with our hearts and hopes high, in a state of unbelievable excitement. Today we would say we were on cloud nine, but that phrase hadn't been invented then.

Jack asked a friend, who was in real estate, to inquire. The land, we learned, was near the Bloomfield-West Hartford line. There were about eighty acres west of Mountain Road and maybe ten east of it. It was owned by a very old lady and her three seemingly almost as elderly children. The son had asthma and could no longer work much about the farm. One sister did what she could about the cows, chickens, and geese. A second sister tended the house. They wanted to sell—not for house lots but to a family who would use the whole place for a home. Their price was plenty high, but the merger of all those companies had been advantageous to us financially; so, after careful thought, weighing the pros and cons of living in the country, where the children would have to be taken to school and everywhere else, we decided the advantages outweighed the disadvantages, and we made an offer to buy. It was accepted.

We agreed that the original owners could live in their house for the time being, thus giving them time to find what they wanted; and we went ahead with plans for a new house on the hill, and with many windows all looking out on something beautiful. Because we were charmed with the home which F. Patterson Smith, a Boston architect, had built for Uncle Fred Snyder and his wife, Nan, we asked him to be our architect. He was a dear man but very slow. To one as efficient as Jack, it was maddening to work with anyone who was so gifted, so utterly artistic and full of creative ideas, but who simply could not get things done on time. The failing was not, however, very apparent until we began building. The conferences about plans were pure joy; and as the house began to take shape on paper, we grew more and more eager to get into it.

Early in 1929, the Bavarian Motor Worken Company (B.M.W.) made overtures to Pratt & Whitney to purchase the franchise to build the Wasp in their plant in Germany. I was horrified. Why should we sell our unique and advanced plans for engines to *any* foreign country? Jack reminded me that the basic design of the Wasp was well known all over the world, and that the plans they wanted were not our latest ones. He also made me see that it was quite possible that we might learn something from B.M.W. It did not cheer me any to learn that Jack was the one selected to go to Germany and meet with the board of B.M.W., see their plant, and act, in effect, as Pratt & Whitney's ambassador. An honor it surely was, but he had more than enough to do, seeing to all the engineering details of development and production—and well, I hated the whole idea.

The day when he was to leave drew inexorably nearer. The plans for our home on Mountain Road were in their final stage. It was almost time for contracts to be drawn. The graceful curving driveway which Jack had designed was complete. The batter-boards for the house were in place, but all the specifications were not nailed down, and I knew I was not smart enough to do that final nailing. I thought of the farm hand whose boss thought he had been working out in the sun too long so put him to sorting potatoes for size in the cool shade of the barn. The boss came back after an hour or so and was puzzled to find him looking haggard and dejected. "What's the trouble?" he asked. "This work shouldn't be hard." "Oh, it isn't the work," answered the farm hand, "it's these terrible decisions." And I knew there would inevitably be "terrible decisions" in the next two months.

About a week before Jack was to leave, officials of United Air-craft and their wives arrived from all over the country. Some stayed at the Bond, but most stayed in various homes. Claire Egtvedt of Boeing and his wife Evelyn stayed with us. Both found the temperatures in Hartford in June very trying after the cool fresh climate of Seattle. Our Westerly Terrace house was bursting at the seams, and we wished that the Mountain Road house were ready instead of just planned—we felt somehow that on the hilltop it would be much cooler and more comfortable. That week it looked as if Hartford was trying to show just how hot a New England city could be. And Mark Twain's old saying, "If you don't like the weather you happen to be having in New England, just wait five minutes" didn't hold true, for it didn't change, even in a week. But it was a full and enjoyable week anyway, and even though I could have wished there wasn't so much going on so that Jack and I could have had more time with each other, it was probably a good thing that the days and evenings were so full with gatherings of various kinds.

On the last day of the conference, Jack and I gave a picnic out at the Mountain Road place. The top of the hill was in a state of mess and confusion, with bulldozers at work, and piles of dirt and rubble. But the back woods, through which Jack had laid out roads and paths, were another matter. They were shady, cool, and calm. Wild flowers carpeted the ground—partridge berry with its tiny twin blossoms, Canada mayflower, wild geranium, etc., and lilies, bishop's mitre, and rue made exclamation points here and there.

While the men played crazy games, such as "Ducky on a Rock," we wives set the picnic out on tables in a little grassy dell, shaded by an old, mostly hollow, butternut tree, where Jack had earlier built a small lean-to cabin and a fireplace with two hip-high brick beds for broiling steaks. As evening came on, everyone assembled in this quiet place—which has been a special spot for three generations of Meads—and sang or just enjoyed the evening sounds. The spell of the sweet summer evening helped to ease the ache in my heart as I thought about the next day and the weeks ahead. Jack and I had discussed my going with him on the trip, but there was no one in either family who could come to be with the children.

The ocean seemed very big and wide as Jack and I packed his things the next morning. We had one final conference with Mr. Smith, the architect, before Jack took the train for New York. As the Ile de France was to sail at midnight, I couldn't see him off, so we said our adieus in Hartford. Then I set about the task of closing the house and taking the children to Rockport, Massachusetts, on Cape Ann. Jack knew how much I loved the ocean and had rented a house for us near Land's End beach, hoping that we would thus have a happier summer and not be so lonesome. It surely did help. There were expeditions to Ipswich to see the keel of a ship laid. It was fascinating to watch the master shipwright working with his adz and shaping the great oaken timber as expertly as a sculptor. We went to Gloucester to see the fishing boats come in. We even went fishing one day with a fisherman named Charlie, but all we caught was a pollack, and Charlie didn't think much of it.

Of course, we spent hours on the beach and in the water. The children would wade out until they were about up to their waists, and either jump the big waves or let them break over them, washing them in to shore. Several friends came at intervals, to spend a week or so, and somehow, the long weeks went by. The children were as brown as Indians. Peyton, with his blue eyes and blond hair, was especially adorable with his super-tan. He became quite a climber that summer, negotiating a certain cliff at the end of the beach with great care and determination.

Helen Jealous and her daughters, Barbara and Frances, were with us the last week before Jack was to return. I wanted to meet him, and Helen suggested she and I could take the night boat down to New York the evening before he was to arrive on the Mauritania. By doing this, we didn't have to cope with the trains, and I wouldn't have to stay at a hotel. It was a great idea, and we had a quick and enjoyable trip.

The next morning I could hardly believe that within a few hours Jack and I would actually be home—after two long months. I had trouble holding my coffee cup steady, but thought nothing of it since my hands were likely to tremble a little when I was excited. The trembling seemed a little worse than usual, but then I was more excited than usual. Finally, the great ship came majestically up the river. As she moved closer and closer, I thought the pounding of my heart would choke me. My knees trembled so I could hardly stand, as I searched for the one face among all those hundreds that lined the rail. Then we saw each other almost at the same moment. It seemed to take forever to let the passengers off, but at last Jack was beside me, and the little matter of waiting to go through customs was of no importance. He was back—safe and sound.

We planned to spend that night in Hartford so he could see what had been accomplished at the Mountain Road place. We found that the foundations and parts of some stone walls had been completed. It was not as much as we wished, but it was something.

As I was getting dinner, Jack noticed my unsteady hands and fast heartbeat. I was sure it was just happiness because he was home. But he said I'd been happy before, and nothing like this had happened. I should see Dr. Witter, but he was on vacation, and the doctor covering for him couldn't find anything to explain the pulse.

So we went on to Rockport the next day, and Jack had a few days with the children before he returned to the plant. He would check on everything there, come back for a week, and then we would all go home together. Once more things didn't work out as planned. When he got back, I had to admit that something was really the matter. I had lost thirty pounds in three weeks, and I had to haul myself up the stairs by the banister. Jack got his Dad, and they put me in the Winchester Hospital. In due time they found out I had a toxic thyroid condition, and the only thing to do was to operate.

What a way to welcome Jack home! They had to fuss around for a couple of weeks to get me in better shape. Then it turned out that the surgeon wouldn't operate anywhere except at Massachusetts General, and Dad didn't want me moved. But he soon found a new surgeon—Dr. Arthur Allen. I'll never forget him. When I started to thank him for being willing to do the job there, he said, "You'd better not thank me yet. I may give you an awful pain in the neck." Well, he didn't, because my neck was numb for weeks, but oh what joy to be able to walk without holding on, and eat without spilling. It was as if he had turned off some poison, and I guess that's just what he did.

My parents had been alarmed at my awful handwriting and had come on to see what the trouble was. They got there the day I went to the hospital. Since Jack couldn't stay in Winchester all the time, he asked a garage owner if he knew a reliable young man who could drive my parents back and forth to the hospital and do various errands. Yes, he did, and introduced us to Harry Bergstrom, who was only eighteen, but a fine, steady driver as well as a fine, steady person. He helped us out then and has helped us out ever since, except for the three years during World War II when he was in the Navy.

While I was in the hospital, Jack received a letter from his friend Ora Brown, who owned the general store in Ashland, New Hampshire, and who also ran a real estate business there. (I might add that he was also active in politics, ran for governor and was nearly elected.) He had learned that a farm on Squam Lake which looked across Sturtevant Bay toward the Sandwich Range had come on the market to settle an estate. Knowing Jack's love for that country, he wondered if he would be interested in buying it. Would he! Jack was thrilled. The place had been more or less abandoned for about twenty years; consequently, even though there were over a hundred acres, gorgeous woods, and considerable shore front, the price was very modest.

I felt somewhat overwhelmed at the thought of embarking on another big undertaking, and I felt a pang as I knew that the Hartford place—every stick and stone of which I loved—would no longer be Jack's first love; but I was certainly not going to be a wet blanket and spoil his fun. We planned to go and see it in October, when presumably I would once more be allowed to behave like a human being, and he would have things under control at the plant.

At last the day came when I could leave the hospital and go home. All the staff were devoted to Dad and had been wonderful to me, and I was grateful for their kindness and friendliness. But oh! the joy to be going home. No piece of Dresden china was ever given such T.L.C. as I. I felt simply great, and also a little bit silly about all the fuss, but it was mighty sweet to be so cherished.

When we reached the house on Westerly Terrace, there were all sorts of big and little surprises. The biggest was a combination record player and radio and glorious records to delight our hearts. I had orders to stay fairly quiet for a while, and not to drive for another month. Therefore, the record player was an especial joy. It was hard to go through the motions of being a semi-invalid, when I didn't feel the least bit like one, but everybody had taken so much trouble to get me well, I figured I should do my best to stay well.

On a golden day in mid-October we went to look at the farm. The town road leading to it said "dead end," and it was "dead" indeed. We felt like a "ship at sea on a night like this" as we lurched over the bumps and into the mud holes. We could only go part way up the drive, when we finally reached it, because it was blocked by fallen trees. The sights that greeted us on every hand were discouraging. Mr. Brown had said it was "somewhat run down," which was a masterpiece of understatement. The lovely old Georgian brick house, with its four chimneys, was almost buried in a horrible gingerbread type of summer-hotel-like cocoon. There were fourteen bedrooms, and all of them had been slept in and *left* for squirrels to bring up their families in (they had quite evidently found the beds delightful).

We went around to the north side where we supposedly looked across Sturtevant Bay to our specially loved mountains. They, at least, greeted us, rearing their majestic heads into the blue sky. We knew the lake was there, but we couldn't see it, because what had probably been lawn twenty years before had grown up in alders and "popples." We finally found a sort of fox run through which we made our way to the place where the ice house had been. The breakwater was still there, and as the lake was low at that time of year, we could walk out on it—and oh! what a piece of heaven on earth. This reach of the lake, which was set like a jewel among the hills of the Squam Range, burst on us. Then beyond, Sandwich Dome, Whiteface, and Passaconoway—Jack's favorites—rose grandly; and Red Hill was close by on our right to keep guard over us. I knew this could be the realization of a dream for Jack, though he had always thought in terms of a New Hampshire camp, not a farm. But this view, though it did not include Chocorua—the miniature Matterhorn of New Hampshire—was the one of all others he loved; and this bay, almost uninhabited, would be sheer heaven to him. It seemed to me that to fix up the brick house and surroundings would be a herculean task, but I would settle for this spot right here.

After retracing our steps, we walked down the farm road beside the big field to the woods, and I fell hard for them. The next day we rented a boat and went all around the shore. There was "good water" all along. This particular part of the lake was simply exquisite, as it turned gracefully around a point, and seemingly went on and on indefinitely. Jack was enchanted—and so was I, to a point—but the practical aspect kept nagging me and dampening my enthusiasm. How could we ever put it into any sort of order? How could we get any good of it when he had to be in

Hartford all but three or four weeks in the summer? And how would we cope with two places anyway? Then I would see that "New Hampshire look" on his face, and all my "good sense" seemed like nonsense. I also knew that if Jack bought the place, he would do so with his eyes wide open, fully aware of all the problems involved, but also fully aware of all the rewards which I, at that time, did not have the "vision" to perceive.

Jack got in touch with another architect friend of his, Richard Derby, of the Boston firm of Derby, Barnes & Champney. Mr. Derby drove up Sunday morning so they could look over the possibilities together, and Jack would not have to make another trip immediately. He also contacted Gene Sturtevant about getting in a crew to clear away the alders, etc., and so give us back the view of, and access to, the lake. Gene was a wonderful man—road-builder, land reclaimer, lumberman—you name it, and he could do it. His ancestor had climbed a great pine, which was still standing in 1929, and had surveyed the surrounding country from its upper branches. "Uncle Si," as he was called, had settled on Pine Hill, and from its summit he could see the five farms belonging to his children. Gene, a grand-nephew, stood about 5′2″, weighed about 180 pounds, was the strongest man I ever knew—and his rugged, weatherbeaten face had nobility written all over it. He was also a regular pied piper as far as children and animals were concerned. They all adored him and would do anything he wanted them to do.

When Mr. Derby came, he and Jack did some investigating and found that the shell of the beautiful old house was intact—just covered up; that the excrescences could be removed, the interior rearranged, and plumbing and heating installed. However, all agreed that modern comforts and conveniences must not detract from the original design and period of the house. There had been an ell on the west side, but Jack knew I would love to have a flower garden there, so we planned to put the ell with the kitchen on the east side, and the garage could go under it, as the land fell away at that point. This would be especially advantageous when we came up in the winter.

By the time we started home, I felt as if we were practically ready to move in. Of course, there were still some little matters to attend to, such as searching titles and actually acquiring the place. But the real decisions were made, and my husband was radiant. In spite of his ability to visualize what could happen, I doubt if even he was able to envision the joy that place would provide for all of us and many friends of several generations. It took several years to evolve from the run-down, over-grown, dilapidated place of 1929 into the beloved home and haven of happiness it has become. Perhaps this slow development was what has made it so very special.

Chapter X

The Crash

The crash had nothing to do with airplanes. October 24, 1929, will go down in history as the day when America came face to face with stark, tragic reality.

For some time, Jack had been deeply concerned about the national economy. The blithe assumption of bankers and brokers—as well as ordinary people—that the stock market would continue rising forever filled him with dismay. How could people be so naive? Couldn't they turn the pages of history and see what lay inevitably ahead? Financiers could converse learnedly about supply and demand, and an era of unprecedented prosperity. Jack knew that paper profits were just exactly that, and would soon be gone with the wind. He knew that there are certain laws which always hold true—such as, that what goes up will inevitably come down.

When the news of this came—the worst financial disaster in our history, and we heard of great fortunes that had been lost, we didn't grieve so much over them. In order to lose millions, you had to have them to lose; and having had the brains to amass fortunes, people should have better sense than to throw a good portion of them away. What did grieve us was the thought of the little people: widows who hoped to make a slender stipend grow; men on small salaries who wanted to buy a home and invested their meager savings in stocks which were "a sure thing"; or the small businesses that had over-expanded and so went bankrupt. Then there were the thousands upon thousands of people who lost jobs because the firms that employed them failed, or because they were in some of the building trades, and almost nobody was building.

I felt we were greedy to go ahead with our happy building plans when so many people had no home at all, no job, no anything. Jack, looking at it from a more practical *and* altruistic viewpoint, said, "But don't you see, Honey, we'll be providing jobs for a good many people who would otherwise not have them—and up country this will be especially vital. It'll make *all* the difference there." He was right, of course, and so we could take added happiness in the building that was going on.

Hugh Chatfield had joined the Wright Aeronautical Company as head of research shortly before Jack and the others left. I had met him once when I had gone over with Jack in the evening to check on a test that was underway. What was my delight, soon after we got home in the late summer of '29, to discover that he and his wife, Grace, had come to Hartford so that he could be in charge of research at United Aircraft. I was equally delighted to hear that the Tillinghasts had come to Hartford so that he could join the aircraft team as executive engineer. The Chatfields, Tillinghasts, Hobbses, and the Willgooses were really our closest friends. We loved the Rentschlers also, but they were away a good deal, so we did not see them as much.

Before going abroad that summer, Jack had characteristically arranged to use some of his equity in the company to set up a trust fund for his parents. He knew that Dad had not been able to put by enough for a comfortable retirement, in spite of their frugal and modest mode of life. Jack wanted his father to be able to retire comfortably so that he and Grammy could have a little fun—*and they did.* After all the grueling years of his heavy practice, he could at last take time out to enjoy life.

It was wonderful to see the difference which freedom from financial worries made to Dad. He and his friend, Alfred Higgins, whom we always called "Lord Alfred" because he had that "landed gentry" look about him, used to go off on jaunts together—and what a high old time they had! They were like two boys out of school, with the devil sporting in their eyes. They had so many projects in mind that they had a hard time deciding which one to embark on first.

Progress on the Mountain Road house was maddeningly slow. However, the walls were pretty much up by November, and the roof began to go on by Christmastime. By good fortune, winter came late that year, so the men were able to work under shelter when snow finally did come. But even that did not speed our progress. It seemed impossible for Mr. Smith to visualize how the wainscoting should be until the moment arrived when it should be put up. Then, he had to sketch it, draw it to scale, go to the mill to select the clear pine—and then we would wait and wait for the wood finish to come. I marveled at Jack's patience. He would needle Mr. Smith a bit—always with a gentle courtesy, and with a smile in his voice. And when F. Patterson Smith would answer with a look from his blue, blue eyes, it was impossible to be angry with him, even though Jack and I were ready to tear our hair out by the roots. Yet, as I look at this house now, after living in it for almost forty years, I still marvel at the charm and artistry of the details; and I thrill at the love and appreciation which our children and grandchildren feel for this home which has sheltered them and welcomed their friends through all these years.

The year 1929 melted into 1930. I rather doubt if there was much of the usual enthusiasm to welcome the new year. As the effects of the crash grew more and more devastating, as money got tighter and banks and companies failed, the only thing that really increased was unemployment. It speaks well for the soundness of United Aircraft management that such a young organization could survive the financial debacle which held the country in its grip. True, the Army and Navy were our largest customers, and of course the air mail part of our business continued unabated. We were grateful that our men did not have to be laid off and that our contracts were not broken at that time.

President Hoover endeavored to bring about a steady, though

slow recovery. It is sad that such a great man and great president could not have had a second term in which to carry through the careful, far-sighted plans by which he hoped to achieve this healthy recovery, and which he had set in motion. He was stymied at every turn by an impatient people and an unfriendly, uncooperative Congress.

Meantime, our purchase of the New Hampshire property had been completed. Jack had arranged with a builder in Center Harbor, Henry Leighton, to remove the hideous excrescences which covered much of the lovely old brick house. Mr. Leighton rigged a sort of tent arrangement to shelter the interior, which would be exposed when he removed the roof and wooden "barnacles," and went to work. There was not too much concern about weather damage because the interior had to be pretty thoroughly removed anyway (the plaster was sagging; the paint had peeled; the woodwork was ugly black oak); but the men had to be sheltered while they got the new roof on. After that, the partitions could be replaced, the plumbing could be roughed in, and the heating installed. Soon after that, plastering would begin. Doors were being made at a good mill, using one beautiful old door as a model. This mill, the name of which I have forgotten, did such excellent work on the doors and door jams that all millwork was entrusted to them. Since we were trying primarily to restore the house to its former dignity and simplicity, the architectural drawings were simple and straightforward, and the work therefore proceeded rather quickly.

Needless to say, through that winter and spring there were frequent trips to Center Harbor to follow up the work. We were able to stay at the Anthon Farm, about a mile from our place, which we had re-christened "Mead Farm." On one of these trips in May, Gene Sturtevant spaded up the spot that was to be my flower garden; and I cultivated it, raked, and planted it. We left late Saturday in order to attend church on Sunday; and Gene must have realized that I would be concerned about the tender little transplants. He said to me just as we were leaving, "I'll water your posy bed for you tomorrow. Ordinarily I don't work on Sunday, but that's kinda like saving a life on the Sabbath, ain't it?" It surely was, and I was touched at his thoughtfulness.

Jack, knowing that there would be many unsolved problems that first year, had planned his work so that he could do most of it in New Hampshire. As I mentioned earlier, the Wasps and Hornets were going through a period of development and refinement; and Jack's work could be done more effectively away from the distractions and interruptions which were an inevitable corollary of working at the plant.

In early July of 1930 the remodeling of the brick house was just about complete. Jack and I planned that the children and I would go up about the 10th. He had gone up a few days earlier to push things along. The movers were engaged; some furnishings from Westerly Terrace were going to New Hampshire, while the rest went to storage until they could go to Mountain Road. Our hearts were light as we drove through the delightful summer day. But again, things did not work out quite as we had planned. The painters had just put the second coat on all the downstairs floors that day! So when the movers finally arrived, all our goods and chattels had to be unloaded on what passed for a front lawn.

Jack had reserved a couple of rooms at the Anthons and had arranged for us to have supper, breakfast, and lunch there. Presumably the paint would be dry by the next day and we could move in. Mercifully it did not rain; the paint did dry; and all was well. When our simple furnishings were finally inside and in place, the house began to take on the look of a home. Outside, the new flower garden against the west wall of the house was beginning to show color, and thanks to Jack's foresight, there was a little beach for the children at the lake. We always liked to think that maybe the place looked pretty much as it had in 1800, when it was built.

So began our first summer on what one of our closest friends described as "the most beautiful lake in the world." There were some problems—ah yes! For instance, electric power had not been brought near us. Anyone within three miles who used electricity had a little generator. So we had one—a small Kohler—the kind that went on whenever a light or the hot water heater or the refrigerator went on. The result was it ran most of the time. It was in the cellar right under our downstairs bedroom and exhausted out of the cellar window and back into our windows. Also, you'd no sooner go to sleep than some appliance would start up. The resulting roar of the generator would have wakened the dead.

The stairs to the second floor were on one side of our bedroom; the kitchen door on the other side; the road over which everything was hauled to grade the lawn north of the house ran right by our south windows; and the children were overhead. Jack was worn out from the unremitting grind of the past few years, and he needed some extra sleep. I had hoped he could have some naps in the afternoons when the children were having theirs, but it didn't work out that way. If we had lain awake nights trying to figure out how to drive ourselves crazy, we couldn't have done a better job. And to compound our problem, Grammy Mead was so happy about our having the place that she frequently rented a boat and brought a half dozen or so of her friends over to see it. Mary was especially devoted to Grammy and could never get enough of her, and when these boatloads would arrive for a short call, she felt she couldn't bear to part with them and urged them to stay for lunch. Since lunch, unless planned for guests, was likely to be the most casual of meals, this habit often filled me with dismay as I frantically cast about in my mind as to what I could produce quickly for so many; but I should have known I could trust Grammy not to put me to the blush.

Mary and Jack had learned to swim, and Peyton, now almost three, seemed to be practically amphibious. We had him wear a little life preserver whenever he was near the lake, and he would jump off the dock into six feet of water without any fear. Jack and Mary, *without* life preservers, were equally at home in the water, though we, of course, never took our eyes or our minds off them for a moment.

Throughout the summer it was necessary for me to go to Hartford nearly every week to follow up the work on the Mountain Road house. Since we had sold the Westerly Terrace house, we *had* to move in when school started in September. By August, it was quite evident that the house would not be finished by mid-September, but at least the bedrooms, baths, and kitchen would be all set, so we could manage. It was certainly fortunate that Mae Beattie had come to help with the children after our illnesses in the summer of 1928. I could not have carried through all the diverse jobs which were now devolving on me, if I had not known they were in such good hands. She had that wonderful Scotch knack of keeping children happy and maintaining discipline, and they adored her.

The men in the engineering department who worked most closely with Jack came to Squam from time to time to wrestle with some of the problems which were always cropping up, because each time they took some big step forward in the design of any of the engines, they would immediately have a still better idea. "Engineering, like woman's work, is never done."

Two lifelong dreams had been fulfilled that summer. One, of course, was the acquisition of Mead Farm, and the other was a sleek Gar Wood motorboat which we christened "Teaser II." It could not, of course, be compared to Mr. Hoyt's boat, but it was a beauty nevertheless. I couldn't resist kidding Jack a little about selecting a "Gar Wood," after all the rivalry there had been a few short years before; but he figured since he couldn't have one built in the Nevin boat yard, this was the next best design. He knew every rock and shoal in the lake "by its first name" and could find his way on the darkest night. I never did learn to run that boat. It was so much more fun to enjoy his matchless knowledge of the lake.

That summer there was certainly never a dull moment. The old farm buildings near the brick house were about to collapse after so many years of neglect, and several farmers were glad to remove them in their spare time for the good material in them. The new barn, sheds, workshop, and garage for truck and tractor and Gene's car were going up on the south side of the neck, and the house that was there was being refurbished and somewhat enlarged for Gene. Some little distance from it was a smaller house for Jack Davidson who would tend the cows when we got them and the vegetable garden.

North of the brick house the grading on the "home lot" was finally done and fertilized and seeded, so that presently a veil of green spread faintly over it and then grew thicker and higher. The children were wonderful about remembering not to walk on the lawn while it was in its extreme infancy. On good days most of the time was spent at the lake, when they weren't eating or sleeping, so it wasn't too hard. How they did love it!

It seemed that the summer simply flew by. August drew inexorably toward its close, and we had to think seriously about going back to Hartford. That involved moving into the house on top of the workmen, school for Mary and Jack, and the demands and problems for Jack at the plant. It had been such an incredibly happy summer, so utterly different from the previous two. As I saw the lines of strain being erased from his face, I could hardly bear for it to end. There were still things he had to see to at the farm, so we planned that I should go down ahead with the children and get them all set, and the house in as much order as possible, and he would join us as soon as he could.

The last evening before we were to leave for Hartford, Jack and I took the canoe for a long paddle after supper. The drowsy notes of the thrushes at the end of the day and the soft night sounds that accompanied the fading of the tender light cast their peaceful spell over us.

Then the lonely, unearthly cry of a loon called us away from this idyll and back to our work. We felt a little solemn as we paddled back. We hated the thought of yet another separation, as we had had to be away from each other so much during the past two years, but we were full of gratitude for all the different kinds of happiness that had been given to us. We were still so young, and we had been given so much, and above all, we had each other.

Chapter XI

"Balbrae"

The first few weeks in the Mountain Road house were something to remember. Dividing the contents of the Westerly Terrace house between two somewhat larger ones took a little doing. We had taken every single kitchen utensil to New Hampshire. There was not so much as a dishmop, saucepan, or mixing bowl in Hartford. We had also taken all blankets, pillows, and some linen. I had made a careful list of the essentials for starting housekeeping again. I thought I kept our needs within reason, but it was still quite a list. The children and I arrived on Friday in the early afternoon. Idamae Hobbs, bless her, went to G. Fox & Company with me and took two pages of the list, while I took the other two, and we put in a busy couple of hours.

The next day Idamae came out bright and early to help us get unpacked and settled. Not only did she work like a Trojan, but she also brought a delicious picnic lunch which we gratefully consumed in the cool shade of an apple tree near what is now the rose garden. Then that evening she had us for dinner.

Our curtains, chosen and arranged for long before, had been put up, and the upstairs furnishings were in place, so it didn't take long to get the bedrooms in order. Downstairs, however, was another matter. True, the kitchen and dining room were finished and could be made ready for use very quickly. We put the sofa and two easy chairs in the dining room. It would have to serve as a sitting room for a while, as the hall, study, and living room were far from complete. There was not even a front door—just some boards held together with some cross-pieces and fastened with an iron hasp. Guests who crossed the threshold during the next few weeks were somewhat taken aback at that door and also the hall, which was the last place to be finished and broke on their astonished gaze with exposed studding, rough flooring and shavings, no light fixtures—about as uninviting an entrance hall as anyone was ever welcomed into.

My parents were coming for a visit the following week, and I was therefore eager to get the noisy work done before they came. In my youthful rashness, I told the carpenters that if they would lay the living room floor on Sunday—it was to be wide boards pegged down—I would cook them a bang-up chicken dinner, with all the fixings. I had plenty of takers. It was before the days of frozen vegetables, of course, and I shelled peas until I thought I would turn into one. I had never used an electric stove and had always heard that a person needed a special training course to use one, but the one we had selected was very cooperative, and the fourteen men who showed up that day surely did justice to the chicken with cream gravy, mashed potatoes, buttered peas, rolls, home-made jelly, ice cream, cake, and coffee. I even got cigars for them, which, since we were non-smokers, was a truly sacrificial act.

But fixing that dinner for them certainly helped a great deal to get the house finished. They not only laid the floor that Sunday, but from then on, they knocked themselves out to get the rest completed. Sometimes we sounded like ten houses being constructed, but each day saw some progress, and before long, the noisy, messy work was done. Of course, there was still waxing and rubbing of the woodwork, and the installing of light fixtures, but that was quiet.

I failed to mention that Mr. Smith had gotten hold of the

pilings which were removed when the North Station in Boston had been rebuilt a year or two before we started our house. These sturdy oak timbers had been under water for forty years and had then been drying for a year before we got them. These he used for the actual framing of the house—the exposed beams extending at least a foot beyond the uprights, making a narrow overhang for the second floor. The ends of these beams were supported by a plain, but beautifully wrought, oak bracket. The uprights for the second floor ended in a pendant dewdrop, also hand hewn.

All these charming touches were the work of a wonderful old carpenter who had, I am sure, been a shipwright, because he worked so expertly with chisel and adz. He had a chisel with a rounded blade, with which he made the groovings on the lower edges of the beams. His were the hands that wrought many of the unique and exquisite touches which, as one grandson remarked recently, "make this home so great." Hand skills have always enthralled me, and during those days of "finishing," I used to love to pause in my own work to watch him for a few minutes as he, with unerring accuracy, carved grooves, brackets, dewdrops, and so forth.

Mamma and Papa were enchanted. They could not believe that the cornfield they had seen less than two years before could have turned into such a gracious home, with lawn, flower garden, and shrubbery, all looking as if they had been there for a long time.

There had been two good-sized elms, an oak, and a maple that were in the swampy places that we had made into a pond. I had wanted to move them to the top of the hill—the very shapely elm and the oak to accent the lovely curve of the driveway, and the other more rangy elm and maple placed casually on the lawn east of the house. The landscape men were dubious about moving them from such a wet to such a dry location, but I argued that we could keep their feet wet until they got used to the change. The men thought there should be a third tree in the curve of the drive and found another elm that looked pretty spindly to me; but since they had done what I asked, I didn't quibble about that. It soon straightened up and "shaped up" nicely and along with the others grew and flourished. They have provided cooling shade for all these years.

Margaret Sayada, a Scotch friend of Mae's, came to help us out for three weeks and stayed for fifteen years and is one of the dearest people I have ever known. No matter how much company we had, she was always smiling and cheerful and helped me plan the most delicious menus; or if I was taken up with the children, or with Jack, she planned them without me. While my parents were with us on that first visit, she coddled them and did all the little extras for their comfort and enjoyment.

The day Jack got home from New Hampshire, it poured. It was only October, but the weather behaved like November. I had wanted him to see the house first in sunshine, but even in the rain it looked warm and inviting. The trees outside were still aflame, as were the fall flowers in the garden. He was delighted that so much was done—and that, of course, made me feel good.

It was just as well there were no headaches at home, because at the plant Jack and everyone in the engineering department needed to be ten people. This was true in all the departments. The struggle to keep new engines coming as fast as they were needed to meet the demand was a continuing challenge. The Wasp Junior had appeared toward the end of 1929, and the department was now working on the Twin Wasp. All these brain children performed better than had been anticipated.

In the meantime, events in the world of aviation had been following one another in rapid succession. Inverted flight was, in the 1920's, one of the unsolved problems of combat flying. It was difficult to work out proper carburetion for the engines because the fueling and lubricating systems of the different planes did not work well upside down. The fact that the pilots had not learned the technique of inverted flight was also a major cause of many accidents.

As late as the spring of 1928, the Navy issued an order prohibiting its pilots from flying upside down or attempting outside loops. However, the Stromberg Company conducted experiments at Wright and McCook Fields, where Jimmy Doolittle was credited with performing the first successful outside loop. Then, Lieutenant Al Williams explored the entire realm of inverted flight in a Wasp-powered Curtiss Hawk at Anacostia. Williams became a thorough master of the art of flying upside down. He worked out an acrobatic routine in which he did outside loops, inverted pylon turns (going round the pylons upside down), and then made his approach for landing in the inverted position until within 200 feet of the ground, whereupon he rolled over and side-slipped to a landing within a chalked circle. It curdles my blood just to think about it.

At San Diego, Admiral Reeves' pilots were experimenting with new aerial maneuvers that might be worked into combat tactics. Lieutenant D. W. Tomlinson (Tommy), who later became the chief pilot of Transcontinental and Western Air, Inc., was also exploring the technique of inverted flight in a Wasp-powered Boeing F-2B. With proper carburetor modifications, the Wasp performed well upside down, and the lower wing-loading of the F-2B made it extremely flexible both in normal and inverted flight. To demonstrate the feasibility of inverted formation flying, Tommy organized a Navy acrobatic trio known as the "Sea Hawks." His wingmen were Lieutenants W. V. Davis, who had navigated the winning plane in the Dole Transpacific air derby, and A. P. Storrs. They gave their first public performance during the racing meet in Los Angeles in 1928.

The performance of the "Sea Hawks" was amazing enough, but the true climax of the Boeing and Wasp performance came on the final day of the races, when the new Boeing XF4B appeared, fresh from the Seattle factory. This experimental Navy fighter was the first plane designed to take full advantage of the Wasp's power and weight. It was a trim, compact plane, which weighed no more than earlier fighters. It featured all-metal control surfaces to withstand the rugged maneuvers made possible by the Wasp.

Lieutenant T. P. Jeter (later Rear Admiral), U.S.N., won the "Aero Digest" Trophy in the military free-for-all, in the XF4B. He averaged 172.6 miles an hour. Even more sensational from a military standpoint was the XF4B's rate of climb. Lieutenant M. T. Seligman flew it in a race to 10,000 feet and back in an elapsed time of 5.92 minutes, compared to the water-cooled Hawk's time of 7.08 minutes. The XF4B was back on the ground before the Hawk even reached 10,000 feet.

Major General James E. Fechet was so impressed with the XF4B performance that he placed a verbal order for the new Boeing fighter then and there, and since the Navy had not as yet placed a production order, the Air Corps got prior deliveries and put the plane into service ahead of the Navy during the summer of 1929 as the P-12A. For nearly a decade the Wasp-powered Boeing fighters were standard equipment for the carrier squadrons of the Navy and Army Air Corps pursuit groups. Boeing built over 500 Wasp-powered fighters for the Army Air Corps alone.

During that period many of the pilots, who were to become the great combat leaders of World War II, put in their flying time behind Wasps in Boeing fighters—Spaatz, Chennault, and many others.

It was in the P-12 and the Wright Apache that the Wasp made another major contribution in exploring the thin, frozen air above 30,000 feet and lifting aerial combat to the levels at which World War II eventually was fought. High-altitude flying in the open-cockpit days of the P-12 and Apache was a brutal job for plane and pilot. The temperatures plunging to 70° below zero froze flight instruments and penetrated to bone marrow through layers of leather and wool. Pilots were thickly bundled in heavy, fleece-lined, leather jackets, pants, boots, and gloves, all so cumbersome they could scarcely walk on the ground. Faces were protected by a leather mask. Tiny pin-holes were bored in goggles so pilots could see after the lens frosted over. Oxygen masks were simply a rubber tube clenched between a pilot's teeth. If the oxygen tube slipped from a pilot's mouth at extreme altitude, he could not retrieve it from the cockpit floor in time to ward off the swift blackout of anoxemia. His only hope was to dive and reach the lower altitudes before he died.

Lieutenant Champion had continued the Wasp's climb to fame in the summer of 1928, when he surpassed the altitude record held by France with a climb to 38,744 feet in the Wasp-powered Apache. With pontoons substituted for the Apache's wheels, he had also set a new seaplane record of 37,995 feet. A fact which had not been noted in the international record books was that Champion made several high altitude flights in the Apache to test his equipment on the same days that he made his record flights.

Champion was succeeded in the engine section of the Bureau of Aeronautics by Apollo Soucek who continued the altitude explorations. He surpassed both of Champion's records in 1929, taking the seaplane Apache to 38,560 feet and the land version to 39,140 feet. This nearly cost him his life, as the temperature even in summer at that altitude is at least 80° *below* zero, and the plane was, of course, an open-cockpit job. The landplane record flight was a bitter battle against this uncharted altitude. Soucek flew with his ears and nose plugged to insure breathing only the pure oxygen flowing to his mouth. Near the peak of his climb over Washington, his goggles frosted, forcing him to remove them to see the flight instruments. With the goggles off, his eyes began to freeze. Holding the goggles a few inches in front of his eyes as a crude windbreak with one hand, Soucek held back with the other hand the supercharger spring that would automatically reduce engine power for a dive if he lost consciousness and flew with the stick between his knees. At the apex of his climb, the Apache fell into a spin for 2,000 feet before Soucek could recover.

A few weeks later a German pilot pushed this record up to 41,794 feet. Soucek spent months preparing to beat that record. His brother, Zeus Soucek, designed electrically heated goggles and gloves and a rubber bulb fastened to the control stick as a crude oxygen regulator when squeezed by hand. With the Wasp-powered Apache, Soucek then struggled up to 43,166 feet over Washington, D.C., and cruised there in a temperature of 85° below zero for twenty-five minutes, trying to push higher. "My engine had plenty of soup," he reported later, "and I didn't use nearly all of it. I believe if I had had one more degree of pitch on that prop, I could have gone considerably higher. In spite of the fact that I kept the engine revved up to 2100 or 2350 all the time, she didn't give a sign of trouble. The prop kept pulling up to 43,000 feet and then it just fanned the air. There was lots of power left, but I couldn't use it." When one stops to think that only twenty-five years had passed since man had first flown machines heavier than air, this is simply phenomenal.

The addition of the Boeing P-12 to Army Air Corps squadrons soon lifted their combat level nearly three miles. The First Pursuit Group began receiving the P-12A in the summer of 1929. It was powered by a new Wasp, rated at 450 horsepower and equipped with a General Electric supercharger impeller for high-altitude performance. A year later an entire squadron of the group flew combat formations at 30,000 feet.

Another P-12A-equipped squadron was soon making routine flights of 400 miles at altitudes of over 25,000 feet, maintaining combat formation all the way. Maintenance needs were so minor that these squadrons could operate at great distances from their permanent bases.

The Hornet was first used in the bomber program in 1928 when each of three planes competing for a production contract was powered by a pair of the early 525-horsepower engines. Although the Air Corps never completely abandoned liquid-cooled-engine development, as did the Navy, virtually all its combat aircraft were powered by air-cooled engines until the eve of World War II.

Both the Wasp and Hornet engines were going steadily up in power during these years. The Wasp had been rated at 450 horsepower in 1928; by 1933 its power was up to 550 and it eventually reached 600. The Hornet, which had originally delivered 525 horsepower, hit 700 in 1933, weighing only 840 pounds, thus giving a ratio of 1.2 pounds per horsepower. This was the lowest then attained by *any* engine. The Hornet eventually climbed to 875 horsepower. The Wasp Junior, which appeared as a 300-horsepower commercial engine in 1929, surpassed the original Wasp with a 425-horsepower rating in 1933.

These increases in power were the result of continuing improvement in the design of components: cooling fins on piston sidewalls; replacement of castings with forgings; improved cylinder cooling fins; improved cowling; automatic power and mixture controls. They were also attributable to the development of better fuels and Pratt & Whitney's basic program of developing and improving the highly stressed engine parts to carry greater loads more safely. The truth of the statement that the development of an engine has only begun when it goes into service has rarely been proved so convincingly.

Jack, Leonard Hobbs, and Andy—really the whole engineering team—labored tirelessly to make these improvements. I often noticed Jack seemingly toying with his pocket slide rule, which almost seemed like a component of himself, and jotting things down in his little notebook. I knew that the wheels were turning, and soon, from those jottings, some significant improvement would emerge.

The tremendous increase in demand for both Wasps and Hornets, necessitating the almost unprecedentedly rapid expansion of Pratt & Whitney's facilities, kept our engineering department's noses pressed to the grindstone. Here we were, scarcely four years old, proud of course that our engines powered a big percentage of both Army and Navy planes, and spanned the country in commercial airlines—but constantly struggling to make it possible for the supply to keep pace with the demand. And my husband, as always, was agonizingly conscious of the fact that human lives depended not only on the accuracy and integrity of his thinking, but on the infinite care, precision, and meticulous workmanship that must go into the manufactured article. It was one thing when engines were being turned out at the rate of fifteen, fifty, and even one hundred per month. But now with thousands being manufactured!

Soon after his inauguration in 1933, President Roosevelt put into effect many "acts" which were designed to restore the country's financial health immediately. In attempting to alleviate the terrible poverty which had stricken so many millions of people following the crash, he set up all the alphabet soup of government agencies which created jobs for the jobless. Millions of dollars were spent to pay men for doing "busy work" when it could have been used to help businesses get back on their feet and so have provided real work for them to do and healthy financial recovery for America.

Soon after Roosevelt took office, the Senate Committee under Senator Hugo Black of Alabama decided to investigate the maritime ship program which had long depended on government subsidies. It did uncover a few small irregularities but nothing startling enough to attract the attention of the press. There was no publicity, and publicity was what the committee wanted. The hearings were called off, without going into the air mail subsidies. (All airlines carrying mail at that time were partially subsidized).

Some eight months later, early in 1934, the investigating committee got hold of the complete financial story of the formation of United Aircraft and Transport Company, which had resulted in some sizeable fortunes for some of the officials. It also learned of a meeting of all the airlines carrying mail that the previous postmaster general had called for the purpose of consolidating and simplifying the country's entire route structure, which had grown up rather haphazardly. Senator Black and his people decided that by using the story of the fortunes which had been acquired right before the crash, largely from government business, they could get the newspaper headlines they had been striving for. Then, by painting the postmaster general's meeting as a monopolistic conspiracy to split up the air transport business among a favored few, they could put across the picture of graft and cheating they had originally attempted to produce.

The theme for the intense publicity that was fed to the press each day before the actual Senatorial hearings took place was the money that had been made and the virtual "criminal conspiracy to allocate the country's air transport system." At this point, the committee almost over-played its hand. As a spectacular to top off the publicity and punish the malefactors, the President ordered all United States air mail contracts cancelled. This, of course, left the country with no air mail service, so he ordered the Army Air Corps to carry the mail. The Army pilots did not have the "know-how" required for carrying the mail. Their training was for completely different types of problems. The result was that a large number of fine young pilots were killed and a number of Army Air Corps planes were wrecked. After a disastrous few weeks, the former operators were asked to help the Air Corps, and did so, but the situation was so bad that the administration had to halt the Air Corps mail delivery and turn the air mail business back to the people whose contracts had been cancelled.

The Senatorial hearings were finally held. I won't go into them too much, as it is all ancient history now. But there are some parts that should be remembered. The day Jack was to testify in Washington was probably one of the hardest days I had ever had to live through at that time. I had thought that anything which questioned his integrity would knock him for a loop. Instead, it merely made him furious, stiffened his spine, and sharpened his wits, so that he completely confounded the Black Committee. Stuart Mapes, Mr. Rentschler's confidential secretary, phoned me from Washington before my husband was free to do so. He was jubilant and overflowing with admiration. He said, "Mr. Mead made a wonderful witness. He was just great. I wish you could have heard him" (So did I!) "He had all the papers with facts and figures in his hands, but he never needed to refer to them. He had them in his head too. He refuted the charges on every count."

Quoting a little from the newspaper accounts of the hearings: "Senator Black tried to prove that the Pratt & Whitney organizers had merely developed an engine that had been under development by the Wright Company when they were still employed there. Mr. Mead gave vigorous denial. Senator Black, 'Do you deny that they had developed this engine in their plant?' Mr. Mead, 'I most certainly do.' He continued, 'The Wright Company did have an engine of 350 horsepower which was completely developed, with which we were neither of us particularly well satisfied.' Then after some more hammering, 'Any engineer will tell you, and the records I am sure will prove, plus the officials from the Bureau of Aeronautics with whom we were working at that time, that the Wasp (Pratt & Whitney) engine was absolutely different in all major particulars from anything we had done at the Wright Company.'

"When accused of designing the Wasp while still an employee of the Wright Company, he said, 'If you knew how hard we worked at the Wright Company, you would know we had no time to design extra engines. You will find, by checking with the people who know, that these are the absolute facts.' Senator Black asked if the Navy had furnished specifications for the Wasp. This also Mr. Mead vigorously denied. He stated that the Navy said, "You go up there and build an engine for us on your own hook, and if it passes its tests, and we find on subsequent test flights that it is satisfactory, we might give you an order for it.'"

Later Jack told me about it in more detail than Mr. Mapes had been able to give over the phone. He also brought the clippings from which I have just quoted. Senator Austin of Vermont had fixed his level gaze on him, and his straight-forward blue eyes seemed to indicate that he would see to it that these hearings were held fairly. His questions were straight and to the point. He, at least, realized the tremendous contribution which these men had made to the development of aviation. Through Senator Austin's questions, Jack was able to bring out the tremendous gamble it had been to leave a company that was established, form another company, and undertake to produce engines so superior that they could compete with his best work to date. He could also bring out that the stock for which he had paid a nominal sum was not worth the paper it was written on at the time he bought it. Furthermore, he could bring out that the company had not dealt in stock manipulations. "We had nothing to do with stock prices. Those prices represent what the public thought of our company."

He went on to say, "In order to be perfectly fair, I should add that we were in a period when we thought commercial aviation was going somewhere, and we happened to be right—we may never be right again." Then he continued, "We have built, over a period of years, an organization of between 4,000 and 5,000 men, and they have definitely contributed to American commercial and military aviation. And I think all our products are internationally famous, and that the men who built such a business in such a short time are due to receive some consideration for that."

These hearings were a pretty disgraceful affair to be perpetrated and condoned by men high in government. Not one single incident involving graft, bribery, robbery of the government, or any illegal act of any kind was uncovered. Not a single individual was proven to be corrupt or to have committed any kind of dishonorable act.

There had to be some face-saving for the Black Committee, so Congress passed a law which had two important features. It barred *for life* the participation of any individual in any transport company carrying air mail, who had attended the postmaster general's meeting. This was probably one of the most unfair things Congress has ever done. None of those individuals had anything to do with calling the meeting, or with the agenda, but were simply there at the request of the postmaster general who had complete authority to do what he did. He had exactly the same authority as the C.A.B. today. The restriction on individuals was rescinded long ago, but too late, as all those men had either died or were too old to be affected.

The other provision made it illegal for any manufacturing company in aviation to own any part of an airline. This caused the break-up of United Aircraft and Transport into United Airlines, United Aircraft, and Boeing. It was probably the complete exoneration of every one of the intended scapegoats that inspired the vindictiveness shown in this law.

On the other hand, the cancellation of the air mail contracts was strictly illegal. They had been obtained in open competitive bidding and had in no way been violated by the transport companies. The administration, again to save its face, compelled the companies to go through the rebidding procedure to get their contracts back. In every case the route went to the previous holder. And more importantly, this illegality was confirmed when the government lost in court the suit the airlines instituted against it, claiming illegality.

It was grand to have my husband safely back in Hartford after the hearings—away from the vindictiveness of those who could not tolerate the idea of a company which succeeded not only in being solvent, but in forging ahead during this depression period.

The adverse publicity generated by the hearings under the Black Committee (it was well named) and the cancelling, even temporarily, of the air-mail contracts had considerably upset the time schedule of the orderly production of our engines in Hartford and the planes in the west. We did not immediately know on what basis we would be permitted to reorganize. It was a headache all round, but our team set to work doggedly to pick up the pieces, rearrange them, and go forward.

To recapitulate a little: the second Wasp Junior to leave the factory had begun its racing career in 1930 in a Laird Racer flown by Charles (Speed) Holman and had won the Thompson Trophy. After several other races, it began a new career on the Sikorsky amphibian used by Martin and Osa Johnson in two years of exploring in Africa and the Dutch East Indies. Its amazing durability under extremely rough usage was equaled only by the fantastic history of Wasp #817. This engine was used by Bernt Balchen in the first aerial exploration of the Antarctic on the Byrd expedition of 1929. It was installed in a Fairchild cabin monoplane. Plane and engine were cached in the Antarctic and buried under snow and ice for *five years.* They were dug out and test flown during Byrd's second expedition in 1934 after merely melting the ice and running hot oil through the engine. The engine started on the first attempt. No. 817 returned to the United States with this expedition after further Antarctic flying and then put in three years service with Pacific Coast barnstormers. It was then sold to the United Fruit Company and was still in use *nine* years later—crop-dusting banana plantations in Honduras.

No engine came anywhere near equaling the performance of the Wasp in the 1932 National Air Races at Cleveland. All of the four finishers in the eight-hour transcontinental grind were powered by Wasps. All the five prize money winners in the "Thompson" race used the Wasp, as did the fastest six planes in the Shell speed dashes. This was the year that Jimmy Doolittle climaxed his long racing career by adding the Thompson Trophy to his Bendix and Schneider Cup victories and setting a new world speed record for land planes. All this was done behind a Wasp engine in a plane which Doolittle had flown only once before the races began. Jimmy Doolittle's name is legend—a dare-devil yes—but the kind of dare-devil who has the courage to try what is difficult and never admit that anything worth doing is impossible.

During these years, planes were becoming more streamlined, and non-stop flights were covering greater distances. In August of 1928, the Lockheed Vega, a standard five-passenger transport which was built by the Loughead brothers, powered by a Wasp, had flown non-stop from Los Angeles to New York City in 18 hours and 58 minutes. Remember that this was one year after the transcontinental air mail route started with planes carrying 100 gallons, and *ten* stops across the country.

In 1928, a businessman named John H. Mears hired an air-mail pilot, Charles B. D. Collyer, to fly him around the world in a Wasp-powered Fairchild monoplane. Collyer and Mears made their trip in 23 days, 15 hours and 3 seconds. The Wasp-Fairchild carried them 11,000 miles across North America, Europe, and Asia, and required eight days. The 8,700 miles of Atlantic and Pacific crossings were made on a boat and required fifteen days. The Wasp functioned flawlessly and required no servicing.

Just two years later, 1930, the adventures of Wiley Post, Wasp #3088, and the Lockheed monoplane, Winnie Mae, began. This stocky one-eyed former oil field roustabout had become one of the finest pilots of his day. He had piloted the Winnie Mae and Wasp #3088 to victory in the Los Angeles–Chicago non-stop air race in 1930. At the end of 245 hours of flying, the Wasp got its first overhaul in preparation for the round-the-world flight of Post and Harold Gatty in the summer of 1931. Post and Gatty set a record of 8 days, 15 hours and 51 minutes for the 15,470-mile trip.

Winnie Mae and the Wasp visited Hartford in the summer of 1932 for another overhaul at the 440-hour mark, and then, 320 hours later got another thorough check in the Braniff Airlines shop in Oklahoma City in preparation for Post's incredible attempt to fly around the world alone.

Ray Peck went to Oklahoma City to supervise this important feat. Wiley, trying to get used to not sleeping, would keep Ray company as he worked far into the night, supervising the installation of a lubricating system that would enable Post to grease his rocker boxes from the cockpit in flight. Other endurance flights had come to grief through lack of in-flight rocker lubrication, and Wiley was taking no chances.

At Floyd Bennett Field, Pratt & Whitney's Lionel Clark gave Wasp #3088 a final check after Post tested out his Sperry autopilot and radio compass. Seven days, 19 hours and 49.5 minutes later, Post, the Wasp, and the mud-spattered Winnie Mae returned to New York from the first successful solo flight around the world in eleven gigantic hops, covering a total of 15,596 miles.

Wasp #3088 and the Winnie Mae went to the Smithsonian Institution in Washington, D.C., where they still hang suspended from the ceiling. Most of the pilots who flew behind Wasps felt about them as did Amelia Earhart. You remember that the plane in which she flew solo across the Atlantic was powered by a Wasp. After successfully completing this flight, in which she became the first woman to fly across the ocean alone, she wired Don Brown from Ireland, "I'd do it again with a Wasp."

The men who had made possible all these gigantic strides forward in the development of the aviation industry had been the targets of the administration's malicious attacks. And some people wondered why I didn't like Roosevelt. It was ironic that years later, after Jack had labored tirelessly and effectively in mobilizing the country's aeronautical resources to carry out the President's 50,000-airplane program in World War II, he (Jack) should receive a photograph from the President inscribed "from your friend, Franklin D. Roosevelt"!

It was in 1932 that Emma and Ray Walsh came to join our ranks. Ray headed up Hamilton Standard. They quickly won the friendship of all and became a most welcome part of the United Aircraft family. They lived in Manchester, Connecticut, but that didn't matter—we'd have gone much farther than that in order to be with and enjoy them. Ray had the same approach to his work that Jack, Andy, Leonard, Tilly, and Wright, and the other engineers had to theirs—meticulous, careful, and tireless. We blessed the day that brought him into the company—and our lives. The Walshes' coming had brought us much happiness and had meant a new and lasting friendship.

Winter melted into spring, and as always our hearts felt lighter as snow and ice yielded to the warmth of sunshine, and the earth stirred in response to it. One day, after a late, fast-melting snow, a giant paint brush spread a coat of green loveliness over the brown fields and lawns. Bulbs and early shrubs spread scarves of color across the landscape, and birds filled the air with song.

In the years since we moved into the Mountain Road house, it had of course lost the raw new look. It was no longer just a charming house but was a comfortable, lived-in home. We had thought long and hard about a name for this home. We wanted to incorporate the hilltop idea, but for a while nothing that really satisfied us occurred to us. Then Alex Brown, Jack's confidential secretary, a devoted and able Scotsman, who had come to work for him in 1929, suggested that since I had some Scots ancestry, we should simply translate "house on a hill" into Scots and call it "Balbrae." This name seemed to fit just right. "Balbrae" it became.

Chapter XII

Our Firecracker

After our problems with Lvoff, we had felt that since we both liked big dogs, we should not attempt to have another one so long as we lived in town. But when we moved to Mountain Road, we lost no time in acquiring a puppy. Airedales did not shed much, and since Lvoff, who adored Jack, had always made a point of depositing his white fur on Jack's meticulously brushed business suits, the choice of an Airedale would certainly be a comfort to him. After some searching, we found a six-weeks old Airedale puppy whom we named "Sandy." He was so small I could hold him on the palm of my hand. He was gay and naturally obedient, and with plenty of loving care and good food, he developed into a most enjoyable family dog. He had a house on the back porch so could live mostly outside until cold weather. He soon grew a handsome coat, with wavy black saddle, and curls on his head and the rest of his body. Having a very short tail, he wagged from his shoulders in order to express his delight at being with us.

As soon as the new barn at the farm in Center Harbor was finished, Gene got some good Guernsey cows from the Ernest Danes, who had a fine herd, and we named the heifer calves for wild flowers. The first two, naturally, were Daisy and Buttercup. They spent their time in a pasture near the house, and when we took Sandy to the farm the summer of 1931, he took a great shine to those calves. He felt, however, that they didn't take proper care of the insides of their ears, and he would get into the pasture and lick their ears assiduously. The calves would stand it just so long, and then the one he was working on would butt him. Nothing daunted, Sandy would go to work on the other. Between them, and some squirrels who tormented him from the pine trees near the garage, chattering and throwing cones, and a certain chipmunk, who lived under a big boulder near the stone wall, Sandy had plenty to entertain him. The chipmunk would sit on the boulder, apparently completely unaware of the careful stalking that was going on, until Sandy got within a few feet of the rock; then he would whisk under it with one swift movement, and Sandy would be left fuming and whining in despair.

The vegetable garden, under Jack Davidson's care, was most prolific, and this provided some useful outdoor occupation for the children and me. They learned to weed and to pick the vegetables carefully. We had a rule that everybody worked most of the morning—Jack, when he was there, in the study developing or creating his brain-children, while the rest of us did whatever most needed to be done. Then we'd all have a swim before lunch. After lunch and the children's rest time, if it wasn't too hot, we'd go on wild flower identification walks, or teach the children to row or paddle, before taking our late afternoon swim.

Jack had suggested to Gene that it would be nice to have some raspberry bushes. Gene never did anything by halves. If Jack wanted raspberries, Gene would make sure he had them. He planted four rows, 100 feet long. When those bushes started bearing—which was fortunately not until the following year—we could have supplied the whole town of Center Harbor. We invited all our friends to bring their pails and help themselves, but even so, picking raspberries, and the blackberries which grew near the end of the hayfield, and the highbush blueberries which fringed the shore of the lake took quite a lot of time. Probably the silliest question anyone ever asked me was that of a New York acquaintance who stopped by one day. She thought the view was gorgeous, "but what on earth do you find to do? You can't swim all the time." Problem—find time to swim at all!

After our rather hectic first two summers, Jack suggested we move the drive farther from the house. By raising a square of lawn near the front door and extending the garden thirty feet or so to form one side of it, we could create a much more attractive approach to the house. This was a wonderful idea, and together we worked out a rearrangement of the beds, so that the garden would not only be roughly twice as big but also far lovelier. By careful, but apparently casual questions, Jack learned the names of the roses I loved best. What was my delight, when we went to the farm in 1933, to discover that the two long beds which ran down the central portion, with a wide grass path between them, were filled with all those specially loved tea roses, and the four little corner triangular beds bloomed with floribundas. The border beds on all four sides next to the wall and little fence blazed with perennials.

Mingled with my delight at all this loveliness was a big lump in my throat as I thought of all the time and thought Jack had put into this project, while constantly carrying a heavy load of responsibility at the plant. There surely never was anyone who got more joy out of making other people happy, and if he could surprise them, that made it all the better.

Working at the house, even with the driveway moved, was somewhat like trying to be creative in the middle of Grand Central Station, because Jack's study was right by the front door. He, therefore, drew a plan for a tiny office by the lake shore—a room about eight feet square, with a minute screened porch, where there was *no telephone.* There was electric light, however, as it was shady under the trees. Here he would go, to work in peace and quiet. The children knew this was off bounds and that if they wanted to play at the beach, which was about 400 feet away, they were to keep their voices down.

From time to time, now that the place was in more or less decent order, various people from the Pratt & Whitney family would come up for a long weekend. We wives caught up on our handwork and the news, while the men put in prodigious hours either in the study or in the office by the lake. Leonard Hobbs and Andy Willgoos worked most closely with Jack on engineering.

The Willgoos daughters were in camp not far from us, so when Andy and Grace were coming to see them, we'd try to synchronize a visit with Idamae and Leonard. Thus Jack, Andy, and Leonard could share, exchange, and crystallize their ideas. These were years of continuing refinement of the Wasp and Hornet engines, but work was also beginning on the "Two Row" or "Twin Wasp." Power continued to climb, as new ideas were put into effect. The minds of those three men worked in such close harmony with each other, that with these intensive conferences as stepping stones, they seemed able between times to catch each other's thoughts from letters, sketches, and phone calls, and translate them into improvements on existing engines or into new designs.

Ray Walsh, as I mentioned earlier, was head of Hamilton Standard, and he and Emmy, sometimes bringing their son Bud, occasionally came up, as well as Margaret and Tilly and Grace and Hugh Chatfield. It was great! So, the summer of 1933 was a time of happiness and refreshment for us all. I was quickly becoming as much of a "Squam-maniac" as the rest of the family. The strength and majesty of the mountains—the delicious crystal-clear water of the lake, which was cool but not cold—the dignified old house which had withstood over a century of hard winters—all conspired to enthrall me and become a part of me.

But we realized we really needed a guest house. So Jack drew plans for a simple bungalow to be set among pines and maples, about 500 feet from the brick house, and focused on a clump of large pure white birches. It was to be a rectangle, composed of a long living room with a huge fireplace in the middle of the inside wall, two comfortable bedrooms, and two baths. There were two large walk-through closets between the chimney and the bathrooms. Theoretically the chimney would keep clothes from getting damp in rainy weather, and in warm dry weather the fire would not be going anyway. There was a big screened porch toward the lake from the living room, and upstairs was open space for a playroom. (This last was not 100% successful because when the children started romping around, it sounded as if the world were coming to an end—fast.)

When the guest house was finished, we fell completely in love with it and decided to move into it ourselves. That left the brick house for the guests. We had many good reasons for this, with which we salved our consciences. The guests wouldn't have raincoats and umbrellas and rubbers (and these were needed frequently). It would be more convenient for our friends and relatives—our parents, for instance—to be in the house where the meals were and not have to negotiate the path between the houses at night. The terrace was screened, and the view of the lake and mountains from it was far more glorious than from the bungalow. All these reasons were good ones. But the plain truth was that we just could not bear for this new and enchanting house to be unoccupied at all during the summer, and we just wanted to live in it. We had lots of fun fixing it up. The two boys were in the other bedroom, and Mary was upstairs except when it was hot, and then she slept on the deep window seat.

Jack had been unhappy about the decision to reduce the size of the Boeing 247 from 16,000 to 12,000 pounds, using Wasps instead of the much more powerful Hornets. I do not have a copy of the telegram he sent to Fred Rentschler, who was in Seattle conferring with Phil Johnson of the Boeing Company, but I recall that it ran as follows: "If you insist on using the Wasp, we will do our utmost to bring it through, so that it will deliver the horsepower required for the 247, but I urge you to use Hornets for these planes, as I do not believe the Wasp can provide sufficient margin of safety, even for the scaled-down model." Jack did not take much stock in the purported ultimatum by the pilots, to the effect that they would not fly the larger planes into the airfields then in existence.

All to no avail. Jack didn't often complain about his colleagues, but this flouting of his carefully thought-out advice upset him. Here he was, supposedly heading up United Aircraft's engineering team, because he was admittedly the ablest man in his field—but, because there was a desire to satisfy one of Boeing's subordinates, his judgment was ignored.

The Wasp *had* reigned supreme on the world's airways through the years that had passed since its first glorious flight in May of 1926. But Jack and Leonard both knew that the time had come for larger planes and, therefore, larger engines. The Wasps would still be required for many types of smaller planes for some years to come, but transport planes needed to be larger.

Jack and Leonard *did* "bring the Wasp through" for the 247. It did deliver the necessary horsepower, but the engines wore out faster than they should have. Thus, by manufacturing the smaller plane, the company lost out. This was a bitter pill to swallow. The board's refusal to accept his verdict on the inadvisability of using the Wasp hurt Jack very deeply, and the wound from this rebuff never quite healed.

Incidentally, it also hurt the company's pocketbook. Shortly after the Boeing 247 went into service in 1933, Douglas came out with a larger transport plane, the DC-3, which was powered by Cyclones and Hornets and took twenty-four passengers. This plane quickly captured the airlines market and acquired an enviable reputation for safety and dependability. Though larger than the 16,000-pound Boeing had been designed to be, it was flying into and out of those same supposedly inadequate airfields. It automatically obsoleted the scaled-down 247. Thus the design, patterns, mock-ups, etc., were all wasted, and the millions of dollars spent on getting the 247 into production went down the drain.

Some further comments made by Leonard Hobbs in the paper quoted at the end of Chapter VII emphasize the gravity of the 247 situation.

> George's (Jack's) power of analysis, another outgrowth of the thoroughness of his thinking, was well illustrated by an incident relating to the second series of Wasp engines to go into the 247 airplane. This was a higher power advance model to replace the original engines which were wearing out. We had been very thorough in its development and thought it to be completely ready for service when it was installed. However, although it was mechanically a good engine in all respects, it soon showed a tendency toward high oil consumption. George (Jack) was absent at this time and although it was not a dangerous situation, it was a very unsatisfactory one, and we did a considerable amount of experimental work and devised several different piston ring combinations which were tried on the airline. However, it appeared that when we got the oil consumption within reasonable limits, the cylinder wear was excessive, and if we got this corrected, the oil consumption went back to being too high. When George (Jack) came back, he immediately got into the problem and called for all the data which, of course, included our test results as well as the airline service experience. By deduction he devised a ring combination which, following some experimental testing, proved to be the solution to the problem.

Jack withdrew for a time from the vice presidency of the company, though he agreed to continue on a consulting basis, but he returned later when Fred urged him to do so. The great truth now came home to the board that it was necessary to design planes *as well as engines* for needs which were far in the future, if they wished to catch up in the airlines race. Jack never said, "I told you so," but I am sure he thought it, and could be forgiven for those thoughts. They—the board—became uncomfortably aware of the length of time it takes for a plane to evolve from drafting board to flight.

To me, and I am sure to his closest associates, my husband grew in moral stature during this time. He had every reason to be angry and a little bitter about this business which caused him so many sleepless nights. But he just went ahead and did his utmost to make the decision work out, even if he did not agree with it.

During the winter of 1933–34, we had many interesting visitors and contacts connected with the work and the international outreach of the company. During this year, the first regular air service to South America was inaugurated. We had a dinner party to honor Igor Sikorsky, who built the ships for this service, to celebrate the first flight. I don't remember what the menu was, but I did make very special hors d'oeuvres, carefully cutting out little airplanes from the whites of hard-boiled eggs. I arranged tiny thread-like bits of pimiento as insignia and four caviar "eggs" as engines. I had spread rounds of toast with cream cheese tinted a pale blue for the sky as a backdrop for these planes. I worked hours over these masterpieces, which of course didn't taste very good, as the toast could not be fresh and crisp; but Jack was delighted and most admiring. When they and the other "nibbles" were passed, and people just ate them without noticing, he called their attention to my works of art. He just was not about to have my efforts taken for granted.

It was on this occasion that I first met Mrs. Sikorsky. She had golden curls which fell around her shoulders. She looked just like a little girl. It was shortly before the birth of one of their sons, and she was so darling talking about Igor who was the youngest child in his large family. She said, "Of course I believe in big families. Just think, if Igor's parents hadn't believed in big families, there would have been no Igor Sikorsky." Her tone indicated that in that event the world might just as well have come to an end then and there.

Just here I would like to tell a bit about Pan American Airlines. From its early days in the Caribbean until it spanned both oceans, its ships were powered by Pratt & Whitney engines. Its chief engineer, Andre Priester, and Charles Lindbergh, its technical consultant, recommended the use of these engines as standard equipment. In 1932 conferences between Priester, Lindbergh, and Juan Trippe, the president of Pan American, had started the conquest of the Pacific. This service from then on, to the opening of the regular passenger service from San Francisco to Manila, and later to Hong Kong, was planned around Pratt & Whitney power and the airframe designing genius of Igor Sikorsky and Glenn Martin. Both Sikorsky and Martin designed special flying clippers for Pan American's Pacific fleet. These ships were incredibly beautiful. The hulls of the "boats" were as graceful and full of symmetry, and as perfectly designed as those of the early "Clipper" ships for which they were named. I have a picture of one about to alight in the bay at Miami, with an exquisite sailing boat nearby. The picture, taken probably about 1935, is a charming study of the old and the new.

When the Sikorsky S-42 took to the air in 1934, powered by four Hornets, with a rating of 750 horsepower each, it established eleven world records for sea planes. Crews for these splendid clippers were trained by Edwin C. Musick, commander, and Frederick J. Noonan, navigational director. These crews became skilled in instrument flying and, after thorough drilling, pioneered the Pacific route to the island stepping-stone bases built by Pan American at Hawaii, Manila, Wake, and Guam. In the fall of 1935 the larger Martin "China Clipper," powered by four Twin Wasps, took over and flew the first air mail from Alameda in San Francisco Bay to Manila. I have the envelope of a letter which was sent to Jack from Manila on the first flight.

For nearly a year the Sikorsky and Martin Clippers were tested with two-ton mail loads over the Pacific route. On October 21, 1936, regular passenger service from San Francisco to Manila began in the China Clippers. Later this service was extended to Hong Kong, where air connections were available with lines serving the Asiatic mainland, Africa, Australia, and Europe.

Late in the winter of 1933 our dog Sandy had died. He had

tangled with a skunk the previous summer, and the skunk squirted him in the face and throat. The effect was similar to that of ether pneumonia. He was a very sick dog, and I nursed him with all the care you would give a human. He lay mostly in the cool shade of the pines, and the squirrels threw sticks and cones at him and chattered and scolded, but he was too sick to care. Somehow I have never felt quite so kindly to squirrels since. He seemed to recover, but late in the winter his heart gave out one day, and Mary found him lying quietly in the snow; then she discovered he wasn't breathing. It was sad that she, the most ardent dog-lover in the family and the most tender-hearted, should have been the one to find him. It was her first experience with death, and Sandy was not just a dog to her, he was our first dog and a member of the family.

Much as we all loved Sandy, Jack felt we should have more of a watchdog type of dog. Since we were in the country, and he often had to be away, this seemed a wise move. "Erno," a beautiful and admirable German Shepherd, came to us in the summer of 1934. He looked fierce and forbidding but was the dearest dog and the handsomest I ever saw. He was mostly black but had tan trimmings on his paws, around his muzzle, and behind his ears. All his underside and ruffled panties were a creamy beige. He always kept himself immaculate, though of course we gave him baths from time to time to give him that extra-clean smell. He was definitely Jack's dog but was not a one-man dog, in that he loved us all, and if he wasn't with Jack, he would attach himself to anyone in the family whom he could find. He particularly loved having Mary sit on the floor so he could put his head in her lap to be stroked.

Later we got a mate for him, Anita. She also was beautiful, her markings much like his. She was gay and full of charm, and she used to badger him to play with her. Sometimes he would forget his dignity long enough for a romp, but his was a more sober nature than hers. He was convinced, however, that the waves in the lake were his own personal enemies, and when a boat sent a wake hurtling in on the beach, he would rush back and forth, barking furiously, and trying to bite them. He was also convinced that no one else could swim and always wanted to rescue us, so we had to tie him up when we wanted to swim. Then he would cry piteously—sure that we would drown.

The original owners gave us a set of commands in German, one of which meant to attack. We had never dared give Erno that command, as we didn't want him to attack anyone, but in case of need, we didn't want him to forget it. One day in the late winter of 1935, we made a very realistic snowman, complete with an old coat and a hat. We gave him the command, which he remembered all right! He leaped on the snowman, the head toppled off, and the whole thing collapsed, and poor Erno came cringing to us, his tail between his legs, as much as to say, "I didn't mean to kill him, honestly I didn't." We comforted him, let him smell the hunks of snow—not the clothes—and told him he was a good dog. Needless to say, we never gave him *that* command again.

On Palm Sunday of 1935 twelve German Shepherd puppies were born. One had a deformed paw, so we put him to sleep, but the other seven males and the four little females were beauties. They were just about the size of a chocolate eclair, and fortunately Anita was not concerned about my care of her and them. I was amazed at the way she knew just what to do for them, and I was also properly humbled, for she would be nursing one or two or three, and so on, until they were all born, lapping the newest one, and perhaps be in the process of giving birth to another one; whereas when July came, I would have one baby, and a doctor and nurse to take care of me.

Yes! About the first week in July our long hoped-for fourth baby would make his or her appearance.

What fun we had with those puppies, and what a lot of work too. Since there were so many, I took the strongest ones away from Anita, most of the time, supplementing their food with a bottle. Their formula was far more complicated than a baby's. We used a protein powder called "Kasek" for a milk modifier. It was wholesome, I dare say, but exasperating to use. If the water you mixed it with was too hot, it turned to rubber and would not mix. If the water wasn't hot enough, it wouldn't dissolve. It was much more aggravating to cope with than yeast, for instance, and I was glad when the "Kasek" stage passed.

Jack used to say plaintively when the alarm would go off at 2:00 a.m. and I would grope for robe and slippers and go down to the "catch-all" room where we had the puppy nursery set up, "When will they get past the midnight feeding?" I wondered about that also. I was surely getting back into the swing of things

A formation of Grumman F3F's powered with Twin Wasp Juniors.

The new East Hartford plant nearing completion, 1930.

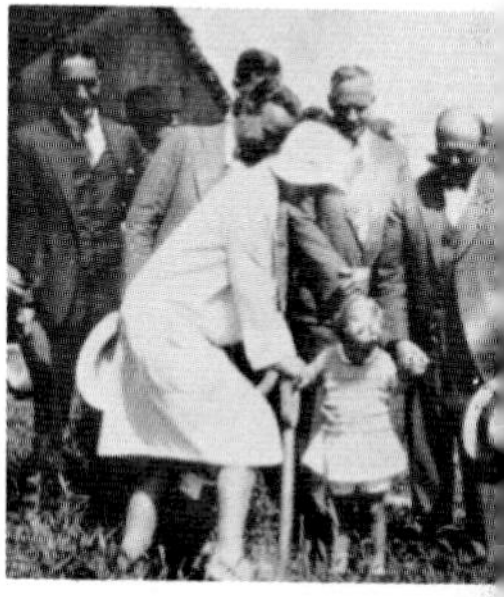

Ground breaking for the East Hartford plant, July 16, 1929.

The world's first modern commercial transport: the Wasp-powered Boeing 247.

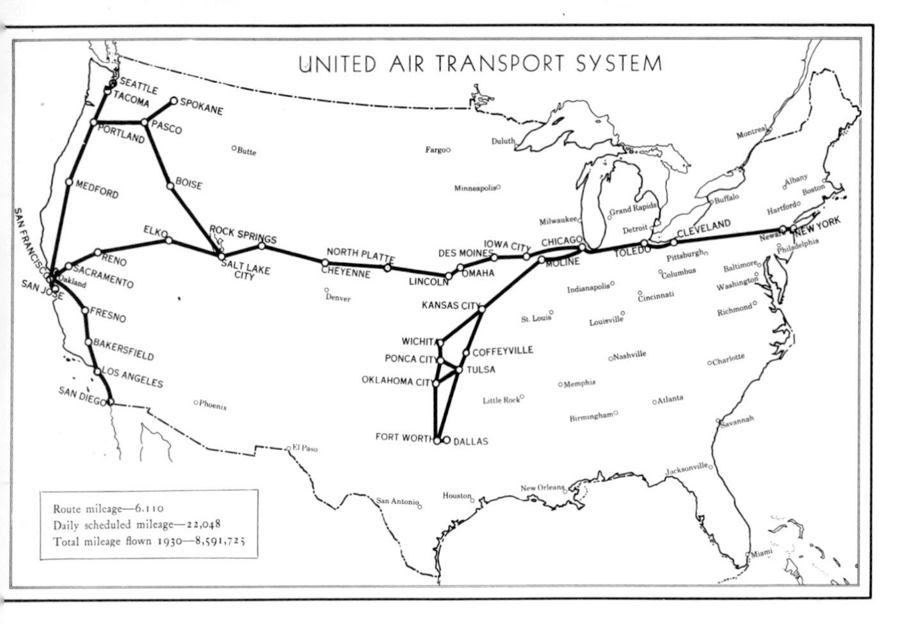

Route map and mileage log of the United Air Transport System in 1930.

United Air Transport officers, 1930.

Air passenger luxury in 1933: the cabin of a Ford Trimotor.

The Boeing Monomail, Hornet powered, was used on United's lines in the early '30's.

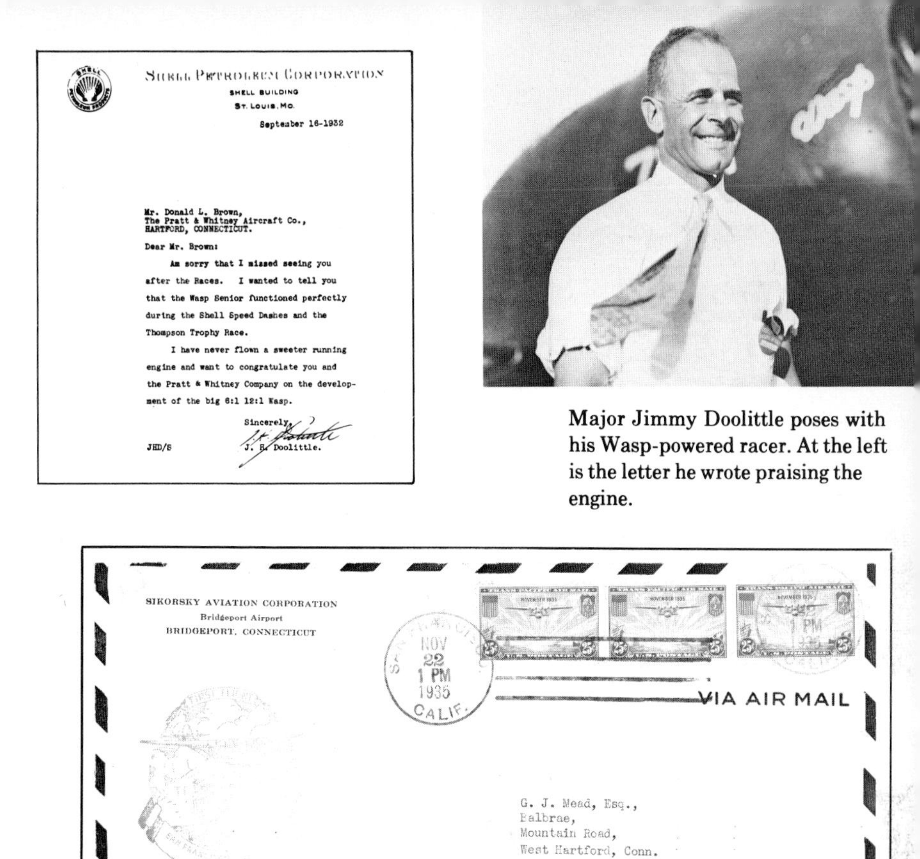

SHELL PETROLEUM CORPORATION
SHELL BUILDING
ST. LOUIS, MO.

September 16-1932

Mr. Donald L. Brown,
The Pratt & Whitney Aircraft Co.,
HARTFORD, CONNECTICUT.

Dear Mr. Brown:

Am sorry that I missed seeing you after the Races. I wanted to tell you that the Wasp Senior functioned perfectly during the Shell Speed Dashes and the Thompson Trophy Race.

I have never flown a sweeter running engine and want to congratulate you and the Pratt & Whitney Company on the development of the big 6:1 12:1 Wasp.

Sincerely,

J. H. Doolittle.

JHD/S

Major Jimmy Doolittle poses with his Wasp-powered racer. At the left is the letter he wrote praising the engine.

A first day cover commemorating the first Clipper flight from San Francisco to Manila.

A Pam Am Clipper winging across the Pacific.

Amelia Earhart prepares her Wasp-powered Lockheed-Vega for her Honolulu-California flight of 1935.

NATIONAL ADVISORY COMMITTEE FOR AERONAUTICS.
MEETING, OCTOBER 19, 1939.

Left to right: Brig. Gen. George H. Brett, Army Air Corps; Clinton M. Hester, Administrator, Civil Aeronautics Authority; Rear Adm. John H. Towers, Chief, Bureau of Aeronautics, Navy Department; Dr. L. J. Briggs, Director, Bureau of Standards; Col. Charles A. Lindbergh; Dr. Orville Wright; Dr. J. C. Hunsaker, Dr. George W. Lewis, Director of Aeronautical Research; Dr. Vannevar Bush, Chairman; Dr. George J. Mead, Vice Chairman; John F. Victory, Secretary; Dr. Charles G. Abbot, Secretary, Smithsonian Institution; Dr. Edward P. Warner; Maj. Gen. Henry H. Arnold, Chief, Army Air Corps; Robert H. Hinckley, Chairman, Civil Aeronautics Authority; Capt. S. M. Kraus, U.S.N.; Dr. F. W. Reichelderfer, Chief, United States Weather Bureau.

The 1940 National Advisory Committee for Aeronautics meeting.

The Altitude Wind Tunnel was designed to study power-plant characteristics and performance at all altitudes of flight. Since its test section of twenty feet diameter admitted an actual fuselage or nacelle with complete power-plant installation, the tunnel was really a full-scale tunnel for engine research. With its wind speed of 500 miles per hour, it rated as a high-speed tunnel. The feature which made it distinctive was its combination of facilities to simulate the conditions of thin air and low temperature corresponding to those at high altitude. Altitudes could be simulated to 50,000 feet and temperatures dropped to −67° F. Many early jet engine studies were conducted in the tunnel including tests of America's first jet aircraft, the Bell P-59. Of all the NACA research tools this probably was the most complicated. The complete altitude wind tunnel, including facilities for refrigeration and air exhaustion cost more than $6,000,000. One of the significant early studies performed in the Altitude Wind Tunnel concerned the problem of the B-29 engine overheating. The information from work in the tunnel and other studies at Lewis led to improvements of the exhaust turbines and elimination of high altitude fuel vaporization problems. This work increased the B-29 payload capacity by 5 1/2 tons and allowed it to fly at high altitudes.

l. to r. George Mead, F. B. Rentschler, Edsel Ford, Eugene Wilson, and Charles Sorensen pose with a Wasp in 1940 when Ford Motor Company became an R-2800 licensee.

A-10

OFFICE OF PRODUCTION MANAGEMENT
WASHINGTON, D. C. 43-077

NAME Mead, George J.

This is to notify you that the following action has been taken in the Office of Production Management concerning your employment.

Nature of Action Presidential Appointment

	FROM	TO
Position		Special Advisor
Grade & Salary		$1.00 Per Annum
Div. Sect. Unit		Office of Director General
Headquarters		West Hartford, Connecticut
Departmental or Field		Field

Effective Date: June 4, 1940 P. C. D. No.

REMARKS:

This appointment is authorized by Presidential Letter dated June 4, 1940.

This action is subject to the provisions of only those paragraphs which are checked below.

(a) *Under this appointment you are subject to the provisions of the Civil Service Retirement Act as amended, and accordingly 3½% will be deducted from your basic salary for deposit to your credit in the Retirement Fund.*

X (b) *This appointment is for such time as your services may be required and funds are available for the work of the Advisory Commission to the Council of National Defense.*

By direction of the Administrative Officer

CHIEF OF PERSONNEL

CAUTION! THIS LETTER, WHILE EVIDENCING AN OFFICIAL ACTION AS OF THE EFFECTIVE DATE SHOWN, IS NOT TO BE ACCEPTED AS AN OFFICIAL CREDENTIAL.

OFFICE OF PRODUCTION MANAGEMENT 10-F
WASHINGTON, D. C.

NAME Mead, George J.

This is to notify you that the following action has been taken in the Office of Production Management concerning your employment.

Nature of Action Termination Without Prejudice

	FROM	TO
Position	Special Advisor	
Grade & Salary	$1.00 per annum	
Div. Sect. Unit	Office of Director General	
Headquarters	West Hartford, Conn.	
Departmental or Field	Field	

Effective Date: June 30, 1941 P. C. D. No.

REMARKS:

To return to private obligations.

This action is subject to the provisions of only those paragraphs which are checked below.

(a) *Under this appointment you are subject to the provisions of the Civil Service Retirement Act as amended, and accordingly 3½% will be deducted from your basic salary for deposit to your credit in the Retirement Fund.*

X (b) *This appointment is for such time as your services may be required and funds are available for the work of the Advisory Commission to the Council of National Defense.*

By direction of the Administrative Officer

CHIEF OF PERSONNEL

CAUTION! THIS LETTER, WHILE EVIDENCING AN OFFICIAL ACTION AS OF THE EFFECTIVE DATE SHOWN, IS NOT TO BE ACCEPTED AS AN OFFICIAL CREDENTIAL.

Government letters concerning George Mead's appointment to the Office of Production Management as a Special Advisor.

TREASURY
DIVISION OF DISBURSEMENT

WASHINGTON, D. C.,

2 Treasurer of the United States

8, 555

JUL -2 1941

15-51

PAY IN DOLLARS $*****0 DOLLARS AND .05 CTS $*****0.05

TO THE ORDER OF George J. Mead

OBJECT FOR WHICH DRAWN: Salary

DEFENSE FUND EXECUTIVE

14 CHIEF DISBURSING OFFICER

220-030

George Mead's paycheck for services as a Special Advisor to the Office of Production Management during 1940–41.

The sprawling Pratt and Whitney plant in East Hartford at the beginning of World War II.

The Boeing Flying Fortress over Mount Rainier, one of many military aircraft powered by Pratt and Whitney engines seeing service in World War II.

World War II's demands brought Wasp and Hornet production up to new levels with engines being produced at several locations throughout the United States.

The scene along the production line at the East Hartford plant during World War II was vastly different from the production line at the original Capitol Ave. plant, sometimes making one wonder how so many changes could take place in less than twenty years. A testimony to George Mead's genius, however, is that the Wasp of the '40's is still as recognizable as the Wasp of the '20's.

ahead of time. Eventually they graduated to Pablum, then scrambled eggs, and finally meat, and the midnight business *and* the Kasek were over.

There was a big dog pen at the edge of the woods. We put a little shelter there for the puppies, and after they were six weeks old and had their preliminary shots, they spent most of their time there. Anita seemed to want to show me her gratitude for my help with her children. Her idea of the most delightful gift she could give me was a dead woodchuck. She would kill one nearly every day and present me with her treasure. It was good to reduce the woodchuck population, but somehow that very hot June they did *not appeal.* I would get the gardener to take them and bury them. There must have been quite a woodchuck cemetery. I didn't know—or want to know—where it was.

Jack had arranged for a group of men from M.I.T. to spend some days in Hartford after July 4th to discuss the future designs of airplanes and maybe make some drawings. I knew that he would put the results of months of thought into this conference and that they would all work long, hard hours. Since it would be some time before I could go to the farm, I urged him to go up and have a few days there at the end of June, to put some physical money in the bank before making such heavy withdrawals. He was hesitant about leaving me right then, especially as our dear Myra was on vacation, and the baby's arrival was imminent. But I persuaded him to go. I was in good hands. Margaret was at the house, and "Crany," a nurse friend, was in town and would come out for the 4th. Lil would come when called. Each evening Jack would be near the phone between 8:30 and 9:00, or he could always call me. I wasn't planning to go anywhere!

Dr. Witter came out the afternoon of July 4th to see the puppy we had picked out for him. Idamae and Grace had taken theirs. They had a cottage at the shore that summer, close enough to Hartford for Leonard and Hugh to commute. After Dr. Witter left, I went back in the house to turn up the hem on a dress I was making for Mary. She stood very patiently, but I couldn't seem to get it straight. So we gave up. Then I realized that "the hour" had come, or was about to. I called Dr. Thompson at his shore cottage, and he came galloping from the beach and said he would be there in an hour. I told him not to hurry, that I wasn't even sure I needed him, but thought it a good idea to know where he was. He said he'd rather come ten times on a false alarm than be one minute late if needed. That was typical of him. He was so very kind and always concerned that each patient should know that her comfort and her baby's safety were a primary concern to him. He had left a bag at our house with everything he would need, for again it seemed best for me to be at home. Crany and I got everything ready, and Dr. Tommy got there about seven, and Charles Cary Mead was born at one minute to eight. He was a fine rugged baby, weighing nine pounds one ounce, strong and well-muscled as Peyton had been, with dark hair and eyes like Mary and Jack instead of blond like Peyton.

We called Jack promptly at 8:30. Dr. Tommy got the number for me. When he answered, the doctor said, "Mrs. Mead wants to speak to you." When I got on the phone, Jack said, "Who is that man?" I said, "You should like him pretty well, he just ushered your third son into the world!" "WHAT?" He couldn't believe that Charlie was safely here. I couldn't either, because I had been so sure he would be a girl. "Are you really all right? Do you feel as well as you sound? Shall I drive home tonight?" "Yes, I am; yes, I do; and no, don't. I am fine, but I'd worry all the hours you were on the road. Have a good sleep tonight, a quiet day tomorrow, and come home Saturday as planned. Remember, next week will be a tough one." So he agreed. Then after Dr. Tommy left, I phoned my parents. Telling Mamma, "Charlie is here," (she thought I meant her youngest brother to whom I was devoted), she said, "How lovely of him to come and spend the holiday with you." I told her I meant his namesake. So we had a joyful gabfest.

There was a pang, of course, that Jack could not be with us to share the wonder of this hour, but I was grateful that he could be in his beloved New Hampshire, drawing the rest and refreshment he so much needed from the lake and mountains, and I knew he was sharing it, even if at a distance. By now it was dark enough for the children's fireworks. Harry had come back from his holiday to set them off for them, as I was a coward about rockets and wouldn't have done it even if Charlie hadn't put in his appearance. So Harry set up operations outside my east windows, at my request, so Charlie and I could enjoy the celebration of *his* birthday as well as the country's. As I looked at the precious little son, asleep in my arms, and watched the showers of "stars"—the "rockets' red glare"—I felt an overwhelming sense of gratitude: for my husband's loving concern—for the faithfulness, skill and care of doctor and nurse—for this blessed new life that had been given into our keeping—and for the free country into which he was born.

After the fireworks were over, the children came back for their goodnight kisses and one more beaming look at *their* baby. And so, the 4th of July, 1935—probably the most significant July 4th of my life—came to a wonderfully happy close.

Chapter XIII

Joys and Troubles—All Kinds of Both

Saturday Jack drove down from New Hampshire, according to plan. What a happy home-coming that was! He was as awed over the perfection of this fine little boy, as if he were our very first. Even though a three-day old baby is not overly attractive, having dropped some weight and rubbed off some of his hair, he was still gorgeous. Our happiness and gratitude knew no bounds. We had wanted him for so long, had about given up hope, and then—he came! What was left of that day was spent mostly in gloating. The other children's rapture over this baby was a delight to see. Once more, as we looked back later, it seemed that especially poignant joys were given us in order to fortify us for anxious days ahead.

Monday morning Jack came in at six to see Charlie and me, as he would be hard at work all the other times that day when the baby would be awake. The time had come to prepare for the hay fever season, so he asked Marion, the night nurse, if she would go down and get the first little vial of hay fever serum out of the box in the refrigerator and give him the first shot. (These inoculations came in a series, the first ampule containing "one pollen" and the others growing progressively stronger, until they worked up to 1,800 pollens.) She did so, gave him the shot expertly, and he went back to watching the baby. Suddenly he turned an awful color and began to gasp and said, "Let me see that vial." Horrified, we all realized the dreadful truth.

There had been a small box in the refrigerator left from last year, containing six vials of the greatest strength. This was on top of the larger box containing the graduated doses. Eighteen hundred pollens had been injected into his arm as a *first dose.* We all knew that this could mean his death if help were not forthcoming almost immediately. Marion discovered despairingly, as she looked in her emergency kit, that her vial of adrenalin was broken. Meantime, I got Gilder Jarvis on the phone; and after calling Dr. David Byrne, a young allergist at the hospital who had worked on antidotes, he came out incredibly quickly and gave Jack the first shot of adrenalin. This undoubtedly saved his life. It all happened so fast we could hardly take in the fact that stark tragedy had stared us in the face, and that almost by a miracle we had escaped it.

Gilder got Jack to go back in the guest room where he could be quiet and Dr. Byrne could work over him, away from the household activities. Gilder stayed on until the worst was over, coming every little while to tell me how everything was going.

Meantime, I was trying to comfort Marion, who was completely shattered. It was not her fault. Those extras from the year before, that hadn't been needed, should have been thrown out. The reason they hadn't been was that I never tampered with Jack's hay fever serums, and he had forgotten all about them. She maintained that no nurse should ever give *any* medication without checking the bottle—and this was true—but she thought she was doing exactly what he asked her to do. We had all learned a tremendous lesson, and we had not had to pay the terrible price we might have; so I pled with her to stop castigating herself and be grateful for our deliverance.

About eleven Jack came in to see me, pale and shaky, but booted and spurred—determined to go through with the day's commitments in spite of the grim experiences of the early morning. I marveled at the iron will and self-discipline which could rise above the illness and weakness he must be feeling, and force his body and his mind to go ahead with their assigned tasks.

Because of the success of the conferences at Squam Lake, away from the distractions and interruptions which were inevitable at the plant, Jack had built an office on our place in West Hartford the previous year, some distance from the house. It comprised a drafting room, model room, and conference room, as well as his own office, and an office for Alex Brown, his able and devoted confidential secretary. It was there that the "study" with the men from M.I.T. and our own engineering crew was to take place in the days ahead.

That July of 1935 was one which broke all heat records day after day. The early mornings were cool and pleasant, and from my east windows I used to love to watch the stately elm, its great arms rising into the blue sky, and then cascading gracefully in lacy festoons toward the ground. But by breakfast time, the heat would strike like a blast from a furnace. Our dear Margaret and Myra valiantly produced luncheon each day for ten or twelve men—as well as the family. Sometimes the men worked on into the evening on this aeroplane of the future; and this meant they were there for dinner also.

Jack had been plugging for planes that were so far beyond anything that had previously been envisioned that nearly everyone thought he was out of his mind. He had maintained that if the airlines really wanted to build up their passenger clientele, it was essential for planes to be comfortable. There must be well-designed seats with enough leg room, adequate washrooms, a galley from which good meals could be served, pressurized cabins so planes could fly high without "ear distress," heating for high altitudes, cooling for hot weather, coat closets, and adequate space for baggage. They must also be a lot faster. Then he really shocked some of his colleagues by suggesting that the transoceanic planes should have berths, and to keep the proportions right, they should be double deckers, with a little spiral staircase leading down to a lounge.

In instigating this study, Jack was undertaking the assignment of retrieving United Aircraft's transport position which the unwise decision of the board in regard to the 247 had cost it. In supervising the specifications and designs for the new four-engine planes he envisioned, he was once more displaying the creative thinking that characterized everything he did throughout his life—whether in the engineering field, or remodeling a home, or bringing up his children.

Igor Sikorsky worked closely with them on this preliminary study. I was aghast when I realized that all this herculean effort was really a *study* of what *should* be done, and not necessarily anything that was going to *be done*—at least any time soon, and probably not by our airframe companies, either Boeing or Sikorsky.

Here I'd like to mention as a sort of footnote that the fine aircraft which evolved from this study for regular airlines planes became the famous DC-4. Jack and Leonard brought through the R-2000 to supply the necessary power. The DC-4, powered by four Pratt & Whitney R-2000 engines, was the basic transport plane for the Air Transport Command and the Naval Transport service through the war; also for the Berlin Airlift in late 1940, and after the war it was the workhorse for the airlines for several years, presenting none of the problems inherent in its immediate successor, the DC-6, which Jack did *not* design, and which had to be grounded for some months until its many defects were corrected. However, it finally worked out to be a workhorse too.

Charlie was an adorable and most responsive baby. He was back to birth weight in one week, and he smiled—really smiled—in response to my whistling a gay little tune to him, at eight days. He was utterly delicious, and I was completely besotted about him. Then trouble hit us, when he was ten days old—not alarmingly at first, but gravely enough for real concern. He began losing his meals, and he seemed to be in almost constant pain. Dr. Witter was still away, and we called in a pediatrician who said it was just the terrible heat, and he indicated that middle-aged mothers were inclined to be over-anxious, etc. Jack was furious. "Any doctor who talks like that should be booted out of the profession. Anyone can see he is a very sick little baby." Dr. Tommy and Dr. Jarvis suggested we call in another pediatrician, Dr. Caulfield. He came several times and was pretty sure what the trouble was, but he couldn't prove it.

Jack went on with his work, his mind faithfully going ahead with his project at the office, while his heart was in that upstairs room at the house where Lil and I took turns walking the floor with Charlie, trying to ease the pain for that precious little fellow.

Anita also walked the floor, keening, and almost driving us wild as she paced behind us, back and forth, back and forth, convinced that we humans knew nothing at all about the care of *our* young.

Charlie's trouble seemed to go in cycles. He would keep his meals down and be fairly free of pain for a day, or maybe two, then the vomiting would start again, increasing in frequency, quantity, and violence, as it worked up toward a climax. This went on for about nine days. The first phase of the "study" at the office was virtually complete. Dr. Caulfield, who was keeping a very close watch over Charlie, assured us that if the trouble was what he felt virtually sure it was, it was not like an acute appendix that had to come out right that minute—there was nothing imminent. So, since Gilder Jarvis was going "on service" at the hospital August 1st, and would not have a single day off for three months, I urged him and Jack to go up to the farm for a few days and drink in "the strength of the hills." The anxiety about Charlie had come hard on the heels of Jack's own dreadful experience, and there had not been a moment's respite since. He had carried the double load of work at the office and anxiety at home, and I knew he *had* to have a break. He refused flatly to go and said he could not leave us with things as they were. But for once, I was adamant, and Gilder backed me up.

A day or so after they left, the "cycle" began to work up to a climax again. Dr. Caulfield came out in the evening to watch until Charlie was fed. The doctor waited as he slept peacefully for a little while after the feeding, then the squirming with pain began, and then sure enough the "projectile" came. The doctor got him onto the bath table immediately and *felt* the small tumor that was partially blocking the outlet to his stomach and told me that now he was sure—it was pyloric stenosis. We should get him to the hospital next day and operate as soon as he had some saline and a blood transfusion.

I phoned Benny Whelan, the company pilot—and a dear friend, I might add—and asked him if he would fly to the farm, leaving at six the next morning. Dr. Caulfield engaged a room at the hospital and reserved Gilder's favorite operating room. This night my prayers were full of thankfulness, for though this was a grave operation, the trouble was something we could *do* something about. We were anxious, but full of hope. In the morning I phoned the farm at six, so that Jack and Gilder would be ready when the plane came. They were back in Hartford by a little after eight, and Gilder confirmed the diagnosis.

Just before we left for the hospital, Idamae Hobbs appeared, coming as always just when she was most needed. She would keep the older children happy, she said, and watch over them so they could go swimming. This has always been typical of her—no phone calls of "Is there anything we can do to help?"—but simply figuring out what would be most helpful and quietly going ahead and doing it. She was our friend in need then and has continued to be all through these many years.

A young Dr. Glass had developed a needle for transfusions for babies that was so tiny it could go into the vein in a baby's ankle. They typed my blood quickly, and it was right, so I could be the "donor" after they had given Charlie all the other intravenous solutions. Dr. Tommy stood by my head while the transfusion was going on, and as I looked into his face, I think I have never seen such compassion written on any countenance. Charlie was, of course, yelling bloody murder, and someone asked me if it was distressing me. I told them I was grateful he had that much strength and spunk.

At last, all was ready, and they took him through all the long ramps and corridors from the Crane Building to the operating room in the Women's Building. While the doctors were working with Charlie, Jack and I discussed the inefficiency of the layout of the hospital which had sort of grown like Topsy—the buildings placed every which way, connected to each other by ramps which involved miles of walking to and fro, wasting time and strength of doctors and nurses. I am sure that the idea of spearheading the building of a new hospital was born that morning as we kept our minds busy waiting for word about Charlie.

After what seemed like a long, long time, but I am sure was not, Dr. Tommy came bounding in to tell us jubilantly that all had gone wonderfully—that it was an absolutely correct diagnosis. They were just closing the incision, and Charlie was fine. Professional formality went to the winds. Dr. Tommy received the full impact of our relief and joy, as we both hugged him, unable to express what we felt in words.

Then Jack started questioning him about the hodgepodge arrangement of outdated buildings, asking for any ideas he might have. His eyes shone at the thought that maybe—just maybe—Jack would be able to kindle in others the concern and enthusiasm which he himself felt. Just then Gilder and the others came in, radiant that now, with careful feeding and nursing, Charlie would be well.

Anita had refused to eat after we left. She just lay by the door, watching for us, sighing deeply from time to time, sometimes whining piteously. After a few days, Jack asked permission to bring her down to the hospital to see for herself that "her" baby was all right. This was possible at the Crane Building, as there was a stairway leading almost to our door, so she need not go near any of the other patients. (When I mentioned this incident to our youngest son, he could hardly believe that this could ever have been permitted. "You mean they let you bring in a dog? And now they won't let the older children see the new baby!")

As she came in the door, she glanced briefly at me, then went straight to the baby's crib and started drawing in long, satisfying whiffs of good, healthy baby. Then she came over to me and settled down quietly. Her every move was, oh, so eloquent. She was satisfied now that at last we stupid humans had learned to take care of this baby for whom she felt such responsibility. She started eating again and also regained her gay spirit.

Charlie had to be under careful supervision all that summer, so we couldn't spend much time at the farm. But when he was really out of the woods, and we found that Lil could stay for an extra two weeks, Jack and the big children and I went up for a fortnight. Short as the visit was, it was wonderful. The children reveled in every minute, and Jack and I began to feel the tensions easing. We got so we could really sleep with both eyes shut.

When we returned to Connecticut, Jack plunged into the more detailed work on the "aeroplane of the future." Precision drawings had been going forward during these few weeks. It was really beginning to "shape up" in fine style. The "team" had done a magnificent job—catching each other's ideas—developing them so they were better. There was the remarkable accord which comes when able men who respect each other, who speak the same scientific language, and who cherish the same standards of workmanship work on a project.

Here I should like to quote the following excerpts from a write-up by a reporter from the Boston Sunday Globe on September 8,

1935. Mr. Louis M. Lyons wrote as follows:

> I have been visiting on a hilltop in Connecticut overlooking the city of Hartford where the future of aviation is charted by young men who thoroughly enjoy their work. It is a New England industry that they are building, the most prophetic of all our industries today. And it is thrilling to a New Englander to watch hundreds of Connecticut mechanics busy on this new wonder of manufacture that is cruising the airways of the world as confidently as the Clipper ships of an earlier New England sailed the seven seas.
>
> They are talking of their 10th anniversary at United Aircraft. Already their airplane factories spread over a square mile in East Hartford and launch their great amphibians on the sea at Bridgeport. Ten years is a long time in aviation. Just listen to George Mead's comments as he strokes his great German Shepherd and talks about his heroes in aviation. "We're none of us 45," he says, "and we're old men in aviation."
>
> "What goes on here is aviation two or three years hence," says Professor Jerome C. Hunsacker of M.I.T. He is here to see George Mead too.
>
> A few years ago George Mead was a curly-headed youngster in Winchester, then a serious engineering student at Tech. Then he built the finest airplane engine in the world. The world's aviation progress has run pretty largely on Mead's engines. . . . His engines fly the great Clipper ships that Sikorsky builds, over South America and over the Pacific to Hawaii. They carry supplies to the gold miners of Alaska and their wings lift men over the jungles of the East Indies. England and France manufacture Mead's engines as soon as the United States Government releases them for foreign copying, which is when Mead has a new design ready for his own Government's army, navy, and mail planes.
>
> Around George Mead's engine has developed an integrated airplane industry that is to aviation, what General Motors is in the automobile field. What Kettering is to General Motors, Mead is to United Aircraft.
>
> "Aviation's going places." George Mead's enthusiasm bubbled as he talked. "Technically we can build them anything they want. We have the mechanical means already to fly to Europe. In five years, commercial flying will be established across the Pacific, and we'll be experimenting with the Atlantic crossing. The ships we're thinking about here,"—and his eye fell to the pad on his desk covered with the curved lines of airplane drawings—"will do Boston to New York in one hour. It isn't outside the possibilities that we'll be

flying from New York to Chicago in two hours. The ship we're thinking about now looks like a bird that folds its feet up under its wings. Just a slick, smooth-looking thing,"—George Mead's eyes sparkled and his hand reached into his dog's fur coat.

"Regular Atlantic crossing is right around the corner," said Mead. "It'll come so soon it'll surprise you. We can carry passengers to Europe in 24 hours. The Pacific will come first because we have the islands for stepping stones. The British have Bermuda and the French the Azores that are the stepping stones in the Atlantic crossing. Ultimately we'll do the Atlantic in one hop. That's the safest way to do it anyway. We can communicate from ship to shore 600 miles off the land. If the weather is bad in England, then land in Spain and a local plane or train will get you to England the same day. You still beat the boats by several days."

"We had to come to Connecticut for the most skilled labor," Mead explains. "In Detroit a man may turn the same bolt all day. But an airplane mechanic has to be able to take a lump of metal and make it into a beautifully machined part."

Later that day I went through the great factories where Mead's engines are joined to other airplane parts so far ahead of current models, that the Government guards the secret while United Aircraft builds 84 bombers for the Navy. I flew down to Bridgeport where Igor Sikorsky, great pioneer of aviation himself, now part of George Mead's engineering organization, is building new amphibians, greater even than his famed Clipper boats that flew to Hawaii. He is ready, he says, wholly ready, to build planes to fly either the Pacific or the Atlantic.

I had a chance to talk for an hour with Frederick B. Rentschler, president of United Aircraft, who had the business genius to organize an airplane industry around Mead's engine.

"All aeronautical development has come as the aftermath of a better engine," Rentschler said. "The engine has received less real credit than any other aspect of aviation. I say that as a manufacturer interested in airplane manufacture as much as in engine manufacture. The keynote of aviation development has been engine development. Today it is taken for granted that the engine doesn't fail."

Mead's prophetic work is done outside the airplane factory, just as Sikorsky's is done mostly at home, and he told me, "plenty at night too."

In his hilltop drafting room, Mead and a little corps of handpicked engineers work with pencils on clean sheets of paper, drawing the airplane of tomorrow.

"How many of our men have you got, George?" asks Hunsaker,

who is head of the department of aeronautical engineering at M.I.T.

"Three or four dozen," says Mead.

"You took a dozen *this* year," says Hunsaker.

Hunsaker himself serves as technical adviser to Mead's engineering group. His predecessor at Tech, C. H. Chatfield, is Mead's first assistant. The greatest of these Tech pioneers in aviation after Mead, I suppose, is Frank Caldwell. "Number one propeller man in the world," Mead calls him. One of the United Aircraft factories is given over to the manufacture of Caldwell's propeller that won the Collier award two years ago for greatest contribution of the year to aviation. Caldwell has improved it since, and the Government won't let me describe it yet. It's of that importance to the most efficient airplane construction. Briefly, what Caldwell has done is to provide a propeller that controls the speed of Mead's engines so that a plane is kept at uniform speed regardless of load or air conditions.

Mead likes to talk about Caldwell, Sikorsky, Hobbs, Willgoos, and the others. "No one person did any of these things," he insists. "The way you do anything as complicated as aviation is through a team. We've got a group over in our plant—boy they're great. If anything makes me provoked, it is to see someone claim credit for anything. Nothing worth-while is done without a team to do it."

But Hunsaker corners me later to make sure I put Mead in the right place in his team.

"This whole group here in Hartford grew out of Mead, who created these engines of astounding precision and power. There are other engines for airplanes. But the best the other fellows can do is to try to catch up with George Mead."

Hunsaker ought to know. He himself designed the Shenandoah and the NC4, first aircraft to fly the Atlantic, in 1919, and he headed the Navy's aircraft design through World War I.

"Historically, the reason that the airplane industry is in Connecticut is this brainchild of Mead's," Hunsaker says. "The manufacture of Mead's engines in the Pratt & Whitney Aircraft Company here attracted other airplane manufacture to Connecticut—the propeller and the planes. It all stems from the best engine built. So now you have these half dozen companies combined here, making everything in an airplane. Then comes the need of engineering control of the product. Mead has built up a central engineering research organization for the whole group of plants looking ahead." . . .

"Two things have held commercial aviation back," Mead went

on. "One is the cramped lack of comfort in the plane. Now, we are talking in terms of cabin planes with cabins as big as this room, with a lounge, two pilots, a couple of stewards, and a navigator—as comfortable as any ship, and quiet and smooth and cool. The second thing that has held flying back is the lack of regular schedules. In some weather we can't fly, but we're getting ships that can climb higher and so fly *above* the weather, and we are getting surer of the weather ahead. It used to take all the power we had to fly at all. If there was a head wind, we were late. If the mail plane was late, the transcontinental plane was late, the business man was late, everything was late. Now we have a big surplus of power, so a plane can make up time, just like a train. Tomorrow the business man can keep his appointment by plane."

"The reliability is up in the 90's now," Hunsaker said.

"Sixteen hours is the flying time between New York and California," Mead went on, and Hunsaker interjected, "It's been done in twelve, and there's no reason they shouldn't clip off an hour every couple of years. Railroad speed is limited by the roadbed. Planes have no limit."

"Cost has held us back," said Mead, "but now the plane fare is just about what the railroad fare plus Pullman is. Do you know that last year planes hauled 400,000 passengers in this country? When planes are of standard design, the transport companies won't need new equipment every year. When we get volume production, it will cut the cost way down. We haven't yet worn out one of our planes."

"We can build bigger and bigger ships and larger engines," said Mead, the builder. "Our biggest engine is 850 horsepower. We can build one with 2000 horsepower anytime anyone wants it."

"There's no limit on power, speed, or size of airplane, except the demand for it," agreed Hunsaker, the scientist.

That afternoon I saw the latest Sikorsky 43 being built at Bridgeport, almost as big as a destroyer, the first of a series for Hawaiian service. Her center spar is the largest piece of extruded aluminum the aluminum company ever made. By changing the duraluminum alloy of her wing composition, Sikorsky's chemists increased the ship load by 40,000 pounds—just one item of return on George Mead's engineering research organization.

In response to my questions, Sikorsky said, "Our present 40,000-ton Clippers that we are building for the Hawaiian service are perfectly satisfactory for crossing the South Atlantic. For a non-stop passage across the North Atlantic—and that is the safest and most reasonable way to cross—we should build ships of 70,000 to

> 100,000 tons to carry 100 passengers. Eventually we will carry several hundred. Such ships can ultimately be self-supporting in competition with other transportation rates."

In the light of present-day trends and developments (1970), it is interesting to note the prophetic vision, which this dedicated and able group of aviation experts voiced in 1935.

That fall found us facing another big hurdle in our family. Our children could not go to West Hartford public schools because our home was just a few hundred feet over the Bloomfield line. The Bloomfield schools were not as good then as they are now. This meant private schools. Mary was at Oxford, a fine girls' school, and that was perfect. Peyton was at the Junior School, a small, good school for children from nursery school through fourth grade, which Jack and I had helped to found. Young Jack was at Kingswood, but this did not seem right for him. He was becoming increasingly discouraged and unsure of himself, and finally, I, who was dead set against boarding schools, suggested that maybe it would be a good idea for him to go to Choate, where each boy was a well-loved individual, whose needs were studied. Jack reluctantly agreed. We went, we saw, and Dr. and Mrs. St. John conquered. We felt that here our boy could find himself, not only scholastically, but in many other ways as well.

Then the awful day came when he was to go. Choate was only thirty miles away, a forty-five minute drive. We could see him anytime; but it was the first break in our family, and as I packed his things, I found myself wiping my eyes every little while. I felt like such a fool, but those idiotic tears kept coming. I *knew* this was the right thing to do, and that we would be glad later that we had taken this step, but still. . . . Furiously, I alternately mopped and packed, and presently when young Jack came in with some more treasures which *couldn't* be left behind, I managed a smile and a little kidding about our taking his knick-knacks—and maybe his clothes, if there was room.

At school, he bade us a cheerful goodbye and plunged into everything with enthusiasm, and immediately improved scholastically, and in other ways too. I am sure he had his homesick moments, but the school officials were very lenient about letting him come home for frequent weekends, and their holidays were long. I was grateful that caring for Charlie kept me busy and happy, in spite of the big hole that Jackie's absence left in the family circle.

The summer of 1936 we could spend at the farm. How grand it was to be together as a family once more. We savored every minute of it, making up for all the enjoyment we had missed the summer before. Choate had done for young Jack just what we hoped it would. He was happy and confident. Along with Mary and Peyton, he could now climb with their father; and this was wonderful for them all, cementing the bonds of understanding and affection which are so vital. Even though Jack usually spent many hours at his little office by the lake, going over any problems that any of the engines might present, exploring new ideas, and refining old ones, he always managed at least a day each week to do something special with the children or me.

In the late winter of 1937 we did a stupendous thing. Jack and I went on a trip purely for pleasure, not to recover from an illness, and not for business. It was to be a real fun trip. Crany would stay with the children, so we knew they would be happy and well cared for, thus there were no worries.

We were going to Jamaica on a United Fruit Line boat. We invested in some giddy clothes, and the florist with whom we dealt sent me a box of flowers in which there was a fresh corsage for each evening. Jack must have seemed very eager and young when he had made our reservations, because when we went aboard, we were ushered into the *bridal suite!* We thought that with four children, and the "40" milestone breathing down my neck, and Jack having recently passed his 45th birthday, we were an unusual bride and groom. It was delightful, however.

At luncheon, we were assigned to a table with a charming couple, Mr. and Mrs. Tip Wilson. We introduced ourselves and soon were discussing the bull we had all been watching in the waist of the ship. We thought how shocked and cold he would be when the waves started really breaking over him. So then we discussed where we lived, and we said we had a farm in New Hampshire with a few cows, and they said they had a ranch in Big Horn, Wyoming, with a few cows. They asked us how many we had, and we said, "Eight," and that we imagined they had a lot more. How many? "Five thousand—more or less." That sort of took our breath. We found many interests in common, and when we met for dinner, we got all dressed up, corsage and all, and had a grand evening.

Next morning I woke bright and early, and though the ship was rolling somewhat, I wasn't going to let that bother me. Jack opened one eye and said that if I were smart, I'd stay put, but I couldn't think of wasting a beautiful morning staying put, so I got up blithely, had my bath, and was happily getting dried and dressed, when I noticed that horrid-looking soapy salt water, sloshing back and forth as it ran slowly out of the tub—and that did it. I scuttled back into my bed and stayed there. Some hours later I woke up, and this time, with no ado, I got into my clothes quickly and went up to the deck.

Standing in the doorway, waiting for a chance to make a dash to a chair between waves (we were going around Cape Hatteras and the ocean was kicking up a storm), I noticed a lovely lady with two empty chairs beside her. I planned to walk over to her and ask if I might sit by her, but just as there seemed to be a lull and I started toward her, the ship lurched madly, and I sprawled ignominiously at her feet, landing almost in her lap. She said, "Oh, am I in your chair?" And I said, "I don't even know where my chair is. I was going to ask if I might sit by you." "By all means," she said cordially, and I picked myself up off the deck, and we had a beautiful morning. She was Mrs. Bronson from Litchfield, Connecticut. Presently, her friend, Mrs. Kingsbury from New Haven, came and sat in the other chair, and we had a beautiful time. After a while a steward came, and Mrs. Bronson said we should have some champagne—that champagne was very good for a slightly queazy tummy—and a chicken sandwich for a bit of nourishment. I couldn't help thinking of a joke my mother had told me about a girl who was seasick, and the steward said, "Do you feel like a little cold chicken?" and she said, "I don't know how a little cold chicken feels, but I feel awful." Well, we had the sandwich and the champagne, and it *was* just what the doctor ordered!

When Jack met Mrs. Bronson later that day, he was simply enchanted with her. She was a true lady of the old school (even wore a dinner dress and evening slippers when she visited us at the farm the next summer), and she was just as sharp as a tack, quick-witted and delightful. She had been to Jamaica many times and gave us helpful hints as to things to see in our short stay, and what not to take time for. She and Mrs. Kingsbury were going on to Montego Bay, as were the Wilsons, so we would not see either of our new-found friends after we disembarked at Kingston. But these friendships grew and flourished during the years that followed.

We were to dock early in the morning, and while it was still dark, we heard a great clanking and much shouting, and we gathered that the pilot had come aboard by means of a chain ladder. Hence the clanks. We quickly got up, dressed, and went out on deck, as we had been told this harbor was exceptionally beautiful. It was. The stars were still bright in the sky, and so close we felt we could touch them, but around the horizon we could see the beginnings of a faint rosy glow. This grew deeper in color as the stars paled, and the sky became more luminous; little by little the land, which partly ringed the harbor, began to be more defined, separated from the clouds we had been watching as they turned from crimson to gold; and then—"Mount Blue," the largest of the 8,000-foot range of mountains which form the real backbone of Jamaica, burst on us. We were awed at its majesty and thankful that the noise of the pilot's coming aboard had enabled us to see the glory of this dawn and the grandeur of the harbor as it all unfolded before us.

We had three wonderful days in Jamaica. We took an interesting trip across the mountains to a different part of the island each day. We were greatly edified to find natives walking along *all* the mountain trails and carrying on their heads their shoes and anything else they needed. We were appalled at the sight of naked children playing in dirty enclosures with goats and donkeys, pigs and cows. Thinking of all the diseases our children came down with in spite of our care, we wondered how any of them survived. Jack was especially horrified at seeing the women working with sledge hammers on the rock piles.

Returning to Kingston, Jack asked me if I wouldn't like to fly to Miami in one of Sikorksy's gorgeous four-engine Clippers and see my parents for a day or so. By flying instead of staying with the ship, we would save two days, and it seemed a shame to be so near them and not see them. I had also been longing to fly in one of these clippers ever since I had seen pictures of them. Jack managed to get us seats, and Mamma and Papa were thrilled with our visit.

That was a glorious flight. We took off over the dimpled water of the harbor. Jack said, "She's on the 'step' now," and then we were air-borne. Straight up over 8,000-foot mountains we went and on to Cuba—on purpose, not because we were forced to. Then at Cienfuegos, the airline handled the deplaning passengers and baggage quickly, and away we went for Miami. The whole flight was one of enchantment for me, as it was my first *long* flight over water, and it was *behind* Jack's engines and *in* Igor's Clipper. Various goodies were served from the galley, but for once I was too excited to eat.

The pilot, seeing Jack's name on the passenger list, sent back to ask if he was related to the George Mead who built the engines, and when he learned that he was *the* one, he invited him to come up in the cockpit—pardon me, to "the bridge"—for a while. Looking down into that crystal-clear water, I was amazed at the almost continuous line of reefs between Cuba and Miami. I guess they were mostly pretty far under water, but even so, I could see how ships would have to keep taking soundings. Alighting in the bay at Miami was fun too, as they had little boat trailers which swimmers went out and attached to the hulls of the Clippers. Then tractors hauled the Clippers up the sandy ramp on to the land. The whole flight was a tremendous experience.

We had two happy days with the family and then, tamely, took the train home. We probably needed that uninspiring trip to unwind.

It was grand to get home. We had loved every minute of the trip but were more hungry for the children than we had realized. They had stayed well while we were gone, so it was a truly happy home-coming.

Chapter XIV

Honors and Problems

Jack had been invited to give a paper before the Royal Aeronautical Society on April 22, 1937. It was to be on "Power Plant Trends," and he labored long and hard over it. He had written many articles for the Society of Automotive Engineers magazine and for other technical journals over the years. One in 1936 for the Technology Review, "Around the Corner in Aviation," was written in collaboration with Dr. Jerome C. Hunsaker. All these articles were excellent. They showed his careful craftsmanship and the clarity of his thinking, and they were highly valued.[1] But to be asked to cross the Atlantic and give a paper before such an august assemblage was an entirely new challenge—*and it had to be tops.*

Jack thought it would be great if Gilder Jarvis could accompany him on this trip. Gilder could visit English hospitals, study their techniques, and see anything else he wished, while Jack was taken up with the Aeronautical responsibilities. Gilder was thrilled, and together they made their plans for a wonderful tour of the continent after they completed the British part of the trip. It was the greatest happiness to Jack to think that for once he had a chance to repay in some small measure a little of all that Gilder had done for us.

Then the axe fell. Mrs. Robbins, Gilder's mother-in-law, was taken seriously ill. Dr. Witter, who had had an alarming case of pneumonia, was convalescing in Florida, so Gilder felt he could not leave. This was a bitter disappointment to Jack and Gilder. This journey together would have been a high point in their lives. But Gilder never hesitated for one moment. All reservations had been confirmed everywhere, and all plans made. Jack asked Hugh Chatfield if he would like to go in Gilder's place. Hugh rearranged his own work schedule and enthusiastically accepted. Jack and Hugh were very close friends, and it was good that he could go, for there was much in this tour that would be of vital use and interest to him.

The paper went well and received much adulation. It was considered so important that the Royal Aeronautical Society agreed that Jack could accept the invitation to give it at the summer meeting of the Society of Automotive Engineers at White Sulphur Springs. For this paper, the Council of the Institute of Aeronautical Engineers awarded him the Taylor Gold Medal. It was considered the most valuable paper that had been submitted or presented up to that time.

Jack was scheduled to reach home in time for our anniversary, but storms at sea delayed him, so he *telephoned from the ship.* The connection was terrible—we could hardly make out anything the other said—but we had heard each other's voices on *our day,* and so the sun was shining and the day was made.

When we went down to meet the Bremen as she came home, she was a bit delayed coming up the river, and the tugs had trouble keeping her on course. A woman standing near us as we waited remarked, "Mebby dey run outta vuell." It was all I could do to keep a straight face at the idea of the Bremen's running out of fuel.

Presently she appeared, coming very slowly because of the current, but she was the most beautiful sight in the world to us who were awaiting her. The tugs were in a tizzy docking her. They carried on like a bevy of hysterical women, squealing with excitement. Peyton was thrilled with all these maneuvers. Jack and Mary watched more quietly, looking for their Dad. Soon he was with us, and Hugh was with Grace, Jack's car was unloaded from the ship, and away we went—a reunited family.

One more honor was to come to Jack in the spring of 1937. Trinity College wished to confer on him the honorary degree of Doctor of Science. He told me this in strictest confidence, and I practically didn't allow myself to *think* about it lest I somehow give a hint to someone.

Dr. Jerome Webster, a noted plastic surgeon at the Presbyterian Hospital in New York, an old friend of the family, and his lovely wife had come out to call the day before the commencement. As he was a Trinity trustee, it was natural he should be there. They asked us if we were going to the commencement, and we said, "Yes, there were several graduates in whom we were interested." We little dreamed he was one of them! Being a trustee, he probably knew about our honorary degree, but we certainly didn't know about his. His citation (given in Latin) wound up with . . . "He is known far and wide for his professional skill, for his collection of old books, *and* his ability to translate them into English. Some people make faces—he *re*makes them. I present to you this distinguished surgeon, Dr. Jerome Pierce Webster."

When it was Jack's turn to receive his citation, it was most heart-wearming. Certainly these citations give a unique opportunity for saying admiring things about people in a most graceful way. I'll quote it in full.

> This gentleman, Mr. President, born in a nearby state, after having received a degree at the Massachusetts Institute of Technology, was busy before the war making aeroplanes, and during the war served his country. Since that time, and especially in the last few years, his reputation has spread throughout our whole country among those who are making flying machines bigger and better than any that Daedalus even dreamed of. An expert he, I present to you, George Jackson Mead.

And with that classic concept of the science of flying, my husband became a doctor.

On May 20, 1937, Amelia Earhart and her navigator, Fred

Noonan, took off from Miami to fly around the world eastward this time, to take advantage of the prevailing tail winds which would follow them. Miss Earhart (Mrs. George Putnam) had been at our house for a short visit earlier, when she was in Hartford to check some details in connection with the engines for her "Electra." She was a tall, slender woman of thirty-nine, with a shock of short, curly hair framing a charming, piquant face. There was a sparkle and an aliveness about her which transcended mere good looks. Idamae and Margaret brought her out. Tilly, Margaret's husband, had been an ace in World War I, had been shot down behind the enemy lines, had somehow escaped from prison and "walked out." Therefore, he and Amelia, America's "first lady of the air," had much to talk about.

Being an air-minded, but mostly an earth-bound person, my admiration and respect for her ability knew no bounds. She and I were about the same age; yet, she had, like "Lindy," soloed across the Atlantic in 1932, had made a new transcontinental record in July of 1932 and had broken her own record in 1933. She had soloed in January of 1935 from Hawaii to California—the first person to fly this stretch alone. Later that year she had flown from Mexico City to Newark, New Jersey, non-stop.

She had also had the courage to follow through on this projected trip, after a terrifying accident on March 19 in Honolulu when she attempted to fly around the world westward. There, as she started down the 3,000-foot runway, a wing dipped. She frantically chopped an engine to straighten the veering plane, but the uneven shear had crumpled the right landing gear. The heavy monoplane, carrying 1,150 gallons of gasoline, ground-looped in a cloud of dust and sparks. The small group of spectators near the hangars waited tensely for the explosion, but it did not come. Miss Earhart, by her presence of mind in cutting the switches, had undoubtedly saved the lives of her navigators, Harry Manning and Fred Noonan, as well as her own.

All these factors added up to a very wonderful person. She was able and knowledgeable, aeronautically speaking, yet she retained her feminine charm and lovableness.

We followed her flight eagerly by radio and newspaper. We did not know that the trailing antenna, which would give her longer and surer communication on the long hops in the Pacific, had been removed, or that she had not been informed of the stronger, longer-range radio station that had been installed on the tiny Howland atoll. We listened constantly for her progress but were not anxious, even though transoceanic flying was still rather new. We were confident she could do what she set out to do.

But on July 3 came word that the "Electra" had not reached Howland Island as expected on July 2. America was not unduly alarmed at first; Amelia Earhart had led a charmed life. The papers suggested that she and her navigator, Fred Noonan, had landed on some other atoll, (though there *were none* anywhere near). We knew that at her last contact with the "Itaska," which was stationed near Howland to lead her in by radio, she had reported that gas was running low. In Washington, Admiral William D. Leahy, Chief of Naval Operations, ordered four destroyers, a battleship, a mine sweeper, and the carrier "Lexington" with its full complement of planes, to the scene.

During the next sixteen days, they set up search patterns around Howland and through the Gilbert and Marshall chains as well. They covered 250,000 square miles. Navy planes scanned 150,000 square miles and logged 1,600 hours. Planes and ships found nothing. A stunned America listened to its radios, hoping each day that a broadcast would tell of the rescue of "Lady Lindy," as she was affectionately called, and her navigator.

The search was finally called off. They passed into mystery. They were never found. Many of us still grieve after all these years that two such gallant people, who had so nearly reached their goal, should have been lost, probably because they lacked the radio antennas for a clear signal to tell them the exact location of Howland.

In 1934 Fred Rentschler found that the demands of the expanded company required that he spend more and more time away from the East Hartford plant. He felt that United Aircraft should have, as its president, a man whose primary interest and responsibility would be the running of the company, and not travelling about. He talked this over first with Jack, who was at that time not only his close friend and associate, but was also vice president and chairman of the executive committees of both Pratt & Whitney and United Aircraft. Fred had considered asking Jack or Don Brown to take over the presidency of United Aircraft Corporation.

Here I will quote a bit from *The Pratt & Whitney Story.*

> . . . Mead, along with his extraordinary engineering talents, combined signal ability as a planner, and even more surprising, he had great skill in production. One of the reasons for Pratt & Whitney's swift growth was the fact that his designs were tempered to manufacturing needs. An associate who worked with Mead for years once said of him, "He was a man who would explore every avenue, every bit of data. In some respects, he came near to being a genius—if indeed he was not a genius."

The book goes on to say:

> He certainly was one, if you take the old definition that genius is nothing more than an infinite capacity for taking pains. However, most people felt he had an extra something plus, which meant that another definition of genius was true in his case—namely, that genius was nine-tenths hard work and one-tenth genius.

Jack was aghast at the thought of Fred's giving up the presidency of United Aircraft. He felt, and rightly, that Fred had the experience and the executive background that fitted him ideally for the presidency of both Pratt & Whitney and the larger United Aircraft Corporation. Moreover, his training as president of Wright Aeronautical had groomed him extraordinarily well for the job he was doing, and it was partly because of this, partly because of the fact that he had grown with the company that it had been so successful. Jack reminded him of the set-up they had planned before even the Pratt & Whitney engine company was started—that he, Fred, would be the president, Jack the vice president of engineering, with Andy as his right hand—Don and Borrup on the production end, with the other key men to round out the organization. He told Fred that each man had a position for which he was ideally suited. He said that he himself would not accept the presidency, even if it were offered to him. He was an engineer and not an executive, and he felt the same was true of Don, who was tops in his production field but had had no experience in the administrative end of the business, and he would be required to plunge into a whole new area of responsibility in a full-grown company without having had the training or experience to fit him for it. Jack pleaded with Fred not to risk putting in a man—even Don—whom he loved and admired sincerely, who did not have the needed experience.

Fred was deaf to all entreaties and carried out his plan of reorganization. Though Jack did not agree, he never let it affect either his work or his friendship.

Meantime, there were troubles. During the early 30's, Wright had gotten itself into the awkward position of developing and refining six different kinds of engines, some air-cooled, some liquid-cooled. Thus, they were dissipating their energy and spreading themselves too thin. But Pratt & Whitney had also spread themselves too thin. In order to keep abreast in the eternal competition with Wright, it seemed necessary for Pratt & Whitney to have an engine to match each engine of the Wright Company. Thus, the company also had a number of engines in the design and development stage. Then the Army Air Corps, after seeing the Allison 1710 flight-tested, strongly urged Pratt & Whitney to develop a liquid-cooled engine. The Army was, for some reason, convinced that the future of fighter aircraft rested with that type of engine. The Army and Navy had been our first customers, and we certainly did not wish to be disobliging, but the Pratt & Whitney men had grave misgivings about the liquid-cooled engines. They had gone all over that problem ten years or more earlier, and it seemed stupid to waste time on it again.

However, Jack went to England to study British developments and came home with high hopes for being able to produce a successful liquid-cooled "H" type engine, with high out-put small cylinders, and the sleeve valves with which he had been experimenting before going abroad. However, after thorough research, Pratt & Whitney men were able to convince the Army that even in the very high-powered engines, the air-cooled engines gave the most satisfactory performance. All believed that the full potential of the air-cooled engines had not been reached. It was obvious also that the liquid-cooled engine, no matter how good, could never get through its development period in time for the emergency which all felt was not too far in the future. When the situation was made clear to General (Hap) Arnold, he agreed that Pratt & Whitney should cancel out on the liquid-cooled and institute the development of a hitherto undreamed-of radial engine, the R-2800.

Arnold said, "You're absolutely right. Why didn't you come to me about this a long time ago? Now, we're getting somewhere. You initiate your papers for cancellation, and I'll see to it they are approved in a hurry." As always, the general fulfilled his promise. The Navy had from the start favored the air-cooled engine, so everybody was satisfied.

Leonard Hobbs, who was on a trip out west, reported to Jack that the 2600, a 14-cylinder engine, was too small, and as Wright was bringing out one about the same size, it would be wise to wash it out and go for something bigger. So, work was started immediately on the R-2800, an 18-cylinder, two-row, which became the most useful aircraft piston engine ever. It powered the P-47—a most vital plane—bombers, fighters, transports, observation planes. With water injection (which controlled detonation when introduced into the cylinders), the team got it up to 3,500 horsepower. Jack started work on that engine before Leonard got back from his trip, but illness intervened, and Leonard completed the development of it. This was their first major joint effort. Leonard was really the one who should receive most of the credit for this great engine.

We enjoyed the farm with especial appreciation that summer of 1937. So much had happened since we had been there as a family the year before. The separation while Jack was abroad, though not really so long in time, seemed more complete because of the ocean which rolled between us.

While Jack and Hugh were on the continent, they had been vividly aware of the careful, thorough, and overwhelmingly sweeping preparations which were being made for war. This mobilizing of Germany's industrial and military manpower was no peacetime defense measure. It was obviously preparation for all-out war—with planes, tanks, guns, all types of munitions, everything being feverishly manufactured for the purpose of conquering all of Europe—and who knows whether they planned to stop there!

France was slumbering peacefully in false security behind her Maginot Line, which was supposed to be the ultimate in defense. (I remember reading an article about this marvel, in which the most crucial details were set forth, literally telling the enemy everything they needed to know.)

Soon after returning from abroad, Jack endeavored to bring

home to officialdom in Washington the gravity of this threat, just as Lindbergh had done not too long before. General Arnold and Admiral Moffett and others in the Army and Navy took these warnings seriously, but Roosevelt and his cohorts were not impressed. They were too busy with their "alphabet soup," the WPA, the OPA, etc. One lesson which peace-loving nations, as well as peace-loving individuals, seem incapable of learning is that eternal vigilance is the price of freedom.

My parents were with us for a visit that summer and so could see Charlie when his conversation was utterly delightful and his independence kept me very agile. Young Jack had come along wonderfully during this year. Choate had proved to be the answer for him, and though we still felt a pang at having him go away to school when he was so young, we were sure that the decision had been a wise one. Mary presented only one problem. She was such an omniverous reader that it was hard to pry her loose from any book until she had finished it, and then, before you could turn around, she had started another. In order to save her eyes, we tried to limit the number of hours she spent reading each day. She tried to do as we asked about it, but would get so enthralled that unless someone reminded her, time meant nothing. It reminded me of my own mother to whom reading was a ruling passion. When we were children and wanted to ask her something when she was reading—permission or whatever—we always had to preface our question with, "Mamma, is your mind turned on?" No permission given without that assurance was valid.

Grammy Mead's eyesight had been ruined by a damaged retina in both eyes. She could see around the perimeter of her eyes—grass, trees, flowers, the mountains, and the sky—but she could not see our faces. Jack was heartsick about this and, as always, set out to do something about it. He got her a car and engaged a chauffeur for her, and managed to get her to sign the registration before she had time to think up reasons why she didn't need it. After she got over her initial objection, she really enjoyed that car. She could take all her friends, whom Dad didn't especially enjoy, on all sorts of trips. I think she ran up more miles than any of us. It thrilled Jack to see how well his idea had worked. Here again was an example of the joy he derived from making others happy.

When my birthday was approaching that summer, Jack asked

me what I would like to do for fun. I told him I'd like to climb Sandwich Dome and go up the Algonquin Trail from the notch which he and Ted Main had cleared as boys in summer camp. I told him I thought maybe I wouldn't feel so old on my 40th birthday if I could climb Sandwich Dome. So we made our plans. The day dawned clear, but very hot. We started up the trail which I don't think anyone had done much about since Jack and Ted first cleared it. It was grown in with raspberry bushes which tore our clothes—and us—and there were trees down which had to be climbed over. Our feet were also sopping wet with heavy dew. It was a long, hard climb, and before we reached the summit, I thought ruefully that I felt about a hundred instead of just forty. However, as we sat on "Black Mountain," which is the first summit of Sandwich Dome, eating—appropriately—our "sandwiches" and oranges and gazing at the magnificent panorama spread before us, it seemed thoroughly worth the effort. I was slow on the long pull between Black Mountain and the real summit. I was mortified to give out so ignominiously, but we finally made it and went down the Noon Peak trail into Waterville Valley.

There Harry met us and was mighty glad to see us. We had taken so long that he had almost given us up. Jack thought I needed a treat, so we stopped at Whitcomb's Drugstore in Ashland where most delicious strawberry sodas were to be had. We were so dirty and disgusting looking that we got Harry to go in and get them for us. Then we saw Grammy across the street. We were ashamed to have her see us indulging in "curb service" and looking so disgraceful, so we scrooched down in the seats, so as not to be visible. We heard her say, "I see Jack's car, but I don't see him." We lay low and said nothing. When we got home, I found a wonderful surprise, which Jack hadn't told me about. My sister, Mary, and her husband, George Houston, were there, having timed a visit to Maine so they could be with us on my birthday evening.

All during that summer we enjoyed visits from some of the Pratt & Whitney family, his closest associates, and our dearest friends. I think more was accomplished engineering-wise during those visits than during many weeks at the plant. The men were rested. They were not interrupted by trivia to derail their trains of thought. They could work creatively and constructively, without battling traffic on their way to and from work.

That fall we started a practice which we were able to continue for the next eleven years. It had always distressed Jack that because of school, I had to miss the gorgeous blaze of autumn color in New Hampshire. So after everybody except Charlie was started in school, I got a nurse friend to look after him, and leaving Margaret, Myra, and Harry to run things, Jack and I would go to the farm for a glorious week of climbing and loafing. We both needed it. My housekeeping activities were more strenuous in summer than in Hartford, what with many guests, and canning, preserving, and jelly-making. His work never stopped. Even in the night, during his sleep, ideas and solutions to problems would come to him, and he would by flashlight set down notes which would keep these ideas from escaping before morning.

Returning to Hartford, things at the plant were becoming increasingly tense and frustrating for Jack. He and Leonard and Andy worked together like parts of a watch. Tilly in his field, Hugh in his, Ray Walsh (president of Hamilton Standard), and Frank Caldwell, the "propeller man of the world"—all were close in their thinking and their association. The friendship of these men grew ever closer. But there were matters of policy which troubled Jack deeply as he saw the war clouds gathering ever more ominously. They preyed on his mind and really taxed his strength. Jack was not only head of engineering for the United Aircraft but was vice president and also chairman of the executive committee. Surely in these capacities, his voice should have been heard—his warnings heeded. This should have been especially true since he had been proved *so right* a few years before in regard to the 247, when the company lost out disastrously because they would not listen to him. He and the group who had worked with him those torrid days of murderous heat in July 1935 had designed planes so superior to anything envisioned up to that time that they marked a completely new era in aviation. Yet, his warnings went unheeded again. Some of those responsible for this unwillingness to face facts have since died, and I therefore do not go into details or name names, but the correspondence over this period displays an almost unforgivable blindness and indifference on the part of some of the officials.

Meantime, Jack had never allowed the matter of the much-needed new Hartford Hospital to be crowded out of his thinking.

Ever since Charlie's illness as a very new baby, when he became poignantly aware of the lack of efficiency in the whole layout, and the extra fatigue for doctors and nurses which the haphazard arrangement of the old buildings caused, he had had it very much on his mind to initiate a drive for funds and to get an able architect to draw up plans. He had been elected to the board of directors of the hospital some time before, so even though he knew that it would take time to get his idea across, and even longer to get it under way, he was now in a position to plant and cultivate some seeds and help them sprout. As in the case of designing aircraft engines, a great deal of preliminary thinking must precede any actual plans.

Here I must digress a little in order to reveal one facet of Jack's character which I have not mentioned before, and also to disclose one more service to his fellow men.

Since Jack had been brought up an Episcopalian, and I had grown up in my father's Presbyterian Church, we had decided when we were married that we would attend several churches of both communions wherever we lived and would join the one which appealed to us most strongly. Before 1925 we had never lived in one place long enough to establish a real church affiliation, but when we moved to Hartford, after visiting several churches, we finally joined a Congregational Church, where a brilliant and dedicated man, Dr. Wyllis Howard Butler, was the minister. We were deeply grieved at his death two years later but hoped the committee would find a worthy successor. After months of searching, they called a man who did well for a while.

Some additions to the church were needed—Sunday School rooms, a modern kitchen, fellowship rooms, ladies' parlor, chapel, etc. Jack was asked to head up the building committee and, as always, did a superb job. He carried through this demanding task on top of his already full schedule at the plant. This was during the late 30's.

We loved the worshipful atmosphere of the sanctuary, and many of the members were cherished friends. The Sunday School curriculum under the new minister left something to be desired, but we supplemented that at home. We missed Dr. Butler's inspiring sermons but were determined to do our part in helping the church he had served so well continue to grow in spiritual strength, influence, and outreach. However, as so often happens, once the new facilities were completed, the incumbent minister seemed not to feel any need to build a church within those walls. The sermons seemed to have little connection with Christian faith, or with helping one be a better person. The children disliked Sunday School, and we were increasingly frustrated as we tried to worship in an atmosphere that was no longer worshipful. Because we had many close friends in the membership, we continued for a long time.

Jack finally suggested that we go to hear Dr. Warren Archibald, who was minister of the South Congregational Church. Jack had met Dr. Archibald in the Twilight Club and had grown to like and admire him very much. The Twilight Club consisted of a group of men who met once a month at the close of their business day, had dinner together, after which one of them presented an interesting paper which was followed by a short discussion. Jack said, "I think you would like Warren. I certainly do, and I hear wonderful things about him as a minister." We went, and from that day on, South Congregational Church was home. There began for us a meaningful church affiliation and one of the closest friendships of our lives. We joined South Church as a family a year later.

The George Houstons had gone to Philadelphia a few years before, so that he could become the president of the Baldwin Locomotive Company and get it onto a more workable basis. Late in the fall we went down to see them—Jack to discuss organizational problems with George, and I to refresh my spirit with a visit to my dearly loved sister. George confirmed Jack's concerns about company policy but urged him to stay with it for a while at least in the hope that *somebody* would see the light and would have the intestinal fortitude to take a firm stand on these vital policy matters. Thanksgiving and Christmas created their oases of happiness during this time of stress and discouragement.

Meantime, we knew that our hopes for a pal for Charlie should be realized in early July of 1938. We had longed for this to come to pass ever since Charlie was born, because he was eight years younger than Peyton. He would, therefore, grow up almost as an only child, unless another child came to us—but we were so lucky, we would be happy anyway. But this promise for July was just the greatest. I was determined that everyone's summer should not be ruined this time, no matter what complications arose, so made careful plans for each one, which I *thought* would take care of all contingencies. But I was wrong.

I thought it would be nice if this baby should also arrive on July 4, but the day came and went with no additional birthday to celebrate. We talked to Mary who was at Pinelands, a girls' camp not far from the farm. She, too, had hoped for news on this day. Tuesday and Wednesday passed, and Thursday morning Jack had an important conference at the plant. I, too, had an important conference—but at the hospital. Our "rocket" opened his eyes on this world at 1:00 p.m. that noontime, so his Daddy could come and see him and me on the way home from the plant. William Randolph Lacy Mead was strong and perfect and very wide awake. He was tall but weighed a bit less than the others, so his dark eyes looked too big for his face. He had a cupid's bow mouth with which he actually kissed me when I had him up on my shoulder, but we didn't tell anybody. Jack came back later for a visit—it was certainly not as chummy as being at home, but it seemed better on the whole, and this certainly proved to be the case.

Next morning early Jack phoned me to say his father, who was traveling around in Maine with his friend "Lord Alfred," had had a heart attack and was laid up at the home of a friend in West Baldwin. He was taking Gilder and Dr. Witter, and they would go up to see him. What Jack did not tell me was that the situation was very grave, that he had gotten permission from police to drive as fast as he felt he could, and they were supplying him with a police escort. The escort couldn't keep up with him, so they stationed officers at various points where there were "No Passing" signs and flagged others out of the way. Notice went out over teletype to make way for "GM 1" so he could zoom north. West Baldwin was about 70 miles from Portland, and I wouldn't like to say after all this time how quickly he got there, but it was plenty fast for those days. I believe he *averaged* over 60 miles an hour (that was *before* we had divided highways).

Dad was glad to see him but couldn't see what all the fuss was about. Jack went back to Portland to get some prescriptions filled, and then they had a hard time making his father take his medicine. He was *not* a good patient. When he seemed better, Jack brought Gilder and Dr. Witter back to Hartford but arranged for Dr. Ralph Durkee, who was to be Dr. Witter's assistant in the fall, to go up and stay at a nearby inn for a week or so, so that a doctor whom we knew and trusted would be within call. I might mention here that first as Dr. Witter's assistant, and later, when Dr. Witter retired, as his successor, he has been our dear friend and well-loved family doctor ever since.

Naturally, I didn't see much of my husband during the ensuing days. Young Jack and Peyton came down when possible. They would stand outside the nursery window, talking to "Brother Bill" and admiring him. Once they brought Charlie to see Bill. He was disappointed that the playmate I had talked about so much didn't seem quite ready to play, but he smothered him with kisses and wanted to hold him right away. I have a priceless picture taken several months later, in which Charlie *is* holding Bill in his arms, and on Bill's face is a look of absolute terror. They got over that, though. Charlie learned to be less violent in showing his love, and Bill learned that these hugs did mean love and not a desire to squeeze him to death.

I had felt perfectly well and strong from the day Bill was born but was required to stay put until he was nine days old. Then I went out on the roof for some sun. This was great! But that was the last day the sun shone for some time. Finally, when Bill was seventeen days old, Benny phoned in the afternoon to say that they could see two hours of clear weather ahead, and if I could get to Brainard Field in fifteen minutes, he could take me up to the farm, drop me, and get back before the clouds closed in again. The rest of the family, except Jack, Sr., were there already.

Everything was ready, and away we went. We had a perfect flight, and the weather got better instead of worse, as they had feared it might. It was another wonderfully happy home-coming. Jack had had two more rooms, which we called "the annex," built on to the bungalow for Charlie and Bill. Dad was better—really out of the woods, though needing to be very careful for some time. Of course, all his delightful plans for exploring every indentation of the coast of Maine had to be abandoned, but he was alive and improving and pleased about that.

Jack had a wonderful surprise for me—an outdoor dining room. It was a room, flagged like the terrace, which had been raised about a foot, about 16 × 24′, and open on all four sides, with just one corner attached to the brick house. Its southern windows looked into the rose garden which was a mass of bloom. The other sides faced the lawn, hillside garden, lake, and mountains, all of which were spread out before us. What rapture to come to this heavenly spot after the hot, steamy days we had been having! That summer was devoted to showing Dad how much he meant to us. As soon as we could, we took Bill over to West Baldwin to show him to Dad.

A few days before we were to return to Hartford, William Farren, the deputy director of research for the British air ministry, came for a visit. Some years before he had been in Hartford, and he and the Chatfields came to our house for dinner. He had shown us some revealing and interesting motion pictures that he had made of air turbulence and its effect on aircraft. I had been fascinated by his exposition, though I could not understand it well. Jack and I were both charmed with him. On this 1938 visit he had come over to a convocation of scientists at Harvard. He had not enjoyed dormitory life too much and spoke appreciatively of having a room to himself and a bath where he could have "a good wallow" in plenty of hot water. We enjoyed him no end, and he was enchanted with the children.

The end of the summer was something else again. The day the children and I left, September 19, was hot and threatening. Before we had gone fifty miles, the rain started. I was driving my car with Bill, Charlie, Myra, and my dog Anita. Harry was driving the "errand" car with all the others. I could just barely see "GM 3" which I was following—the rain was coming down in such sheets. We didn't dare stop, lest the plugs get wet and the engines "drown," so we kept going forward at a rather sedate pace. It was a long trip but we made it home finally. Margaret had everything in readiness, charming and inviting for us. It was good not to have to go anywhere at all the rest of that day.

The next day, when all the pre-school things had to be done, it was still pouring. On Wednesday, Mary and Peyton went back to school. Some friends came for lunch. The wind was blowing, the clouds seemed to be lifting, and we all thought it was clearing. After the guests left, young Jack and I went up in the playroom to amuse Charlie after his nap. Myra called from the foot of the stairs, "The apple tree's down." There it was—uprooted—our dear apple tree that bloomed so beautifully that Peyton used to think it was a Christmas tree each May! It looked so pitiful as it lay broken and twisted, its roots sticking up uselessly.

Then we noticed that trees were uprooted everywhere—great pines at the edges of the woods and all the cedars around the rose garden. I could hardly believe that so much devastation could have occurred within a matter of minutes, when we weren't even aware that the storm was so bad. Then the phone gave up, and so did the electricity. This meant no water, no refrigerator, no stove. Harry thought he'd better go get Mary and Peyton, and I suggested he bring back some ice to keep the milk, as well as an oil stove and kerosene. The city water system was all right, so there was still water at the foot of the hill. It was just our booster pump that needed electric power.

For ten days we managed with water brought up in five-gallon milk cans. We used the living room fireplace and that three-burner oil stove for cooking everything, including Billy's formula. The worst thing, however, was that Jack and I could not communicate with each other. The day after the hurricane, Andy came out to tell us that WTIC had announced that when people needed to get in touch with one another, they would broadcast messages brought to them. This was an answer to prayer, and I wrote out a message for Andy to take to the station, telling Jack that we had a stove, ice, water, and were managing all right.

That evening a neighbor, listening to his car radio, sent me word that he had gotten an answer to my message, and that my message was received, and my husband was all right. This was most reassuring, and I went blithely about my improvised housekeeping, thinking that we *had* communicated, only to find out later that it was *my* message the neighbor had received—not one from Jack at all. It developed that the storm had hit New Hampshire with ferocity equal to that in Connecticut and Massachusetts. Thousands of miles of telephone and electric wires were down. A thousand trees at least had gone down on our own place in New Hampshire.

New England was in a state of emergency, and as soon as the wind and rain had abated, Jack and the men on the farm had gone out in "Teaser" with axes and ropes and a rowboat for places where "Teaser" couldn't dock. The lake was usually low after the 10th of September, but it had gone up *22 inches* during the hurricane. Jack went systematically around the lake, going first to the houses or camps where he knew people had not gone to their winter homes. He was particularly concerned for those on islands whose boats might have been washed away or where trees might have fallen in such a way as to imprison them. So, for about three days, he was hardly ever in our house, except for breakfast and dinner and sleep; and when he was there, he wasn't listening to the radio.

One of Jack's doctor friends who owned a Beechcraft plane decided he would take Sunday afternoon off and fly to New Hampshire to see him. He told me that if I left a letter to Jack at his home Sunday morning, he would take it with him. This was a heaven-sent opportunity; and I wrote him at length and dropped the letter by on my way to church.

About 2 a.m. the next morning, I awoke to the beam of a flashlight shining in the window next to the drive. Thinking it must be Jack, though I didn't see how it could be, I ran to the window. There he was, looking up at me. He hadn't wanted to make a sound or come in, for fear of startling me and starting Anita barking. A minute later, we were in each other's arms. It was little more than a week since we had parted, but it seemed like a year. The doctor had apparently forgotten to take my letter to him, and he just couldn't stand going without first-hand news of us any longer. So after his friend left, he got in the car and drove down. It had taken much longer than usual because so many trees were down across the roads that there were lots of detours.

We talked and talked. He was proud of us for managing so well, amused at some of our improvisations, and appalled by some of our makeshifts. The next morning some heads rolled, I guess, as he went to the phone company and electric company and told them just what he thought about letting us go without service for ten days, when all over Hartford electricity and phones were back in service after 24 hours or less. Then he decided he wouldn't risk having this happen again, so he had two of the six burners on the stove converted from electricity to canned gas. He also installed an emergency generator.

One amusing incident occurred when the man came to put in the pipe to connect the stove to the tanks of gas which were to be in the basement area-way below the kitchen. He came to me in great distress, telling me he thought the drawing that had been given him was wrong, and he must be drilling into an upright, as he had gone down six inches and hadn't come through. I told him just to go on down another six inches, that there was a reinforced concrete slab a foot thick over the boiler room. He looked completely undone and ejaculated, "My gawd, this foundation could hold up Fox's store!" We found later that he had renewed his flagging strength by consuming all the cooking sherry in the storeroom by the kitchen.

Electric service was restored to us almost miraculously. I asked Jack what he did to bring this about. "Oh, I just gave them a good sob-story about your having to make the baby's formula over the living room fireplace, and having to bring water up the hill, and heat water in the kitchen over a kerosene stove, and carry it to the laundry to do the baby's washing. I was a real 'squeaky wheel.'"

After getting us all back in working order, and after working with Leonard and Andy on some urgent problems at the plant, Jack went back to New Hampshire to see about getting the fallen timber cleaned up. By the time the color in New Hampshire was at its height, I was able to arrange things at home so I could go up for our October "honeymoon." There may not have been quite as many leaves as usual, but the color was glorious anyway. The weather, having unleashed its fury in the hurricane, seemed to have used up all its bad temper. It was a time of serene, golden days with warm sunshine which we soaked up for hours on end. The lake was calm and blue, the mountains clear and silhouetted against the blue sky, and along the whole shoreline of the lake, aflame with brilliant color, the trees were all looking at themselves as they were reflected in the quiet waters. This time of renewal fortified us for the two years ahead.

Chapter XV

Decisions

The year 1939 seemed to come in just like any other year. True, there were ominous war clouds, but there had been war clouds for a long time. There were tensions at the plant, but this also had been true for several years.

But, beginning in January, evidences of deepening trouble at the plant began to be apparent. Always careful and orderly in everything that he did, Jack had been troubled by the fact that in order to please one customer or another, the engineering department had been more or less required to over-extend itself. Too many engines were being developed. There is a big file of correspondence between Jack and several of the officials in which he set down his recommendations. These pointed out the high cost of developing new engines and called for greater care in deciding which were most urgently needed. He also emphasized the need for more effective sales techniques. Each of his memos and letters was clearly and forcefully expressed and complete with facts and figures to back up his recommendations. He wasn't just airing his opinions; he was endeavoring to get a well thought-out plan of action set up so that he and Leonard and Andy could go ahead with their work.

As I have already said, Jack was theoretically head of the engineering department. Up to a certain point, the different departments were autonomous, but they naturally cooperated with one another on all matters of mutual concern; and they deferred, of course, to the directives handed down by the officials who had the administrative responsibility of the company. When asked to produce an engine of a given horsepower for a special type of plane, all departments naturally went to work on it; but *too little thought was given to how many different models were requested.*

Unfortunately Jack's letters did not evoke any real response. There was not even any evidence of interest in the statements they contained, or any intention of doing anything about them. In the afore-mentioned file of correspondence, I came across a draft of a letter in Jack's own handwriting, written to Fred during this year of 1939, which I will quote in part, for it points up the situation with great clarity.

> Fourteen years ago I came to Hartford with you at your urgent request, because I had an ambition to carry out certain business and engineering ideals. For several years thereafter, we together developed a strong, well-managed company along lines I believed in. Then came changes over which I had no control, and the consequences of which I could not foresee. Finally, in 1933, I realized I could no longer go along whole-heartedly with the enterprise and regretfully withdrew, though I agreed to continue on a consulting basis.
>
> A year or so later, at your request, I returned. At that time, you will recall, it was agreed that certain business procedures of our original venture should be restored to management. Now, after some five years, it is evident that these principles are not going to be restored, and under these circumstances, it seems best to withdraw once more. . . .

It was the same old story of battering his head against a stone wall of rather arrogant stubbornness. He hated the thought of resigning. He loved the company and most of his associates. He even loved those who had brushed aside his suggestions so unthinkingly. He felt that to cut himself off from the company that he had worked so hard and so creatively to help establish would be like cutting off a piece of himself. Yet, what choice was left to him? He simply could not and would not go along with wasting the stockholders' money and downgrading the quality of the company because of the lack of meticulous business management.

When the children were asleep, we used to thrash this all out, pro and con. Should he or should he not resign . . .? It was hard for me to be tolerant of those who owed so much of their success to Jack, yet took him and his work so much for granted. Even after all these years, it is hard for me to think about it or write about it objectively. Neither his parents nor the children knew of the unhappiness and disillusion he was enduring. Generally, when things are not going well with a husband's job, the family is very much aware of the trouble, in varying degrees, according to the personality of the husband. But Jack did not allow his anxieties and concerns to mar our family's happiness. There was the same fun time before supper if he got home early enough—otherwise afterwards. Either he would read aloud, always putting in some delightful nonsense just at the crucial climax in the story when we were all on the edges of our chairs, or he would play one of the games which he made up. These trained the children to be observant and have fun at the same time. As an example, he used to draw a picture of some article of furniture or an ornament that was visible. For instance, he would select the seven-branch candlestick on the piano and draw one arm, then maybe a candle flame on the farthest branch. The picture might be sidewise or upside down. All the parts in the drawing were well separated from each other to begin with, and the game was to see which child could first guess from these pieces what the article he was drawing was destined to be. He would continue filling in the various sections until someone guessed it.

Having grown up as an only child, except for the four short years of Doris' life, the very fact of our family was a source of unending wonder and enjoyment to Jack. Each member was especially precious to him for some individual reason, and I am sure that these times of happiness and comradeship with his children helped him through this hard time more than either of us perhaps realized at the time.

February came, and with it plans for Dr. Mead's 81st birthday on the 18th. Dad had recovered sufficiently to come to Boston to spend the winter in the apartment of a friend who was going to spend the following months in Florida. The loan of the apartment was a blessing, since Dad was not allowed to go up and down stairs and, therefore, could not live in the Winchester home. We pondered long and hard, trying to come up with a way to celebrate his birthday without risking his health. Since he could not come to us, we finally decided to bring the birthday dinner to him in Winchester, all ready except for the finishing touches. It would include a cake from S. S. Pierce decorated by a real "frosting artist." I gave her the instructions for this masterpiece over the telephone, and she carried them out delightfully. On top of the cake there was to be a station wagon, with two older men in it, traveling along a tree-lined road flanked by mountains on one side and a lake on the other. On the sides of the cake the artist had made several small pictures—a fisherman just pulling in a fish—the two men on a golf course—also one of them in a canoe. There was also one of a sailboat heeling over in the wind, although I don't think Dad or Mr. Higgins ever did much sailing, but it looked pretty anyway.

"Lord Alfred" joined us, and Dad was as happy as a boy. When it was time to cut the cake, he was very particular about who got which picture. One got a wheel of the station wagon, another got the successful cast of the fish being reeled in, I got a piece of Dad's beard, Grammy said she'd take "the back seat." We told her, "All right, but never '*a* back seat.'" We had lots of fun over the whole visit and then obediently went home when the nurse said Dad should take a rest in what had been his office, before his drive back to the Boston apartment. Our plans had worked out well. It had been a happy day for Dad, and he hadn't gotten overtired. Simple as the celebration was, he knew that loving thought had gone into it. And just having Jack with him made it a red-letter day.

One other noteworthy event occurred in February of that year. On the 22nd, quite a blizzard was raging, and Jack was watching the snow blow across the garden. Suddenly he called me to come quickly. "What is that gorgeous red bird?" He flew to a lilac bush, and there he posed—a glorious male cardinal. I had not realized how much I had missed their brilliant plumage and the clear notes of their song. We quickly put out more suet and wild bird food to welcome him, and he took up his abode *in* one of the covered bird feeders and seemed to settle down and make himself very much at home. We had never seen a cardinal this far north, and having him brave this severe snowstorm made his coming that much more special. My Kentucky home seemed to be following me to New England.

February passed into March. Still there was no action on Jack's recommendations. There was apparently no awareness of the lack of any plan of action, no facing up to the fact that the company was losing business to its competitors. This was partly because the prices of our engines were higher per horsepower than those of other companies. This had not been true at the time of the Senate investigations, and there was no reason for it to be true now. Admittedly our engines were better than the others, but good sales techniques are needed to convince the customer that the merchandise is worth the difference in price, *and there was no adequate sales program.*

At the March meeting of the board, Jack declined re-election as a director. He stated simply that he was an engineer and wanted to devote his time and energy to engineering. He said that the discussions of business details at the board meetings were time-consuming and distracting, and he therefore hoped they would understand and accept his decision. The other board members expressed dismay at this, and with one accord they begged him to reconsider. Finally, after much urging, he agreed that his resignation as a director need not be made public for the time being. The announcement was eventually made on June 27.

The correspondence continued. Jack received assurances of the high esteem in which his work was held—of the company's need for his genius. There were pleas for him to continue as a director. *But,* nothing was done about the problems which were clear as crystal to him and should have been to those who could so easily have solved them.

March was drawing to a close. It had been a hard winter in many ways, and Jack suggested we take Mary and Peyton to Bermuda during their vacation. We needed no urging. The only trouble was that young Jack's spring vacation was nearly over, which meant he would have to go back to Choate just when we would leave for Bermuda. He was a good sport about it, but we felt sad.

Then, once again, things went awry. There was to be some rearrangement of the uses of the various buildings at the plant. Whether the persons who were assigned to carry out the move got sick or had to go out of town I don't remember; but all who could have directed the move were away, except Jack and Ray Walsh, so they took on the task. The move was scheduled to go forward just when we were to leave. Jack wouldn't hear of our cancelling our plans. He called up my sister, Mary Houston, and persuaded her to let her daughter, Mary Stuart, go in his place. We loved having her, but we surely hated not having him, and he surely needed the vacation more than anyone.

It was a rare and wonderful trip. As the ship entered St. George's harbor, it was really thrilling. We seemed to be entering a gateway, and a not-too-wide gateway at that. The harbor was beautiful. We loved every moment of our passage through its waters and could hardly bear for the ship to dock. At last we finished with the formalities of entering a British possession and got on the funny little train that was to take us to Hamilton, after which we would proceed to the hotel in a horse-drawn "bus." Peyton had, amazingly, never been on a train, and he was excited at the prospect, but somewhat taken aback at this poky, little, narrow-gauge affair, which was at that time Bermuda's "rapid transit."

We couldn't get over the flowers! They were everywhere—climbing up telephone poles, covering any little vacant spots, or cascading down embankments. The gardens around the houses were a breath-taking mass of color. I just couldn't bear for Jack not to see all this beauty. The beach was wonderful, the water so clear it was like swimming in an aquamarine. The air was crisp, but not too cool. We felt full of vim and vigor, but not at all chilly.

Those ten days in Bermuda were almost pure joy. I say almost, because whenever some glorious sight ravished our eyes, like the lily fields in full bloom on St. David's Island, stretching as far as the eye could see; or the sweep of ocean, blue, purple, or turquoise from some high eminence, there was a pang because Jack wasn't seeing it too. He phoned us four or five times while we were there, and this was fine, because our letters to each other seemed to take forever to reach us.

Mary Stuart had to go back ahead of us, and we arranged for her to fly. One passenger missed the little steamer that was to take us to the island that served at that time as a landing field for the Clippers. He came roaring out in a launch which he had hired, just as the other passengers were finishing being "weighed in" with their baggage. We waited a while longer, and then the announcement came that there would be no service that day. It was too windy! Dismay was written on nearly every countenance, but a crew member reminded them that it was their lives Pan Am was being careful of, and also they would have an extra day in Bermuda at Pan Am's expense. But I'll bet the man who hired the launch wished he hadn't been quite so efficient.

The next day we did it all over again, and this time the great beautiful ship—equipped with landing gear instead of the former pontoons—did take off, and Stuey wrote us ecstatically about the wonderful trip and the delicious four-course meal which Pan Am called their 600-mile luncheon, since it lasted nearly all the way home. Elegant meals in the air were an innovation in 1939.

(The change from flying boats to land planes for transoceanic crossings had reduced both weight and parasite resistance and had thus increased both speed and payload.)

We reached home the Thursday after Easter which came on April 9 that year. It had snowed on Easter Sunday, Jack told me, and this had discouraged the cardinal, which had left us. He seemed to feel, and we agreed, that there should be no snowstorms after March. It was several years before we heard the clear, unmistakable notes of the cardinal's song again.

All was springlike and beautiful now, the snow, as it melted, having seemed to leave a miraculous green carpet. Jack was sure that the lovely day and the crocuses had come on purpose to tell us that New England as well as Bermuda could be beautiful.

When Jack and I were alone together and could talk things over, I wished more earnestly than ever that he had been free to go with us. I felt that if he could have had a complete change of scene, he could have viewed the whole plant situation in a more detached way; that if he had not been right in the midst of it all, maybe it would not have hurt so much.

Things had certainly gotten no better. Don Brown, who had heretofore been a strong, healthy person, had been having some recurring spells of illness, which the doctors could neither diagnose nor explain. With Fred away and Don ill, this brought administrative matters to a standstill. Everything was pretty well stymied.

In May a thrilling event took place. Jack told me in strictest confidence that Lindbergh was coming to Hartford on May 27, and that he, Jack, would like to have him for lunch with a group of men whom Lindbergh would find particularly congenial—probably fourteen in all. This was joyful news to me—doubly so, because it seemed as if some of the sadness that had been in the background of our lives ever since January had lifted. It was also quite an assignment for me. No on, *but no one,* was to know Lindy was coming. He had had his fill of publicity, and he wanted simply to come and see the plant, talk with some of the men, discuss the growing problems of airports, air traffic, etc., *and* he would be happy to have lunch with Jack and some of the men.

My task was to plan and help produce this special luncheon and have Margaret and Myra literally on their toes, so that everything would be perfect for this very special guest. But even to them I could not disclose who the special guest was. Lindbergh was almost a legend in our household. We had rejoiced over his successful flight across the ocean, had gloried in the reception he had received abroad, at the way he had won the hearts of all everywhere he went. Then we had all grieved when little Charles Lindbergh was kidnapped and had suffered through the anguished weeks that followed. So I knew, that if they knew who was coming, it would literally give wings to their feet and add to their pleasure, *but* I had promised not to tell anyone, so that was that.

May 27 dawned warm, clear, and beautiful. The grass and trees still had their lush springtime greenness. It was one of those exquisite days when spring is slipping into summer but is still very decidedly herself. The tulips in the planting pockets on the terrace south of the living room had gone by, so that morning we took them up, to store and dry, and planted pansies in their place. We gave them an extra sprinkling after the loose dirt was swept up, and I left Billy in his pen, and Charlie riding his tricycle up and down the terrace while I went out in the garden north of the house to cut flowers for the table. It was sort of between seasons, so it took me a little longer than I had anticipated. Then I arranged them and went to check to see that the children were happy, and when I reached the terrace, the sight that greeted me was—well, appalling!

Charlie had decided to do a little transplanting himself, but it was mostly trans and almost no planting. The terrace was a shambles of muddy, squashed pansy plants. He—now aged four—took one look at my horrified face and decided he had gone too far, even for him. He clasped his muddy little hands over his equally muddy little shirt front and said with an ineffably innocent look, "God in heaven, give me patience." This broke me up—and I knew I must not laugh—I counted to ten and then told him quietly to go and wash his hands *without touching anything* on the way, and then to wait in his room until I had time to give him a bath. All this time, I was mentally calculating how long it would take me to clean up the mess, find the gardener, get more pansies and plant them—and—and—and!!

Somehow everything got done so that by the time Jack, Lindbergh, and the others got there, no one would have dreamed that two short hours before we had had such a crisis. Billy was now full of his lunch and happily playing in his pen once more; and Charlie, freshly—and not too gently—scrubbed, was his most beguiling self—having had a few little home truths brought to his attention while the scrubbing and dressing were going on. The children and I joined the men only during coffee which, because of the beautiful day, I served outside.

Lindbergh proved to be the quiet, unassuming young man we had envisioned—tall, slender, immaculate, and handsome. He played with the children, absent-mindedly stroked the dogs, who immediately decided he was their kind of person, while talking shop with the men. My ears waggled as I heard references to ways for making night flying more feasible, or comments on instrument flying so as not to be so dependent on weather, or discussions of de-icing devices for wings and fuselage in winter flights. All the men were eager to share ideas and hear Lindy's suggestions for more adequate airports. The emphasis was not so much on stunt flying as on the need for greater safety and reliability, so that people could make realistic plans for appointments after a flight.

I would have loved to stay and listen to their discussion, but this was a man's party, so I slipped away to put Charlie and Billy down for their naps. I think it was, for Jack, the happiest day there had been in 1939.

The announcement of Jack's resignation first appeared in a summer issue of the British magazine, "Aeroplane": "Mr. George J. Mead, vice president, director, and member of the executive committee of the United Aircraft Corporation, and chief engineer and founder of Pratt & Whitney Division of United Aircraft, resigned on June 27." This concise statement of facts does not reveal all of the heart-searching involved in this crucial decision. The most creative years of his life had gone into the building of aircraft engines, which would change aviation from an experiment into a reliable means of transportation. He had given of his best and most meticulous craftsmanship to his work as chief engineer of the Wright Company, and then had surpassed it when he and Fred founded Pratt & Whitney. He had continued to surpass his best work ever since. Though constantly plagued with ill health, his work had never been allowed to suffer.

The writer of the article in "Aeroplane" may have sensed some of the pain of Jack's action, for he went on to tell, in his reserved British way, of some of Jack's accomplishments, and of some of the honors he had received; and he mentioned especially how very gratified the members of the Royal Aeronautical Society were to have had him "come to lecture to us on April 22, 1937."

The severance of any cherished relationship is always a cruelly bleak experience, whether it be the loss of a friend, or the termination of a professional partnership which had been deeply satisfying and rewarding. In this case it was doubly hard, because treasured friendships were involved, and Jack was breaking with the company he had helped to found, in which his hopes and dreams were inextricably bound up. In spite of his modest estimate of his own ability, there had been countless proofs that the spectacular success of the company had been due in large measure to his engineering ability. Fred's administrative genius could not have spelled such success without the vastly superior products Jack gave him to sell. Fred himself said as much in a tribute he wrote some years later.

I will draw the curtain on this sad moment in our lives. A wonderful chapter had closed. Although Jack's professional tie with the company was severed, most of his associates proved the depth and sincerity of their friendship for him. There was never a moment when we were not heart-warmingly aware of the loyalty and devotion of all with whom he had worked so closely. When we were discussing with Idamae and Leonard our happiness that he, Leonard, was to succeed Jack in the top post in the engineering department, Idamae said, "But Cary, you know my Papa can't fill your Papa's shoes." We assured her he could and would. And he surely *did.* It was he, Leonard Hobbs, who later brought out the great jet engines which have made aviation history since 1950—just as the Wasp and Hornet and their successors had done in the preceding twenty-four years.*

Here I must insert a little parenthesis. In an address given before the Newcomen Society, H. M. Horner, chairman of the board of United Aircraft Corporation, made the following statement: "In 1953 Leonard Hobbs was awarded the Collier Trophy in recognition of his tremendous achievement in bringing out in 1950 the J-57, which more than doubled the 5,000 pounds' thrust of any existing jet, and on top of that offered a fuel economy thirty per cent better than any other jet engine in service. It is noteworthy that aircraft powered by the J-57 won the award three out of the next four Collier trophies. Like the Wasp, the J-57 has been the progenitor of a family of engines, and it has set many of the criteria for performance in the modern jet age that the Wasp did for the piston engine."

July brought some very heart-warming letters to Jack from many people both inside and outside the company—people like William B. Mayo, Harry Stoddard, Gordon Rentschler, Jack Northrop, and many others. Then there were visits or letters from those who had worked with him over the years. One man, who happened to come when Jack was not at home, visited with me and poured out his grief over his resignation. He wound up with, "Well, to me, the company is *his* company. It always has been, and as far as I am concerned, it always will be." A letter from Joseph McCarthy, the comptroller, written in long-hand, was most eloquent, because it expressed affection and admiration so simply and sincerely.

*These engines power the sleek, swept-wing transport planes DC-8, 707, 727, etc.

Jack had felt certain for many months that resignation from the company was inevitable. Partly because of this, and partly because that was the way he did things, he made sure that to the very last day, the utmost of his ability went into his work. Since these months of frustration and working against odds had taken their toll, his physical reserves were badly depleted. However, once the decision, over which he had agonized all those months, was made and publicized, he characteristically stopped worrying about it and started rebuilding his life. The first thing to do was to get back into good physical condition. We went up to the farm early in July, so that he might hopefully start doing just that. It always seemed that once we crossed the line into New Hampshire, "the air was different"; and when he could see his beloved mountains, his spirits began to lift. This summer especially, all our spirits lifted.

I have already mentioned his love of the mountains. He loved to climb them, pitting his strength against the difficulties that climbing them presented. He loved the great trees which clothed their shoulders below the timber line. I can still see his lithe figure as he nimbly scaled steep slopes and great boulders, urging me on to the next lookout point. When he cut trails, which he loved to do, so as to encourage more people to climb and revel in the glorious views thus revealed, he always aimed to cut as few good trees as possible, and find as many lookout points as he could, to cheer us on.

One day, toward the end of July, Billy and I were on the porch at the bungalow. Billy was practicing his newly acquired skill in walking. The two Jacks had gone off that morning to clear the Algonquin Trail on Sandwich Dome. I expected them to come home between five and six, tired but happy, *and* ravenous. Suddenly—this was about four—I saw them coming across the path from the brick house—Jack, Sr., hopping and young Jack steadying him. The story came out painfully, as we eased the blood-soaked boot and sock from the injured foot. As they were working, Jack, Sr.'s axe had glanced off a dead log and sliced down the center of his instep, right through his heavy shoe and sock. Luckily they were not too far up the mountain, but even going a short distance on that rough trail, with such a deep wound, must have been a dreadful ordeal. Then he had to drive home over the notch road (which was, and is, the worst road that ever was), because young Jack, though he had learned to drive, did not yet have his license. It was the right foot that was injured, which of course made the boulders and ruts doubly painful, as he used the brake and accelerator pedals.

I bathed the foot in a solution of warm water, witch hazel, and salt, that being the most antiseptic solution I could think of that wouldn't hurt too much. Then we got him into bed, and I ran over to the other house to phone Gilder for advice. He gave me some instructions about bathing it, then soaking it in warm epsom salts, and then *bed. He must keep off of it.* Fortunately, neither the big vein nor the tendon was hurt, *but he must not walk on it.*

No sooner had we gotten him back into bed, with some aspirin to ease the pain, than John, Grammy's chauffeur, came over to tell us that she was quite ill, was not eating, and he was worried about her; would Jack please come and get her and bring her over so we could take care of her. I pleaded with him to stay quiet and let me go—I was sure I could persuade her: she and I were always very close—and I thought I could put it to her as doing something for Jack's sake. But he felt he must go, and go he did, using Dad's cane, which he had left one time, and John's shoulder.

Despairingly, I got things ready for Grammy in the downstairs bedroom at the brick house, gave Charlie and Billy their supper, and waited. Finally they returned, and I think that for once Grammy was happy to be cared for; but as I helped her into bed, rubbed her back, and then fed her her supper, it seemed too cruel that this valiant little soldier should have to be dependent on anyone. She had accepted her increasing blindness without complaint and had managed to do for herself remarkably well in spite of it. I knew this loss of independence, even temporarily, was a bitter pill for her to take. Her trouble was mostly that she just hadn't been able to see well enough to prepare proper meals for herself, and she had been unwilling for *anyone* to do it for her. After a few days of TLC and the companionship of the children, and a diet of her favorite foods, she began to pick up.

My days were well taken up between my two invalids, but it was a joy to see them both improving. Jack's foot responded well to the "green soap, epsom salt" treatment. We got some crutches so he could hobble out to a long chair on the porch. I also brought his meals over to him, so that there was a minimum of locomotion. Grammy insisted on going back to her camp, which was seven miles away, as soon as she was better, but in order to avoid a repetition of the emergency, we prepared her main meal for her each day and took it over to her. Jack's foot took longer, but it was finally healed enough for him to move around freely, but not take any real walks.

August brought a letter from Lindbergh, one paragraph of which I will quote, as it has a bearing on events soon to take place.

> I have been much encouraged by the designs of new types of military aircraft submitted by various American manufacturers. From a military standpoint, our weakness still seems to be lack of high-speed engines. I would have no concern about our standing in aviation in the future, if it were not for the continued tendency for it to become involved in politics, and for the fact that the industry cannot be certain of adequate and balanced support. Putting it briefly, I am encouraged from a technical standpoint, and very much concerned from a political one.

A wonderful letter from Mr. Farren, who was active in the Air Ministry in England, was equally timely and significant. In alluding to Jack's resignation, he said: "I am sure you will find work to do in aviation. . . . I hope you will be able to devote most of your time and thought to making the world a better and happier place to live in, rather than to the kind of purpose with which I am now concerned. We, ourselves, have reached a point where we feel that in spite of the needs of the immediate situation, we can and must devote an appreciable part of our energies to thinking and working for the future. . . ."

For my birthday that year Jack created the "picnic ground," which he knew was the spot I loved most dearly on the place. It was down on the point, about three-quarters of a mile from the house, where the pines soared nearly two hundred feet. Two of us could not reach around their trunks. Jack cut a trail from the point road to the lake, and the men cleared the small weed trees away to create a charming woodland dell. They built a fireplace for cooking hamburgers and such, and knocked together some rough but comfortable benches with wide arms so that when eating we could set down our beverages. It was close enough to the lake to dip up water for boiling corn, etc. It was a thrilling and delightful birthday gift. Then, without telling me, Jack invited all my favorite people for a cookout, had arranged about the food and everything. The whole project, including the "new look" of the picnic ground, was a complete surprise and made for me a birthday which stands out with especial clarity, for it followed so soon after the sad and disillusioning events of the past months, and was followed so soon by the tragic events of September which plunged the whole world into sorrow.

No one who was alive and old enough to be aware of events that were going on in the world will ever forget the horrifying news which stunned the free world on September 1, 1939. The war that every thinking person had dreaded for some time, and which was to plunge the world into a holocaust of anguish for nearly six years, had begun. Within four weeks Poland had been conquered, and Hitler turned his attention to the Scandinavian countries. During this all-too-brief respite, England and France tried to prepare for their turn which they knew would come soon. But even then, preparation for war took a long time.

A very sober Mead family returned to Hartford from New Hampshire that autumn. Young Jack was almost seventeen. He would be starting his senior year at Choate. There were several cousins in England who were eligible for service. We felt that the British people had not had time to recover fully from World War I. We knew that a whole generation of wonderful men and boys would be sacrificed on Hitler's altar. We just could not believe that anything so terrible, as we knew this war would be, was actually coming to pass.

On October 12, Dr. Joseph Ames, chairman of the National Advisory Committee for Aeronautics, resigned because of poor health. He had celebrated his 85th birthday on July 3. He said, "I regret that at this critical time I am physically unable to take a sufficiently active part in the work that confronts the committee, to justify my continuing as a member."

On October 13, Jack was asked to succeed him. The Hartford Courant said in an editorial, "Hartford will take a very natural pride in the fact that the President has come to this area for the appointment of a member of the National Advisory Committee for Aeronautics to succeed Dr. Joseph Ames. Satisfaction that George J. Mead, formerly vice president in charge of engineering of the United Aircraft Corporation, has been chosen for the post will not represent merely local pride. Certainly if anyone in the country is qualified to act in an advisory capacity upon aeronautics, with respect to mechanical and engineering developments, it is Mr. Mead. As chief engineer of the Wright Aeronautical Corporation and later as vice president in charge of engineering of Pratt & Whitney and United Aircraft, Mr. Mead has had an important part in the development of airplanes. He is alert to the needs of the industry and to the possibilities the future holds. It would have been difficult to find a man better qualified by thorough familiarity with aviation and by expert technical understanding of the industry."

Most of us who went through World War I will remember that at that time very little was known about the science of aeronautics. In order to encourage both manufacturers of aircraft and the government of the United States to coordinate their efforts, and to study and overcome the problems involved, the National Advisory Committee for Aeronautics was established. Dr. Ames, who had been recognized among scientists as a great authority on aerodynamics, had served as chairman of the N.A.C.A. since its beginning in 1915, when Woodrow Wilson appointed him to that post. During the ensuing twenty-four years, the N.A.C.A. had been served by many distinguished scientists—men who stood high in aviation circles and had helped immeasurably in the significant advances aviation had achieved during that period.

I am sure, though he never said so, that when the war actually started, Jack grieved over not being actively involved in getting war materiel ready to help the allies. I don't mean that he regretted his resignation. That was unavoidable. But I knew that the fact that it was necessary hurt worse because of the war. But now, after that particular door had closed, another door had opened on a wider field of endeavor. Just who was responsible for opening that door we never knew, though we had a strong suspicion as to who it might be; but in any case, it was a wise move.

Here was a more comprehensive opportunity for Jack to help and, I thought, a chance to use his extraordinary planning skill—his knack for evaluating planes and engines, and coordinating production. This preliminary experience with the N.A.C.A., working with Dr. Jerome C. Hunsaker, was an ideal preparation for the even more challenging service he was to render some months later.

The whole committee, consisting of 18 to 20 distinguished men, high in their professions, plunged into the details of the multiplicity of problems that confronted them with all the zeal and determination which had speeded up the development of the aviation industry in the years immediately preceding.[1]

Dad wasn't well enough to come to us for Thanksgiving. It seemed strange and forlorn not to be making ready for the grandparents' arrival. The children could not understand how this could be. He had been so much better through the summer of '39 that they thought we were back to normal. We went ahead with preparations for Christmas with something less than our usual enthusiasm. Somehow Dad's condition took from these preparations the joyous anticipation that was so much a part of this season. There was a feeling of impending sorrow that hung like a pall over all that we did, and then, as we were having dinner the evening of December 14, the phone rang, and it was Grammy telling us that Dad had had a stroke and the doctors thought it was very serious.

Quickly we made arrangements about the children, cancelled our own appointments, packed the necessities for a night or so, and were on the road within a half hour. Never did Jack drive more magnificently—no super highways then, but rather narrow and curving roads, blind turns, and hills. The car covered the miles swiftly and surely but under perfect and complete control every minute. I longed to be able to say some word of comfort, but I knew that words meant nothing just then. The warm communication of sympathetic silence was better, and he needed his whole attention for what he was doing.

When we reached the apartment, John was waiting for us and took care of parking the car. Grammy took us into Dad's room, and there he lay in his last sleep, the twinkling blue eyes closed, the lips in repose that had so often been curved in a smile. The end had come swiftly and quietly. He had not been conscious, even when Grammy had phoned, but I had hoped so hard that we could get there in time. I felt somehow that if he were still breathing, he would know when Jack touched his hand, and so would be comforted and strengthened by our presence and our love.

He had been wrapping his Christmas gifts that day. There they were—an eloquent reminder of his loving thought for each one of us. As I looked at him, I thought that his last day on earth had been spent in a way that was typical of him—for his whole life had been one of service, of thought for others. Only a few of the more spectacular honors came his way, for his was not a spectacular life, but he received the greatest honor a man could have—the love and esteem and confidence of those in whose service he spent his life.

Christmas was not exactly merry in 1939. We were concerned for the plight of people in many parts of the world for whom there could be no joy that year, and there was of course our own personal sense of loss; but since Christmas was not just a time for merry-making, but a time when all Christians remembered *why* it was a day of joy, we did not allow it to be a day of sadness. We knew that Dad would grieve if we did—so, even though opening his gifts brought tears, we tried to make it as happy a day for Grammy and the children as we could.

And so the year 1939, probably the hardest we had lived through up to that time, came at last to an end.

Chapter XVI

Honors—Opportunities—Service

The year 1940 was filled with varied and tremendous experiences. We were naturally concerned for Jack's English cousins and their young children. We felt sure that this "sitskrieg," as some called the interval following the fall of Poland, would prove to be only a short and *very* inadequate "breather" preceding the unleashing of the fury of Hitler's forces. We did not know how meager the preparations for war in France and England were, but we felt virtually sure that there was nothing that could meet the onslaught which would inevitably come. Our surmises were tragically accurate.

During the first week of the new year, Jack was asked to accept a position on the Board of Commissioners of the Metropolitan District. (This board also included the Water Bureau.) There were many people on this board whom he greatly admired, and he was especially fond of Charles Goodwin, the chairman. Jack was, however, doubtful about accepting, in view of his work on the

National Advisory Committee for Aeronautics, but they assured him that under no circumstances would they ever want him to let this appointment interfere with his work for the country. He still questioned his right to accept, as he was never willing to receive any honor without accepting the responsibility that went with it. However, they made him see that his planning ability, his good common sense, and his wisdom and knowledge about water resources would be valuable to them, even if he could not always attend meetings, and so he finally agreed.

Therefore, in the Hartford Courant for January 9 there was this headline: "Mead Named to District Commission." The article went on to tell of his achievements. It also mentioned that he succeeded Philip Gale. Mr. Gale was a man whom Jack admired most sincerely, and the fact that he was to succeed him made this honor doubly precious.

Then on January 10 a headline in the New York Times announced: "George J. Mead, engineer, has been selected for aviation award." The article stated further that the Institute of Aeronautical Sciences had announced that George J. Mead, vice chairman of the National Advisory Committee for Aeronautics, had been selected to receive the Sylvanus Albert Reed Award for 1939. Quoting from the article, "Given annually since 1933 for outstanding achievement in the aeronautical sciences, the award was conferred on Mr. Mead partly for his participation in the development of radial aircraft engines for military and commercial services. Presentation of the award will be at the Institute's honors night dinner on January 26."

It went on to tell in more detail of his twenty-four years of experience in building aircraft engines, of his work for Wright-Martin, then at McCook Field, and later at Wright Aeronautical. The article concluded with, "He was a founder of Pratt & Whitney Aircraft Company and became vice president and chief engineer of the United Aircraft Corporation."

Our happiness over these two wonderful honors was shadowed by our sorrow that Dad could not have lived just a little longer, so he could have been with us to rejoice over them. A day or so later came a letter from Dr. Jerome C. Hunsaker, part of which I will quote:

> Dear George, My New York Times today says the fellows of the I.A.S. have done what was suggested to them about the Reed

award, and I am naturally pleased at their good sense. This is the *one* award that can't be jockeyed, or bestowed because of friendship or favoritism. The fellows of the I.A.S. vote by mail and independently. They never get together and nobody can make a speech or a political harangue. . . .

I therefore congratulate you on the position you evidently hold among the people who really know what has gone on in the past twenty years.

How Jack's eyes shone when he showed me this letter. These thoughts, expressed by a man of such eminence and stature as Dr. Hunsaker, meant more to him than volumes from a lesser man could have.

On January 26 it was Rear Admiral J. H. Towers, chief of the Bureau of Aeronautics, Navy Department, who read the citation before Latham G. Reed, brother of Sylvanus Albert Reed, made the actual presentation. I will quote Admiral Towers' remarks in full as they show the high regard in which Jack was held by men who knew the value of his work, and I will also quote in full Jack's speech of acceptance because it expresses briefly and clearly the graciousness, the sound thinking and the sincere humility that undergirded all that he did.

Rear Adm. J. H. Towers' Presentation to George Jackson Mead of the Sylvanus Albert Reed Award

It is wholly unnecessary to point out to most of this assemblage that the outstanding position attained by the United States in civil and in military aeronautics has been built largely around the development of highly efficient air-cooled radial aircraft engines. Tonight we honor a man who has been a leader in that development from its beginning. At 28, he was engineer-in-charge of the power plant laboratories of the United States Army Air Corps at what was then McCook Field. Only a few years later he became chief engineer of the Wright Aeronautical Corporation. His rapidly expanding interest in engineering and business problems connected with aviation power plants led him in 1925 to take part in the founding of a project at Hartford, which has been the scene of his activities up to the recent past. As vice president and as chief engineer of Pratt & Whitney Aircraft, he has been responsible for developing the series of Wasp and Hornet engines now in use in civil and military aircraft all over the world. In 1929 he was elected vice president, director, and chief engineer of the United Aircraft Group, which includes Pratt & Whitney, Vought-Sikorsky and Hamilton Standard Propellers. His whole career has been one of rapid and continuous progress in his chosen field.

Dr. George Jackson Mead is a New Englander. He was born in Everett, Massachusetts, 48 years ago. He attended the Massachusetts Institute of Technology, class of 1916, and after a tour of duty as an experimental engineer with the old Wright-Martin Corporation, he launched out on the career that I have described, a road which led him to that position of eminence in the industry for which we are honoring him tonight.

Other well-earned honors have come to Dr. Mead in recent years. In 1937 he was invited to lecture before the British Royal Aeronautical Society on "Power Plant Trends." The same year he received an honorary degree of Doctor of Science from Trinity College. He is an Honorary Fellow of the Institute of the Aeronautical Sciences, an Associate Fellow of the Royal Aeronautical Society, a member of the Society of Automotive Engineers, and a member of the American Society of Mechanical Engineers. In 1939 Dr. Mead retired from the vice presidency of United Aircraft, and in October the President of the United States appointed him to serve as a member of the National Advisory Committee for Aeronautics to succeed Dr. Joseph S. Ames, retired. At the following meeting of the National Advisory Committee, Dr. Mead was unanimously elected vice chairman of that distinguished group.

Aviation in America is proud to recognize its debt to Dr. Mead, and I consider it a great privilege to present to him, in the name of the Institute of the Aeronautical Sciences, the Sylvanus Albert Reed Award "for the design and development of high-output engines for commercial and military aircraft."

Jack's speech of acceptance is quoted below:

Mr. President, Honored Guests and Members of the Institute:

First of all, I wish to thank Admiral Towers for his most generous remarks and the tribute he has seen fit to pay my work. It is particularly gratifying to know, after more than twenty years' association with the Navy, that the chief of the Bureau of Aeronautics can commend me so highly. Next, I desire especially to thank Mr. Reed for coming this evening and personally presenting the award founded by his brother, which has become one of the greatest honors open to an engineer in the aeronautical field. To the fellows of the Institute who have seen fit to confer this honor upon me, I wish to express my sincere appreciation and extend to you, each and every one, my heartfelt thanks. I am proud of the record of American engines, both at home and abroad, and for that reason I am vitally interested in their continued leadership. This will depend upon wise, courageous and far-sighted planning, the necessity for which is more apt to be lost sight of with plants running to capacity than when competition is rife. Nevertheless, constant thought and work along these lines are essential if the self-same facilities are to furnish the outstanding engines of tomorrow.

The success of commercial aviation is bound up with economics of operation, while our national defense depends more and more on superior plane performance. The future development of our aeronautical power plants then becomes of vital importance. Engines are not as yet standardized to the extent that the airplane is. Furthermore, the problems incident to the design and refinement of larger and more powerful units are becoming increasingly difficult, with the result that four to five years is required to develop thoroughly a new type, adequately service-test it and put it to work in reasonable quantities. The engineering and development expense may easily run from a million to two million dollars a year. Even the original Wasp engine of 400 horsepower, the first of which was designed and built in five months, required some three years to become firmly established. Price alone will not sell aeronautical equipment upon which the safety of the individual and the nation may depend. The skill of our designers is unexcelled, our manufacturing genius is acknowledged, and we have, in our far-flung airways, the best proving grounds in the world. These assets, despite their importance, may prove of little value unless directed into the proper channels with sufficient foresight. Unfortunately, our countrymen are apt to give the engineer undue credit in believing that he can rise to any emergency, which we know is true only within limits. As a matter of fact, we are forced to rely on what we have in a crisis, as it is impossible in a brief period to develop new engine types of value.

Such programs, involving as they do increasingly large expenditures and periods of time, should, of course, be based on the most complete and reliable information possible. The industry, therefore, is justified in plowing back into well-directed experimental and development work a reasonably large percentage of its profits. Fortunately, American executives are beginning to appreciate the value of such an investment, even though the results are not necessarily apparent to begin with. This work frequently provides the knowledge that makes possible the product that keeps the plant going in the years to come and is, therefore, the best possible insurance. Our government should do likewise; only in this case the funds should be used for fundamental investigation. Certain foreign governments have already appreciated the far-reaching significance of aviation, with the result that they have seen the wisdom and necessity of providing adequate national research facilities to supplement those of industry. In this country the National Advisory Committee for Aeronautics has done outstanding work in aerodynamics, but as yet we have no comparable facilities devoted to engine research. It has been said that our engines lead the world, which may be true now, but I know only too well what an increasingly difficult task our designers must face unless we can furnish them the kind of fundamental information that is becoming available abroad.

Our safety as a nation does not so much depend on huge quantities of military equipment produced spasmodically under pressure, but rather on a sufficient uniformity in government orders from year to year to permit maintaining the necessary trained and experienced engineering and manufacturing staffs at the various industrial plants. These men can be relied upon to produce better and better prototype equipment from year to year, under the stimulation of active competition, and thus put the industry in a position to supply almost any quantity of really outstanding equipment whenever it is required. There is no reason why our aeronautical industry should not lead the world in the same way that our automobile industry does. We now have an opportunity to establish ourselves firmly in such a position, and for this reason I wish to stress again the need for long-range planning, more and more fundamental research and a greater uniformity in procurement to stabilize the industry.

Nobody realizes better than I what a small share one person can have in the development of a modern power plant, involving, as it does, so much diversified and highly technical work. I therefore desire at this time to pay sincere and well-deserved tribute to the host of loyal workers who have made possible whatever success you may attribute to me. In closing, I wish to express my sincere appreciation of our honored secretary whose enthusiasm and hard work have made possible what to me will always be a memorable occasion. Thank you.

Letters poured in congratulating Jack on the Reed Award. They were not only gratifying, but they proved the esteem and respect which key officials in the armed services and men of stature in industry accorded him. I will quote one letter from the vice president of Wright Aeronautical and my husband's answer; both are revealing.

> Dear George: I was unable to attend the last meeting of the Institute of the Aeronautical Sciences on account of illness in my family, which I regretted very much, as I would like to have been there to witness the presentation of the Sylvanus Albert Reed Award to you on that evening.
>
> In my opinion the recognition for the work which you have done in the design and construction of aircraft engines has been too long in being acknowledged by the industry. The widespread use of the product with which you had so much to do is sufficient evidence of its importance in the aircraft industry.
>
> It pleases me very much to see you as the recipient of this award. With heartiest congratulations. Sincerely, Arthur Nutt.

> Dear Arthur: Many thanks for your congratulations on the Sylvanus Albert Reed Award. I particularly appreciate them, coming from you who have so long been a leader in our chosen field. It is embarrassing, however, to be singled out for such recognition when I realize there are others more deserving than I. Aside from that, no one knows better than I how little an individual can contribute to engine development nowadays. The finished product, as we both know, has become the work of many minds. With heartfelt thanks, I am, Sincerely yours, George J. Mead.

The happiness over the events of the evening of January 26 was short-lived. As had happened several times before, sorrow followed this high spot in our lives, swiftly and poignantly. The morning of the 27th we received word that Don Brown, who had been under treatment for about a month at the Doctors' Hospital in New York, had been operated on; the trouble was malignant and had progressed so far that there was no hope of recovery. He might live a week, or even a month, but the doctors could do nothing for him. He was only 49 and had always been so strong and vital that we could not believe this was really true. He and Jack had been closely associated since 1921, when Don had become assistant factory manager at Wright Aeronautical. He was one of the original group that had come to Hartford in 1925. His boy and our Jack were close in age, so there was that added bond.

Don was interested in, and devoted to, all his associates and their families. Friendliness radiated from him. It didn't seem possible that soon we'd have to learn to do without his warm handshake and bright smile. . . . The next day, word came that he had died.

The big sanctuary of the Asylum Hill Congregational Church was filled on January 30 with friends and associates who had come to pay him this final tribute. They had come not because he was president of the company and it was the proper thing to do, but because they loved him. That surely is the finest tribute anyone could ever receive.

The winter of 1940 was, of course, filled with work on the National Advisory Committee for Aeronautics. There is a big file of correspondence between Jack and Dr. Hunsaker, in which plans for improving the effectiveness of the committee were discussed and refined. Much of this was an amplification of some of the suggestions Jack had made in his speech of acceptance of the Sylvanus Albert Reed Award. He and Dr. Hunsaker had many conferences in between meetings, and sometimes Mrs. Hunsaker (Lady Alice, as we called her) would come with him. This was, of course, a great pleasure for me. She was a beautiful and charming lady, and we all loved her very much

This winter was also young Jack's senior year at Choate. We were painfully aware that a new era in our family would soon begin. It seemed impossible that in another year we would have a boy in college, and Mary and Peyton would follow along at two-year intervals. There would be a respite before Charlie and Billy went off, but it seemed suddenly that our family was growing up much too fast, that the closely knit family unit would soon be expanding in many directions, and with the war situation, we could have no idea what those directions might include.

Toward spring a letter came from Dr. Baxter, president of Williams College, saying that the trustees would like to confer on Jack the degree of Doctor of Science. This was a real accolade. He loved Williams and all that it stood for. If they wanted to give him a degree, the feeling must be mutual. I had always hoped that one of our boys might attend Williams, but now Jack would be an alumnus whether or not any of our sons were fortunate enough to have it as their alma mater.

Then on May 18, our anniversary, we were having a quiet family dinner. With the war situation overseas as tense and tragic as it was, our hearts were full of concern for the allies. We were discussing young Jack's approaching graduation. He was to receive an award that made us very proud of him. He was cited for the most consistent effort to improve scholastically, the most faithful and conscientious fulfillment of his responsibilities in all facets of school life, and for excellent citizenship as a member of the Choate student body. We felt that having won this award, he had also won a tool which would be of inestimable value throughout his life (and this has certainly proved to be the case). He had been accepted at Princeton with honors in math and physics, and we were glowing with pride in him and happiness for him.

Suddenly the phone rang. It was a call for Jack from Washington. When he came back to the table, he seemed utterly dumbfounded. The call had been from the office of Henry Morgenthau, Secretary of the Treasury, and the substance of it was that President Roosevelt wanted him, Jack, to work with Morgenthau on the National Defense Commission. He was to be a special assistant to the Secretary of the Treasury and to serve as an advisor in the procurement of materiel for national defense. One particular concern would be the 50,000-airplane program. We were stunned. A bombshell had indeed been dropped into our lives.

The beautiful May evening simply faded into insignificance. Whatever plans we had were abandoned. Suddenly we were all electrified into activity. Jack phoned his secretary, Alex Brown, to make reservations for him on the midnight train for Washington and engage a room for him at a hotel. While Jack collected and arranged the papers he wanted to take in his brief case, I laid out the clothes I thought he would need. I deliberately closed my mind to the immediate future. I knew that as soon as he got over the shock of this newest assignment, he would think through our family plans, and we would work out what was best. I realized that this appointment would mean that for the weeks or months ahead he would have to make his headquarters in Washington and would probably have to do considerable traveling. If he were to be responsible for procurement of war materiel, he would have to make personal contact with manufacturers all around the country and evaluate their plants, products and personnel.

Would he want us to come to Washington, or what? Already I was thinking in terms of schools for the children, a place to live, and . . . !! I had concentrated on getting things ready for this sudden trip and had not voiced any of my questions, but, as if he had read my mind, he said as we were driving to the station, "I don't know exactly what I'll be doing these next months, but I know this job will mean grueling work, morning, noon and night. There would be no point in moving the family to Washington, disrupting everything for all of you. I hope I'll be able to get home from time to time for a weekend, and I'd like to have the peace and happiness of our own home to come to when I can have twenty-four or forty-eight hours free." In the midst of the complete upheaval of his own life, his mind had leaped ahead to think of what would be best for all those who were closest to his heart.

I was oh so proud of this assignment, probably the most significant opportunity that ever could come to him, or anyone. There was being placed in his hands the chance to serve his country in the most vital way anyone could serve her. The fate not only of our own armed forces, but of those of our allies, would depend on the thoroughness of his investigations, the clarity of his thinking, and the accuracy of his evaluation of the skill and ability of those who would produce the needed materiel.

But mingled with my pride in him—my feeling of awe that he was *the* man selected by the government for this crucial task—was a deep concern for his health. I had no illusions as to what the strain of this responsibility, and the pressures it entailed, would do to him physically and nervously. He had always maintained that nobody could be right all the time. Yet this was one time when he would *have* to be right and would have to *know* he was right. Hundreds of thousands of lives would depend on his being right. He would need to do his investigating, make his studies, be sure of his facts, and then plunge ahead, battering his head against the stone wall of a stubborn and lethargic Congress, while untangling miles of governmental red tape.

It later developed that William S. Knudsen, president of General Motors, instead of Secretary Morgenthau, was to head up the National Defense Commission. Jack would be directly under him.

The Hartford Courant for May 25, 1940, carried an editorial entitled "A Gratifying Appointment." I will quote a few sentences from it:

> The Secretary of the Treasury has announced the appointment of George Jackson Mead of West Hartford as a "special assistant"

to get the Administration's program for fifty thousand warplanes underway. It is a selection that will commend itself to the entire industry, which will find pleasure in cooperating as fully as possible with this highly-qualified aeronautical engineer. The task that confronts Mr. Mead is one of almost staggering proportions, but no one knows better than he what is required and how to get things done in the shortest space of time.

Much of the development of aircraft engines is directly due to Mr. Mead's inventive genius. His mastery of technical science in this field was not gained from books alone but from his own methods of experimentation as well. Nothing more delights him than to take an intricate piece of mechanism apart, put it together again, and try to see wherein it could be improved. Along with an inquiring mind he possesses executive ability of a high order.

It is to such men as he that we must look if the Administration is to achieve its purpose with respect to the quickest possible expansion of all our military defenses.

On June 17 Jack wrote to M. S. Sherman, editor of the Hartford Courant, as follows:

Thanks for your recent note and especially for the good wishes it contained. I greatly appreciated your editorial and only hope I can live up to your estimation of me.

I am convinced that it is of vital importance for this country to be prepared and, therefore, am only too glad to do whatever I can towards this end. Unfortunately, allowing even the minimum periods of time required to produce equipment under ideal conditions, it is impossible to arm as rapidly as we might wish. Furthermore, there is a definite shortage of experienced personnel, which will be felt with greater and greater intensity as the rate of production is stepped up. Our people, I am afraid, are going to expect miracles to be performed, but it is obviously impossible to make up from three to five years overnight. As you know, some very able industrialists and experts in various fields are now devoting their entire time to problems of national defense, so that I feel a good start is at last being made on the gigantic task that lies before us. The most serious problem just now is to awaken the nation to the very real and urgent need for preparedness. Many still think "it cannot happen here," as did my acquaintances abroad not so long ago. With best wishes and many thanks for your thought of me.

Mr. Sherman's words meant a great deal to Jack, as did the

letters from many associates who wrote him expressing relief that he had been selected and had accepted the appointment to the National Defense Commission. One letter dated May 24 from Gordon S. Rentschler, president of the National City Bank in New York, was much to the point:

> You have a big job on your hands now, and I am delighted that you are the fellow that is picked to do it. Nobody in the country can do it so well. Mary and I felt greatly relieved when we saw the announcement, because we know what a fine job you will do. I will be glad to help in any way I can.

Jack's answer several days later along the same lines that he had written to Mr. Sherman, summed up the situation clearly and graphically. He was under no illusions as to the magnitude of the problems that had to be faced and solved. A subsequent letter to Gordon, dated July 15, shows how much was accomplished in less than two months.

> I feel that our aviation program is really beginning to move now that we have gotten over the first two hurdles, namely, determining what the program should consist of in detail and then asking for the necessary funds. Twenty-five thousand airplanes in two years is really a gigantic task, and it would have been most unwise to have unduly rushed the decisions which have now been reached. We are now in a position to put pressure on the industry for results and continue to help them by removing handicaps, etc.

Jack settled into a small apartment which Alex Brown had found for him, and in a matter of days he laid out a program that covered the whole engine procurement and production field for the next five years. Quoting from one of his associates, "It was an astonishingly far-sighted and detailed performance, a work that was in retrospect of incalculable importance to the nation. Nor was he content to rest with the merits of the plan's precision and scope. He was now ready to take a major share in its implementation."

One of the first problems that needed to be tackled was how the government proposed to go about *procuring* the 50,000 planes the President had called for, and manufacturing the engines for them.

Jack insisted that the chiefs of staff in the services should sit down and think out what types of planes would be needed—bombers, transport, fighters, pursuit planes, flying box cars for the paratroopers, planes for carriers, etc.—and how many of each. No one apparently had given much thought to this crucial question. For the power plants or engines, Jack's idea was to have as few models as possible—some in each horsepower category. The more standardization there could be, the simpler would be the tooling up. Therefore, each model must be scrutinized with the utmost care to be sure it was the best available.

The defense commission lost no time in sending all available war materiel to help the allies. The surrender of Belgium, and consequent trapping of 300,000 British troops, and the tense drama of Dunkerque, had shaken the American people as well as the government into an awareness of the gravity of the situation. On June 14 there was a huge shipment of planes and engines on the docks, ready to go to France. When word came that the Germans had entered Paris, Edward Stettinius, who had the responsibility of expediting shipments, rushed down to the docks and managed to divert the shipment to England. His prompt action not only meant much needed help for England at this time when Hitler was boasting he would be in London by August, but it kept our most recent models from falling into the wrong hands.

Somehow, Jack managed to get away from Washington for the Williams commencement on June 17. We left early in the morning for the ten o'clock commencement exercises, allowing time enough to drive over the shoulder of Mount Greylock. Jack was ecstatic over this detour. The delicious early morning air gave a breath of the mountains to an already joyous day.

Damon Everett Hall, LL.D., of the class of 1897, was the commencement speaker. His address was completely free of histrionics but full of pertinent historical references. It was tremendous. At its conclusion the whole student body rose and cheered until the rafters rang. Then they solemnly pledged themselves to enter their country's service; the members of the graduating class would enlist immediately, the undergraduates would plan to go ahead with their studies but would engage in defense work during vacations. It was a stirring and deeply moving experience.

Dr. Baxter's citation was graphic and straight-forward. In a letter to Jack the next day, he said in part, "Enclosed is a copy of the citation which it gave me so much pleasure to write and pronounce." The citation is as follows:

> George Jackson Mead, vice chairman of the National Advisory Committee for Aeronautics, an engineering genius whose great technical skill and administrative abilities have carried him to top rank in the aviation industry. Internationally known as a pioneer in aeronautical science, he has recently been called to Washington to undertake the all-important task of speeding up the production of American airplanes. He stands in the front line of our country's defense.

Following the respite afforded by the Williams commencement, the grueling work began once more. This was Jack's schedule. At 4:30 a.m. he would get up, make some tea and a piece of toast, and, in the uninterrupted early morning hours, lay out the work for the day. Following an eight o'clock breakfast, he and the members of the council would gather in the office at 8:30, ready to tackle their jobs. A sandwich lunch was brought in at noon, and work was resumed at 1:00 p.m. After three more hours of concentrated effort, there was another break at 4:00, then more work until 6:30 when the work day officially ended. Jack would take a good walk after dinner, to unwind a bit, then organize and tabulate his notes from the day's discussions, explorations and decisions.

After deciding on the country's needs, there was the task of persuading the aeronautical companies to expand and standardize. Jack would also have to persuade certain key automobile manufacturers to convert to the building of aeronautical engines. These undertakings required personal contacts, and for these trips he was provided with an old bomber and its crew, in which he flew all over the country to visit and talk with the different industrialists. He flew thousands and thousands of miles in that plane, the speed of which was perhaps 150 to 200 miles an hour *if* there was a tail wind.

One of the great difficulties in getting the companies to expand or convert was that everyone in industry was still acutely conscious of the administration's punitive attitude toward any organization which had succeeded in keeping "in the black" during the depression years. But because everyone in the industry knew and trusted Jack, those who were urged to expand or convert agreed to do so. The question then was, *where* was the money coming from to pay for all this? (It is interesting to note just here that it took longer for the bill authorizing the funds to finance the program for national defense to get through Congress, than for the Germans to over-run France.)

Here again, Jack's rapport not only with industry but with the armed services bore fruit. The Army and Navy always had certain funds allocated to them for research, etc. At Jack's suggestion, they wrote "letters of intent" to the effect that the companies were to go ahead and tool up. *If the expected contracts were not awarded to them,* they would be reimbursed from these funds. This confidence in Jack, exhibited by industry *and* services, was a real tribute to him. The time thus gained in speeding up production of aircraft for the allies made it possible to ship them to England in time to withstand the blitz.

One of his greatest achievements during this period was to persuade the Ford Motor Company to convert. He had conferred with Edsel Ford on several occasions, but nothing had been decided. When it came time to put the matter squarely to the Ford company, Jack asked that Leonard Hobbs should accompany him on his visit to the Ford plant. Together they convinced the heads of the organization that the Ford Company should enter the aircraft engine field as Pratt & Whitney's first licensee. Charles Sorensen, Ford's general manager, phoned Fred Rentschler for permission to send a team of experts to Pratt & Whitney to analyze the tooling up for building the R-2800, our most powerful engine, and to analyze the engine itself. Fifteen experts arrived next day by plane, and for two solid weeks they explored every facet of production at the Pratt & Whitney plant. They were amazed at the preoccupation with precision displayed by every machinist. The salvage tables held their attention the longest. The fact that a crankshaft, machined so exquisitely that it glistened like a jewel, was rejected because of a microscopic imperfection which could not even be seen by the naked eye, sent them into a soft-spoken huddle. The Pratt & Whitney people said among themselves that the Ford boys reminded them of doctors in a clinic.

When their studies were complete, Mr. Sorensen, spokesman for Ford, stated that he and Edsel Ford had gone over the report of the team and had studied their plan of procedure. Their judgment was that Ford had neither the techniques nor the facilities for producing the R-2800 double Wasp. Therefore, if Pratt & Whitney would be kind enough to supply blueprints not only of the engine, but of the entire factory, Ford would reproduce the Pratt & Whitney plant, tool it precisely to Pratt & Whitney specifications, and model its production exactly according to Pratt & Whitney standards. "What we propose to do," Sorensen said, "is to duplicate your whole operation from the floor up." This they proceeded to do with incredible speed. Twenty-two months later, the new Ford plant was turning out 400 R-2800 engines a month.

A letter from Fred Rentschler to Jack, dated August 22, 1940, is appropriate just here:

> I have already told you so personally, but I again want to congratulate you for what I think is a splendid job with Ford. I am sure that they really want to go ahead with the job and I am equally sure are the best fitted in the country to do so.
>
> Incidentally, it certainly seemed like old times to have you on the job out through the shop—it might just as well have been fifteen years ago with a group of Naval officers rather than Ford officials. At any rate you never did a better job than yesterday.
>
> I thoroughly dislike the idea of seeing you running around the plant with a green tag tied on you. We have just received for distribution our fifteen-year Pratt & Whitney pins, and no one is more entitled to one than yourself. It is going forward under separate cover and the next time you have occasion to go through the plant, I am sure it will serve a useful purpose.

Similar programs, almost identical in detail and execution to Ford's, were put through under Jack's direction with Buick, which built the R-1830 Twin Wasp and the advanced R-2000 Twin Wasp. Nash-Kelvinator, Chevrolet and Continental Motors all converted to the manufacture of aircraft engines. In the original plans drawn up by Jack, and endorsed by Major General Oliver Echols, procurement chief of the Army Air Corps, and Rear Admiral Towers, chief of the Navy's Bureau of Aeronautics, Pratt & Whitney Aircraft was requested to manufacture 50% of the nation's engine needs (35,000 engines) in the two-year period ending July 1, 1942. Thereafter, a good share of the load would fall on the licensees. By December 1940, Pratt & Whitney was shipping 1,000,000 horsepower per month. Eleven months later, monthly shipments reached 2,000,000 horsepower. Production increases continued until in 1943 the shipments were finally stabilized at 4,500,000 horsepower each month.

The above figures are no doubt dull reading, but they were vital in 1940 to 1945. They spelled the difference between being vanquished or victorious. Dr. Baxter's statement that Jack was in the front line of our country's defense was no figure of speech.

Chapter XVII

Service to Country

Our glimpses of Jack that summer were few and far between. When he phoned us, he always wanted to talk to each one, so the calls were rather lengthy. When Billy, who was two years old, had his turn, he would start off with, "Daddy, the plane's in the hangar, come home, I miss you." When he did come, the family knew that rest was essential and all were considerate, but there was family fun too.

Mary Stuart Houston, the niece whom Jack had adored from babyhood, was to be married in Greenwich, Connecticut, to John W. Meriwether on October 12, and Jack arranged his work so that he could attend their wedding. At the last moment, a problem with one of the companies on the West Coast required his presence there. This was a blow to us all, but especially to him and to Mary Stuart. It was to be a precious wedding. She and John had been in love for a long time. The bridal party were not only all cousins of hers or John's, but were devoted to each other, as well as to the bride and groom. My father could not perform the ceremony, as he was not licensed in Connecticut, but he was to share in the service. Our Jack came up from Princeton. Except for our disappointment about Jack Senior's absence, we were as lighthearted as people could be in wartime. There was no premonition of personal sorrow. The sunny Indian summer day was like a benediction.

When the minister of the church came in, Father was not with him. I whispered a question to my sister in the pew in front of me. She answered, "Father didn't feel well and it seemed best for him not to try to take part in the service." Neither of us thought it was anything but an upset to which he had been subject from time to time since a serious illness thirty-one years before. We were just awfully sad that it had occurred right then. After the service, we learned that he had been taken to the hospital. We still were not alarmed. Mamma insisted that Mary and George Houston should go immediately to do their part as hosts at the reception. She and I and my brother William and Uncle Charlie Holladay (Mamma's youngest brother) would go to the hospital and see Father and cheer him up.

When we got there, the young doctor who was to have been one of the ushers told us that Father had had a fatal heart attack. They had done everything to save him, but he had died in the minister's study. After a moment of stunned silence, Mamma said, "Now he'll never be totally blind." Then, "Cary, you and William must go to that reception, and Charlie and I will stay here and make the arrangements." We said we couldn't, we just absolutely could not do that. But she was firm. "If you don't, you are not worthy to be your father's children. Nothing would grieve him more than to have any shadow fall on Mary Stuart's wedding day. You can say that Father is not suffering, and that Charlie and I are with him."

Our parents' courage in facing whatever came had always been an inspiration to us, but this immediate concern for the undimmed happiness of her granddaughter's wedding day, when her own life had suddenly lost its meaning, transcended everything.

When we reached the house, the first question that greeted us was, "Was he conscious when you got to the hospital?" We had not been briefed for this, but for once the right answer came, "Oh, was he unconscious?" Somehow we got through that afternoon, though I often wondered what would happen if my smile came unglued, and Mary Stuart and John left on their wedding trip with their joy unmarred by sorrow.

Jack phoned me from California that night and was stricken to think he could not be with me in my hour of loss, as I had been with him less than a year before when his father died suddenly. He could not come home. We would not have wanted him to. His work for defense had to take precedence over everything. He knew we wanted him to do his utmost for the war effort even more than we wanted him near us.

A letter from Dr. Hunsaker, dated September 23, 1940, and Jack's answer of October 2 give a picture of the interlocking of his work on the National Advisory Committee for Aeronautics and the Defense Commission.

> About the production control matter. We agreed that this winter you should be more useful with the N.A.C.A. provided, before shifting across the street, arrangements were made to open a contact between the Defense Commission and N.A.C.A. through yourself as the active member and vice chairman.
>
> Bush wants to limit himself to policy and to act only as presiding officer. It will suit him fine to have you handle and organize the coordination of our advice-giving and research functions.
>
> The suggestion of Bush is that your best relief on the Commission might be Doherty, a recently retired vice president of Sears Roebuck, who is a real expert on production control. He is the sort of man who can keep a lot of balls in the air at once and lose sight of none of them.
>
> My own idea is that the plan to establish contact with the N.A.C.A. for advice, etc., should be fixed with Knudsen, Towers, Arnold, and Bush."

Jack's reply to Hunsaker follows:

> I am decidedly of the opinion that the N.A.C.A. is not occupying its proper place in government councils at the present time. During the last war it served as an unbiased technical advisor to any branch of the government on aeronautical matters, and I believe that is its proper function. I have talked to Van (Bush) of the necessity for bringing this matter to the attention of the Secretaries of War and Navy, as they may otherwise endeavor to surround

themselves with experts on matters that our group are better qualified to assist them with. Naturally, some of us will have to be available to give help when needed and I believe that you and I could be of considerable assistance along these lines.

As I told you over the telephone, the National Defense group is really a production outfit and not a defense commission as its name implies. Aside from this, the preliminary cycle of placing the work in competent hands and arranging for the necessary plant expansions is drawing to a close. Not only will the contracts soon be placed for all the appropriations, but the job will have been scheduled for the Army, the Navy, and the British requirements. It then becomes a follow-up job in which production people would be of much more assistance than I. Under these circumstances, it seems best for me to return to N.A.C.A. and render what assistance I can as a member of that group rather than to continue with the Defense Commission. Under no circumstances do I want to take over active direction of the Committee, as I am not fitted for that job. I would, however, be glad to lend a hand with the things that my experience would enable me to be helpful with. There is one job in particular that I feel we can and should do together, and that is to give advice as to the new types of equipment that should be developed for production two years hence. Certainly that is a function of N.A.C.A. and we could render really valuable aid in this connection.

His work was certainly going on at a break-neck pace. He called Captain Kraus on October 18, giving him his itinerary for the next ten days or so. Kraus made a transcript of it, which is quoted below, for Mr. Knudsen, Alex Brown, and others who would need to know his whereabouts.

Mr. Mead called from Santa Monica at 10:10 a.m. 18 October 1940. He advised that he was continuing his visits to aircraft factories in the Los Angeles area and that his address would be the Del Mar Hotel, Santa Monica, until Tuesday, 22 October, when he would leave by air for Sunnydale (Mountain View, California). He will be in the San Francisco area until sometime on Wednesday when he will leave for Seattle, arriving at that point late Wednesday. He will spend part of Wednesday and all day Thursday in Seattle, where his address will be the Olympia Hotel. On his present schedule, Mr. Mead expects to arrive in Hartford probably late in the afternoon or early evening of Saturday, the 26th of October, will remain in Hartford over the weekend and through Monday,

> and according to his present plans will be in the office on Tuesday, the 29th of October.

Each stop required him to shift gears mentally. Each company he visited presented different problems. So much flying in that uncomfortable bomber would be exhausting, without the need to solve problems the minute he landed anywhere. The mental and physical stamina required for this task was tremendous.

He had thought his work for the Council of National Defense would be completed by November 1. Nearly all the orders were placed and the work scheduled. He felt that he should devote his time to the affairs of the National Advisory Committee for Aeronautics. He told Mr. Knudsen that as vice chairman of N.A.C.A. he would be available to advise the commission on aeronautical matters, as that was the function of the committee. However, Mr. Knudsen urged him to take full charge of the bomber program. A letter dated November 2, 1940, from J. C. Nichols, Director of Miscellaneous Equipment Division, together with Jack's response on November 8, are significant.

> I was concerned when I heard you were resigning as head of the aeronautical section, but I was greatly relieved when I heard you had become directly associated with Mr. Knudsen in full charge of the coordination of the bomber program and its relation to the airplane and automobile industry.
>
> I take it that this is even greater responsibility than your work in the aeronautical section of the Defense Commission, and I know you will do as well as any man in the world could do with all of the difficulties and speed requirements.

Jack's response on November 8 was as follows:

> Thank you for your kind thoughts of me as expressed in your recent note. I had fully expected to return to my duties with the National Advisory Committee for Aeronautics on the first day of November, but could hardly refuse Mr. Knudsen's request that I stay on and help him with certain new problems. Hoping that this will give me the opportunity of seeing you from time to time. . . .

A memo to Mr. Knudsen from Jack on November 4 spelled out exactly what he understood his responsibilities in this connection to be, and the need for appropriations by the government to pay for the bombers, and for planning ahead by the services for their probable needs after 1942.

> It is my understanding, as a result of our discussions last week, that you wish me to take charge of the following matters:
>
> 1. Work out a plan to provide for additional capacity of 700 airplanes a month with engines and propellers. Two government plants, later to be used as depots, with a capacity of 100 heavy and 200 medium bombers per month are to be considered as a part of this capacity.
> 2. Determine how the automotive industry can best assist with the production of 12,000 additional bombers.
> 3. Schedule the releases beyond the present program and make a tentative distribution of production between our services and the British subsequent to April 1, 1942.
>
> In order to go ahead intelligently with this work, I need definite instructions on the following points:
>
> a. Ultimate size of Army depots required and location of same.
> b. Date to be assumed upon which funds will be available for the new bombers and the amount of such appropriations.
> c. The ratio of capacity to be allotted to our services and the British for the period following that covered by the present program, and the estimated monthly requirements by quantities and types for the Army, Navy and British.
>
> It is important to point out in connection with the above that the peak of production based on the manufacturers' deliveries will be reached in the spring of 1942 and that deliveries will fall off rapidly thereafter unless further orders are placed early in the coming year. Additional funds will therefore be necessary by that time and a final decision on the types of equipment to be purchased.

The task of persuading leading automobile manufacturers to build the bombers was as demanding as the efforts to enlist the help of Ford, Buick and Chevrolet in building aircraft engines had been. A letter to I. M. Laddon, vice president and chief engineer of Consolidated Aircraft Corporation in San Diego, dated December 24, 1940, gives a partial outline of the plans for accomplishing this.

> I am writing you quite unofficially as a friend in order that you may have a better picture of the bomber situation as it pertains to

the depot plants. Further consideration of the matter has led to the belief that the only way we can get the maximum assistance from the automobile group is to have the three largest companies each sponsor one type of bomber which the Army requires. This makes available the management, supervision and experience of the strongest companies, who, in turn, can subcontract the work as their experience dictates among the parts makers and others in the automotive field. Each of these large companies will then be responsible to furnish the necessary subassemblies and parts to the depot plants for the particular type of plane they are concerned with. I am glad to say that Chrysler, Ford and General Motors have tentatively agreed to take educational contracts looking toward carrying through such a procedure. We have asked Ford to take on the B-24, but before committing themselves, they naturally wish to know more about the job. Mr. Sorensen has, consequently, agreed to visit the coast with me, arriving in San Diego on the 8th. I called Fleet regarding this and gather this will be satisfactory to him. It is, of course, essential to work out the details of such a procedure as soon as possible, so that I am coming along with the hope of expediting matters.

What I hope we can arrange is for Mr. Sorensen to become familiar with the construction of the B-24 and your shop methods with the hope that he will agree to become responsible to furnish the material required by the depots building this type of plane. We really have a selling job to do and I don't know of anyone else who could do it as well as you can. The situation abroad is so serious that we certainly shouldn't let company or personal opinions deter us from going forward rapidly and efficiently towards setting up the best possible secondary source of supply of bomber parts. The safety of our country may well depend upon doing so. I surely hope the industry will cooperate in this regard as whole-heartedly as they have so far with everything else we have tried to do. Incidentally, I feel this procedure will take the minimum amount of your time in the end and that the aircraft industry cannot expand any more at present without seriously interfering with the deliveries required by our present program.

Money is now available for the educational contracts and the Air Corps is moving right ahead to place these as fast as possible with the three companies indicated. Management contracts for the depots are also in the works, which will provide not only for the necessary supervision by the parent companies, but for such assistance as they may render the educational program. In other words, you will be reimbursed for engineering services, drawings, parts,

> and out-of-pocket expense that may be involved. To expedite matters, we hope to issue letters of intent on this situation, which will cover you until suitable contracts can be drawn up. With best wishes for the new year and hoping to see you soon. . . .

As 1940 passed into history, the future looked black indeed. The new year was greeted by a partially awakened nation. Italy had joined the Axis powers, which were constantly attacking on new fronts: Africa, the Balkans and Greece. Meantime, the Soviets had attacked Finland. The Finns had fought valiantly but were helpless against the might of Russia. It seemed that nothing could check the deadly forces of Hitler's and Mussolini's war machines.

America's industries had stepped up production to an amazing degree. Plants were running three shifts a day, seven days a week, with a staggered schedule so that each employee would get one day off each week. By February all the orders were placed and contracts drawn. The time had come when Jack, having fulfilled his responsibilities for the Defense Commission, could relinquish the reins to a follow-up man.

In going over my records for 1942, I found a speech entitled "Something of the Beginnings" which he evidently gave March 27, 1942. It gives a vivid and authentic account of the problems faced in 1940 by the Defense Commission. The expansion achieved during this period and the mobilization of our country's industrial resources in time of emergency are almost incredible, and I am, therefore, quoting all of this particular speech, even though it involves some repetition.

"Something of the Beginnings"

"It is hardly possible that the Wright Brothers, less than forty years ago, could have conceived the dominant influence their new invention was so soon to have over world affairs. Today we realize that air power may win this war. That means the quantities and the performance of our own aircraft may well be vital to our very existence. The successful evacuation of Dunkirk and the inability of the Germans to date to gain control of the air over the British Isles has adequately proven that superiority in numbers alone is of little value compared with superiority in performance, even giving due credit to the courage of the RAF pilots. The mere appropriation of huge funds will not win the war either, as was well illustrated by the President's report on the Lend-Lease activities of last year. To win, we must have the maximum number of superior planes at the front at the earliest possible date. Appropriated for, "on order" or minus some vital equipment, won't do. As I was closely identified with the beginnings of the present aircraft program, it occurred to me you might be interested to know something of what was involved to make possible our present production.

"Early in May 1940 President Roosevelt announced his 50,000-plane program. Most people, laymen as well as executives in the aircraft industry, raised a questioning eyebrow at such a stupendous quantity. Regardless of our political faith, we must at least concede the wisdom of President Roosevelt's vision in this particular. Shortly after the program was announced, I was called to Washington to act as Secretary Morgenthau's adviser on aviation. At that time large orders were being placed for American-built planes by Great Britain and France, and Mr. Morgenthau was virtually the administration's chief of aircraft production. This seemed quite illogical offhand, but was apparently due to Roosevelt's desire to aid the allies as far as possible, which included facilitating the large financial transactions involved. Although I was in the Treasury but a few weeks, I could not help but admire the earnestness and hard work of the Secretary as well as the efficiency of the Treasury organization.

"The 50,000-plane objective having been set, it was next essential to know the division of this quantity between the Army and the Navy and the breakdown into the various types of aircraft required by each service. Fortunately, General Arnold and Admiral Towers, the respective heads of the service air arms, were well known to me, and we quickly arrived at an amicable division of the total. Then followed the preliminary breakdown into types and a cost estimate, all of which was accomplished in a few days. When this job was done, I carried the results into Mr. Morgenthau who immediately took the memorandum and left for the White House just across the street, remarking: "That's our program!" A month was to go by, however, before the final program was agreed upon. Meanwhile the Defense Commission came into being and I was transferred to it as head of the aeronautical section.

"Mr. Knudsen, my new boss, although known to me by reputation, was also a stranger. I found him in a large office in the gorgeous Federal Reserve Building. Just before we parted he said, 'Come on over and bring your gang,' which I did. That began an association that was to last some eight months and brought me into daily contact with the Army and Navy air arms as well as both the aviation and automobile industries.

"The choice of planes with superior performance for immediate production was limited to prototypes that were flying experimentally or to orthodox new designs which were well along towards experimental construction. Military aircraft are custom-built to Army and Navy requirements, as you no doubt know, and cannot be taken off the shelf. Fortunately the Army had two fighter types and a long-range bomber which had had limited service tests, while two new medium bombers and another long-range bomber were coming through experimentally. The Navy were in comparable shape with shipboard fighters, medium and long-range patrol planes and a dive bomber which, incidentally, is a type our Navy developed. These various planes compared favorably with the best the Germans and Italians then had in production. It was somewhat of a gamble to order into large-scale production several planes which had not then been service-tested, but to do otherwise would have given us inferior aircraft. Practically all of our ships were deficient as regards armament and protection of the crew and the fuel supply, due largely to the rapidity with which these features had been developed in actual warfare. This necessitated adding guns, increasing their caliber, and providing power turrets to guard the bombers from attack in the rear. It also meant adding bullet-proof tanks which, although used in the last war, had been discarded, and protecting the pilot and some of the crew with armor running up to a half-inch thick. These changes necessitated major structural modifications in the airplanes, which all took time.

"The President's decision to send our latest military types abroad under the Lend-Lease agreement was fortunate, even though contrary to the wishes of the air arms. Their point was that this policy would give our secrets to the enemy in advance of our entering the conflict. We have gained immeasurably, however, since most of our plane types were combat-tested a year or more before we entered the conflict. This gave the opportunity of making any other necessary changes at an early date, which benefited both ourselves and our allies.

"My first job with the Defense Commission was to get from the Army and Navy their final programs, so that these might be approved by the President and the necessary funds requested from Congress. Actually this took a month of bickering as to the correct proportion of training planes, fighters and two- and four-engine bombers, etc. Finally General Arnold and I interrupted a general staff conference and insisted that the almost daily change of requirements cease, as no one—I might add not even God himself—could tell the exact quantities required, for the simple reason that no one knew whom, where or when we were to fight. General Marshall fortunately agreed with us. It was but a comparatively simple job to evaluate the cost of the Army's share and add it to the Navy's. I shall never forget taking the estimate, as it emerged from the typewriter, on a hot July day and rushing to the White House, there to put it in my chief's hands just as he went into a conference with the President. On my way back I commenced to marvel at the magnitude of the total cost—over two billion dollars. Until then it was only a number that I had gradually built up, but all of a sudden I realized it was a real Amos and Andy figure!

"While this was going forward, I had a chance to become somewhat acquainted with the Commission which, as you will recall, consisted of Messrs. Knudsen, chairman and in charge of production; Stettinius—industrial materials; Hillman—labor; Henderson—prices; Budd—transportation; Davis—agriculture; and Miss Harriet Elliott—consumer protection; with Donald Nelson—coordinator of purchases. In our production group were John Biggers, president of Libbey-Owens Glass, deputy commissioner and in charge of tanks, trucks and tractors; Harold Vance, chairman of the Studebaker Corporation—machine tools and heavy ordnance; E. F. Johnson, retired from General Motors and previously with du Pont—ammunition and light ordnance; Admiral Land, chairman of the Maritime Commission—shipbuilding; Bill Harrison, vice president and chief engineer of A.T.&T.—construction; George Moffett, president of Corn Products Refining Company—food and food products; J. C. Nichols, a business man from Kansas—miscellaneous equipment; and myself—aircraft.

"As soon as the program was approved, estimates of the raw and semi-finished materials required were made and the necessary rates of production estimated. There has been so much talk of aluminum shortage that you might be interested to know that an aluminum estimate was made in July 1940 and turned over to the Metals Division of the Defense Commission. Subsequent events seem to indicate this did not get the attention it might have at the time. On the other hand, a single company, the Aluminum Company of America, was being asked to produce practically all the aluminum for the entire war effort. Reynolds Metals was finally brought in, but in all fairness they are new at the game. I have the greatest admiration for the Aluminum Company, which has accomplished wonders despite the fact they were formerly damned up and down by the administration.

"The next job was to allocate the work among the various plants. As we had but seven major plane companies and needed three times the floor area and five times the personnel then available, this was a difficult problem. Consideration had to be given the size of the existing plants, the orders on hand, labor available, transportation and even housing. Obviously all existing plants had to be expanded, but how, where and by whom? First, we provided for doubling the plant of each company that had originated a design. This was done in the main regardless of the geographical location of the original plant in the interest of speed. The point was that each parent company, with its relatively small organization, could expand more and faster at home without interfering with its production, than further away. It was easier, and quicker too, to train mechanics in the older plant alongside. The next move was to work toward an ultimate centralization of our facilities in the mid-continent area. To this end we insisted that the other third of the production capacity needed was to be located between the mountains. This policy was designed to establish seven large new self-contained plants inland and force the majority of subcontracting for parts away from the seaboards. The factories started in this way are practically all in production now and are largely staffed by key men trained in the parent factories. To further safeguard our production, I feel we can and should gradually move at least half of the machinery and men from the coastal plants to these inland plants which could be readily expanded for the purpose. The cost would be relatively small compared with the increased safety, and the necessary buildings could be erected in less than three months. This would place two-thirds to three-quarters of our plane capacity between the mountains. Some coastal plants are desirable both to provide the necessary flying boats which cannot well be built inland due to the time that would be lost when most lakes are frozen and because, after all, a large volume of skilled labor is to be found along our seaboards.

"Making provision for the engine requirements was decidedly more difficult, since there were but two large companies, namely, Wright and Pratt & Whitney, who, besides doing the majority of the domestic business, also had large orders for engines to be installed in foreign-built planes. A third, General Motors' Allison Company, was in the making, but at the time of which I speak—July 1940—was still small. To begin with, each existing engine plant was enlarged first to balance its equipment and then to at least double its output. This, however, still left us far short. Wright was willing to double again and we agreed on a huge plant at Cincinnati. Pratt & Whitney felt they would be unable to provide management for an inland plant, so Ford was approached to build one of their designs and Buick the other.

"The volume of Allison engines required was not so great, as these were used in fighters only, so that expansion at Indianapolis was sufficient. As the Allison engine was more or less untried in service, it seemed wise not to have all our pursuit eggs in one basket. The only interchangeable engine was the English Rolls-Royce which had been thoroughly proven by the RAF. The British were in great need of more of these engines and consequently were only too glad to cooperate with us in setting up an additional source here. We first asked Ford but were turned down. Next we turned to Packard, largely due to the fact that this company had successfully built Liberty engines during the last war. They took on the job and by rehabilitating parts of their plant and putting up a few new buildings are doing a creditable piece of work.

"Our engine capacity in particular was materially increased too by subcontracting the parts. Pratt & Whitney had always followed this policy in order to keep down its investment in plant and machinery. Now we extended it to the limit as a means of stepping up production and spreading the work both geographically and physically. To do this successfully requires careful selection of sources, excellent liaison work with the prime contractor, and good inspection; otherwise the parts will not go together.

"The next step was to build up a master schedule for planes, engines and propellers, so that the various contract delivery requirements could be coordinated and the production of the component parts brought into step with one another. This scheduling had to reflect the plans for increased production; first, from existing facilities, then from the new plants at the dates when it was estimated these would come into production. It was soon evident that scheduling of an industry could hardly accomplish the desired results unless it were to cover all customers. During the period of which I speak the American aircraft industry was practically sold out to Great Britain and France. Furthermore, these countries had put up funds for large plant additions that were thus obligated to their work. The defeat of France failed to ease the situation, as the British promptly took over the French orders. What was even more embarrassing was that the late Henry Purvis, the head of the British Purchasing Commission, set out to take up all the aircraft and machine tool capacity in the country for an indefinite period. It was evident that at any given time there would be a certain maximum production available, so that Knudsen ruled the British might have a certain percentage of the total, the balance going to fill our needs, while both countries should benefit from the facilities regardless of who paid for them. With this point settled, it was next agreed that we should schedule all the orders in the aeronautical section and that no new orders could be placed without our sanction.

"We were now ready to get at the job of placing the contracts. The actual paper work was done by the services, who had the funds, but under our general supervision. Knudsen measured the efficiency of our efforts by the dollar volume of contracts placed. The first stumbling block was that Congress did not appropriate the required funds for a considerable period after the estimates were in their hands. It runs in my mind that it took decidedly longer to get our first aircraft appropriation than it did for the Germans to conquer France. While waiting impatiently for Congress, it finally occurred to some of us that the services had sufficient unobligated funds to guarantee payments of the patterns, dies, jigs and materials required to start the big program, and, furthermore, the President had some unassigned funds we could draw on. That started the idea of "letters of intent" which advised a manufacturer the Army or Navy would place an order with him for such and such equipment as soon as Congress authorized the funds. Meanwhile the services would guarantee the cost of tools and materials and would also agree to take these over in the event a contract was not finally negotiated. Immediately there was a hue and cry from "across the street," meaning the Army and Navy. This was illegal and could not be done, but we did it with the help of their own judge advocates and thereby speeded up production anywhere from one to two or three months.

"It was essential to institute shortcuts, as you can well imagine the complication of expanding a whole industry more or less overnight when it involved going right back to the source of the raw materials. There just weren't enough people in Washington to do the job. To simplify matters, I decided that we should only deal with the prime contractors and have them, in turn, deal with their subcontractors, except in cases where a subcontractor furnished a large number of prime contractors. This procedure cut down our work in Washington and spread the load thoughout the organizations of the larger companies who were well able to carry it. Their requests for additional facilities, both buildings and machinery, included therefore those of their principal subcontractors. To further simplify matters, it was agreed that the service having the most work in a particular plant should deal exclusively with that plant and should include the requirements of the other service with its own. This meant the manufacturers had only to deal with one service instead of two in negotiating contracts and making the final arrangements for new facilities. It was another of those things which couldn't be done, but we did it. I won't bore you with the details of financing the plants and the various plans that were adopted. Briefly, each manufacturer was encouraged to expand his own plant as far as he was willing. Beyond that, the government stood ready to finance the additional facilities, and we tried in general to lease these to the manufacturer who had the equipment contract, with provision that he operate them throughout the emergency.

"The magnitude of the task unfolded from day to day. Normally it would have been a comparatively simple matter to choose the types of planes, decide on the quantities, place the contracts, and let the manufacturers do the rest. In this case, because of the huge quantities involved, the customer had to provide land, factories and machinery, as well as make provision for training labor and housing. This would not have been so difficult if it had applied only to the aircraft industry. However, the needs of this one industry fanned out and reached back eventually to many others and to the raw material supply through their direct and subcontracting needs. Not only did we have to consider making planes, engines and propellers, but raw materials such as steel, aluminum, magnesium, etc., as well. There were also the semi-finished parts to be considered, including bar stock, tubing, structural shapes, castings and forgings of steel, aluminum and magnesium. Finally, consideration had to be given to parts normally purchased finished, such as wheels, brakes, tires, landing gear struts, navigation instruments, radios, ball and roller bearings, piston rings, spark plugs, wire, starters, generators, fuel pumps, gun synchronizers, and myriads of other things. The manufacturers of all these items invariably had plant, machinery and material requirements that had to be considered if completely equipped planes were to be made available on time. The modern engine has upwards of three thousand separate parts, while a good-sized airplane may easily have forty thousand pieces, not to mention rivets. By the way, you might like to know that a long-range bomber has some 450,000 rivets. All this may give you some idea of the number of problems involved in such a program.

"Early in the fall of 1940, before the original program had been fairly launched, it was decided that the bomber requirements should be materially increased. This was a fortunate decision, as things have turned out, but it seemed like the straw that might break the camel's back at the time. The fact was that the aircraft industry had all it could possibly do, so that insisting on further expansion at this time would very probably have resulted in fewer rather than more planes. The only other group who had the requisite mechanical experience and managerial ability was the automobile industry. It is true that an automobile manufacturer could not turn readily from cars to planes, but he understands the handling of metals as well as the scheduling and following of innumerable parts which must all come together at predetermined times if the completed product is to roll continuously off the end of the assembly line. It was management more than anything else that limited the amount of work that could be undertaken by the aircraft industry, as the industry itself was small and there were relatively few executives. To bring in outsiders and especially potential competitors was a delicate task, since the whole-hearted cooperation of the plane manufacturers was necessary for success. The latter, generally speaking, were disinclined to give over their designs to the financially powerful motor car manufacturers, since they felt they had nothing to gain and everything to lose. As things have turned out, each group has found the other able to teach invaluable lessons. The aviation industry is learning the secret of mass production from masters of the art, while the automobile manufacturer is being shown cheaper methods of handling sheet metal and how to use light metals, which may well revolutionize the post-war motor cars.

"While the increased bomber requirements were being discussed, the Air Corps proposed to establish four mid-continent depots for plane repair and maintenance. It was suggested that these depots be used to assemble bomber parts to be built by the automotive industry and that the parent plane organizations should staff and operate the depots in order to insure an experienced organization at each. The great disadvantage of the plan was transportation, since the parts were large and hollow and could not be nested.

"About this same time it was proposed that all the automotive manufacturers in the Detroit area be allowed to choose the parts of the several bombers they were willing to make, depending on their experience and equipment. On the face of it, this seemed like a good plan to utilize large and small shops alike. The danger I saw in both of these schemes was that no financially responsible group could be looked to for a complete airplane and the great difficulty, if not practical impossibility, of making the parts fit when brought together for final assembly. I therefore worked toward contracting with the three large automobile companies, namely, Ford, General Motors and Chrysler, for each of the three types of plane and letting them subcontract as they saw fit among their reliable vendors. This spread the work and made a reliable and financially strong company responsible for the results. The scheme worked out, with General Motors taking the North American bomber, Chrysler the Martin, and Ford the Consolidated. Chrysler, because of their commitments on tanks and the fact that they were a smaller organization than the other two, were not willing to be entirely responsible for the complete plane, but they did agree to general supervision of the project as a whole.

"The biggest job of all was the Consolidated bomber, twice the size of either of the others, and I very much wanted Ford to undertake this. It was a colossal task, but I had every confidence in the organization and believed they could handle it despite their other war work. A year ago last January I met with Edsel Ford, his two sons, Henry II and Benson, and Charles Sorensen, his general manager, at San Diego. We spent five days together on the coast, first in the Consolidated plant so they might become familiar with the problem, and finally in a rapid tour of the principal plane plants in the Los Angeles area, which included Douglas, Lockheed and North American, so they might see the various methods used by other manufacturers.

"Soon after my return to Washington, I was advised they would take on the job and proposed to build a big plant, now known as Willow Run, at Ypsilanti, Michigan. As a matter of fact, Sorensen had sat up most of one night while we were in San Diego, laying out this plant on the backs of envelopes, a fact I learned when I discovered him in his pajamas, still working away at breakfast time. His layout involved an assembly line over six thousand feet long and probably the single largest building in the world. Mr. Sorensen is a compatriot of Mr. Knudsen. They were both born in Copenhagen. He has a dynamic personality and is without question one of the world's greatest production men.

"More bombers meant more engines, and here again we had to turn to the automobile industry. The additional quantities of Pratt & Whitney engines were provided for by increasing the facilities of Ford and Buick. Bringing Studebaker into the picture supplied the additional Wright engines. This arrangement had the further advantage of increasing our engine production between the mountains and, incidentally, reducing the transportation both to the west coast and midwest plants.

"A number of cure-alls have been suggested from time to time in connection with the aircraft program. There has been a lot of talk of 'standardization' to win the war, and automotive executives are apt to be partial to this idea, as it has been a contributing factor to their industrial success. For example, dies for one type of body satisfy the needs of Chevrolet, Pontiac, Buick and sometimes Cadillac, while a single wheel base takes a great variety of bodies, etc. The military requirements are so entirely different for each type that no such compromise is feasible; consequently, no comparable standardization is possible. The best that can be done is to reduce the number of types, such as trainers, fighters, bombers, etc., to a minimum and then the number of models of each type put in production. Generally speaking, aside from training planes, two models of each type were ordered. This spread the load between two parent organizations, which let us get going much faster and, furthermore, provided some assurance of having at least one good airplane of the required type. There is some merit to going further than this now, although it is doubtful if the advantages would be great. It is only possible to achieve the automotive type of standardization in the case of equipment, such as gun mounts, radios, brakes, tires, wheels, landing gear struts, starters, etc.

"Conversion of the automobile plants has been another favorite topic. Reuther proposed by this means to produce five hundred planes a day, etc. The fact is very little machinery in an automobile plant is suitable for making aircraft parts. The reason is that the machines are what we call 'special,' that is, built for a particular job. Unfortunately the aircraft parts are not of the right shape nor size to fit into these tools. Even the buildings themselves are not adapted to airplane construction, because of their low ceilings and multiple-post construction. As I said before, the big thing the automobile industry had to contribute was management and their skilled labor. There can be no question that it would have been better to have started curtailing automobile production earlier, but, as you will remember, the President himself promised we would arm without reducing our standard of living.

"The automobile manufacturers, as a rule, were at first contemptuous of the manufacturing methods used by the plane people. Instead of massive steel dies for making the sheet metal parts, the airplane man used lead dies and rubber sheets which are both inexpensive and very satisfactory for working aluminum. One of the foremost automotive production men advocated spending millions of dollars to make steel dies on the theory that this would speed up plane production assembly, before he completely understood the problem. As a matter of fact, the man-hours required for all the die work on an airplane does not exceed ten percent of the total, so that an improvement in this figure could hardly be expected to accomplish wonders. Against this, it takes 25% of the man-hours to install the equipment alone in a modern military airplane! Naturally, once the automobile people understood the problem, their good sense dictated largely following the practice of the airplane manufacturers as far as dies were concerned.

"Before closing my paper, I wish to say a few words about why the rate of aircraft production cannot be increased more rapidly. To begin with, it is not a question of money nor of buildings which can be quickly provided almost anywhere. The job is to procure or train management and supervision and provide at increasing rates the necessary machinery and raw materials. This process takes time, which is something money can't buy. We are suffering now from unbalanced production, as the expansion has not been uniform throughout all the plants and industries. This can only be prevented by a step-by-step growth, completing each step and balancing the facilities before attempting another. It is easy for the President to set new goals, but there is a practical limit to how fast these can be achieved. An effort to force production to a higher rate is quite apt to result in the reverse effect, as materials commence to be absorbed by the machinery, for example, required for the expanded production, which deprives the airplane manufacturer of the material for current parts.

"Our present effort could be materially accelerated by a few simple expedients such as any large commercial enterprise requires for success. First of all, our war needs should be surveyed to determine the types, quantities and deliveries of the necessary equipment. Editorials from time to time bear out what I believe to be the case—that there is no master plan nor any group, such as a war council, who can review the job as a whole and decide whether airplanes are more important than battleships, whether we should have tanks or anti-aircraft guns and the required quantities of each. So far there has been more or less shotgun ordering—a lot of everything because it might be needed. Obviously, we cannot make the best possible progress in filling our vital needs if man-hours, machines and materials are thus to be squandered. It is just as important to overhaul our defense orders as to curtail and slow down civilian production.

"Next, clearly defined jobs are essential to efficiency, and so is the grouping of all kindred work under one responsible head. For example, no one person is responsible for aircraft production, but instead a large number of agencies and individuals. England has a Minister of Aircraft Production and Germany has a single head, as no doubt do Italy and Japan. We should not tolerate our present setup, as it does not provide for the direct action so necessary to make up the lost time before it is too late. All these major wartime jobs are stupendous in size, but the same sound business principles normally applied to our industrial effort will, I feel sure, solve the problems involved.

"The selection of able, experienced executives for each job is vital and may require some sacrifice on the part of industry, as there are relatively few good men on the loose. The men we need are not interested as a rule in dropping an essential task to take up a poorly defined government job with greatly subdivided authority, and you can hardly blame them. Such an attitude may sound unpatriotic, but unless a man is free to accomplish something worth-while, it is quite likely he can contribute more to the defense effort as a whole by sticking to his present job. A way should be found, however, to properly compensate such executives and specialists, as their private means are frequently inadequate for them to live on civil service salaries. Unless this can be done, an inferior class of man is apt to be found in positions of great responsibility just at a time when we need those best qualified. The right key men will go a long way to win the war providing they are given adequate authority. The greatest handicap to speeding production right now is in Washington and not in industry.

"Too long as this paper has been, it has only been possible even then to sketch the outline of what was done during the first eight months to make the 50,000-plane program a reality. We could undoubtedly have accomplished a good deal more had we been working under war conditions, the principal difference being we could then have ordered things done, while during that period we had to request them, with very little chance of enforcing our will on the manufacturers. To the credit of American industry I should add that none of the executives of the large companies failed to carry out our wishes, although it sometimes took a good deal of discussion. I cannot close my remarks without paying sincere and heartfelt tribute to the executive officers in both branches of the air services for their whole-hearted and efficient cooperation. The loyal, earnest work of these men has largely made possible whatever air strength we may now have. The foundations have been laid for a tremendous output of planes and in less than a year and a half, production has increased tenfold. An enormous industry has been built up in an incredibly short period and it is delivering the goods. Thank you." March 27, 1942.

Chapter XVIII

Service to Community and Country

In this chapter it will be impossible to stick to one facet of Jack's service to his fellowmen, whether through working for the community or the nation, for during these particular years these two compelling concerns in his life were carried on almost simultaneously. It will also be necessary to backtrack to some extent.

Since the summer of 1935, when we had that eye-opening experience at the Hartford Hospital when Charlie was a baby, Jack had been increasingly troubled about its outdated buildings and inefficient layout. Their haphazard arrangement, due to the lack of a master plan in locating them, meant extra fatigue for doctors and nurses, as well as precious time lost, as they negotiated the long ramps which connected the buildings.

During the years since their friendship had become so close, Jack and Gilder (Dr. Jarvis) had made a practice of going off early on Sunday morning so as to get in a good walk before church. On these walks they discussed their hopes and dreams for

The DC-4, a prewar dream of George Mead, became a reality in 1946 and ushered in a new age of commercial aviation.

George J. Mead receives the Medal for Merit, the highest honor given to a civilian, from Major General E. M. Powers. With General Powers is Dr. John P. Victory, Executive Secretary of the National Advisory Committee for Aeronautics.

THE UNITED STATES OF AMERICA

TO ALL WHO SHALL SEE THESE PRESENTS, GREETING:

THIS IS TO CERTIFY THAT
THE PRESIDENT OF THE UNITED STATES OF AMERICA
IN ACCORDANCE WITH THE ORDER ISSUED BY GENERAL
GEORGE WASHINGTON AT HEADQUARTERS, NEWBURGH,
NEW YORK, ON AUGUST 7, 1782, AND PURSUANT TO ACT
OF CONGRESS, HAS AWARDED THE MEDAL

FOR MERIT

TO

DR. GEORGE JACKSON MEAD

FOR EXTRAORDINARY FIDELITY AND EXCEPTIONALLY
MERITORIOUS CONDUCT

GIVEN UNDER MY HAND IN THE CITY OF WASHINGTON
THIS FIFTEENTH DAY OF APRIL 1946

James F. Byrnes
SECRETARY OF STATE

Harry S. Truman
COMMANDER-IN-CHIEF

CITATION TO ACCOMPANY THE AWARD OF

THE MEDAL FOR MERIT

TO

DR. GEORGE JACKSON MEAD

DR. GEORGE JACKSON MEAD, for exceptionally meritorious conduct in the performance of outstanding services to the United States. Dr. Mead, as Chairman of the NACA Power Plants Committee, initiated, planned and energetically promoted the establishment of the Aircraft Engine Research Laboratory at Cleveland, Ohio, which laboratory has become the most advanced installation of its kind in the world. Through his insistence, over objections of others, the Altitude Wind Tunnel at the Aircraft Engine Research Laboratory was made adequate for research and test work on full-size airplane power plants under a wide range of controlled, simulated service conditions. Because of the capacity of that tunnel and the availability of the other facilities at the Laboratory, the bomber program of the United States was substantially accelerated. Dr. Mead was responsible in large measure for bringing into the airplane-engine program, the vast engineering potentialities of the automobile manufacturers.

Harry S. Truman

Dr. and Mrs. Peyton H. Hoge, Cary's parents holding Charles Cary Mead, aged 18 months.

Captain Jago.

The Pewee Valley Presbyterian Church, Kentucky, where George J. Mead and Cary Hoge were married on May 18, 1921.

Cary Mead and Gene Sturtevant, 1930.

Jackie Mead at the first Mead home in Montclair, New Jersey.

George J. Mead with his first born son, Jackie.

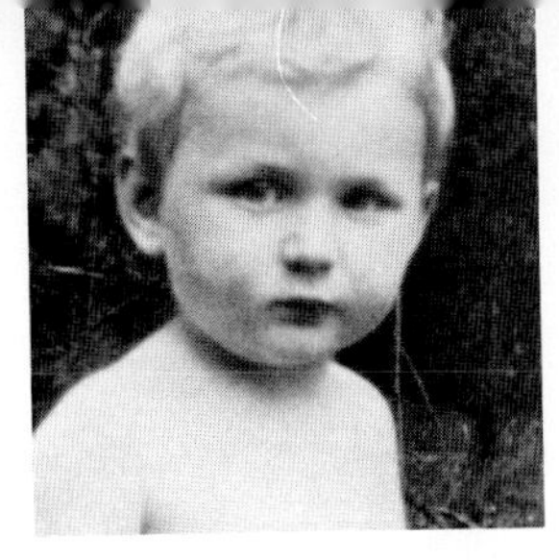

Peyton Mead, 1928.

Mary Mead, 1925.

Charlie Mead with his mother, 1936.

Charlie and his father. With them is Mary Stuart Houston.

Bill Mead, 1939.

Jackie, Mary, Charlie, Peyton, 1936.

Balbrae, West Hartford, 1930.

Erno, 1935.

Mead Farm, Center Harbor, New Hampshire, as it was when purchased and after restoration to its original New England simplicity and beauty.

Christmas, 1945.

Christmas, 1947.

Christmas, 1946.

Mead family grandchildren at Squam Lake, 1965.

The view of the New Hampshire mountains from Mead Farm, Center Harbor, New Hampshire.

George J. Mead and the mountains he climbed and loved.

a modern, efficient and well-planned hospital. In 1937 Jack was elected to the board of directors of the Hartford Hospital. Soon afterwards he gave a dinner for the board members at which he laid the need for a new hospital squarely before them all. He reminded them that for years many public-spirited citizens of Hartford, including some board members, had been stressing the need for a new hospital, but that so far nothing had been done, and he thought it was time to take action. To back up his words, he made his own pledge then and there and urged the other board members to decide promptly on the amounts of their pledges.

In a letter to James Lester Goodwin, chairman of the executive committee of the Hartford Hospital, dated December 22, 1937, Jack pointed out the urgency of the need for a modern, well-conceived, new building. He said in part, "There can be no question as to the importance of the hospital to the community nor its urgent need. It is evident from the increase in admissions and the resulting shortage of beds that our facilities will soon be unable to meet all the demands made upon them. Aside from this, one can readily see from any realistic examination that the present plant seriously handicaps the staff, due to its uncoordinated and decidedly inconvenient layout. We have good reason, therefore, to start the building fund regardless of the times. I am convinced that this community can and will furnish the necessary money. It can hardly do otherwise if the hospital is to stand ready to render to *each and every one of us* the service that we expect in time of need."

This letter was discussed with the board and tentative plans to go ahead were made. After careful consideration, Henry R. Shepley of the Boston firm of Coolidge, Shepley, Bullfinch and Abbott was selected as the architect. Jack, who was asked to serve as chairman of the building committee from the board of directors, worked long hours with Mr. Shepley. These consultations were often in collaboration with Dr. Jarvis, who was chairman of the building committee from the medical and surgical staff. Fund-raising went along quietly. Progress was slow during those years immediately preceding World War II, but there was progress.

A property acquisition committee had been appointed and had obtained options on a number of pieces of property to augment the amount of land already owned by the hospital. There are several exchanges of letters between Jack and Mr. Goodwin which show that plans for the new hospital building occupied a major part of the discussions of the meetings of the board.

Jack, Dr. Jarvis, Mr. Shepley and other members of the building committee had gone ahead with their work. Preliminary plans were completed and a model of the structure they hoped to build was ready as a "visual aid" for the 1940 January meeting. This model was the spark needed to kindle the enthusiasm of the board members. By April the directors were ready to move forward. At the meeting of the board on April 25, the minutes of the executive committee show that Mr. Gale introduced a motion regarding the solicitation of funds to finance the construction of the new hospital building. In seconding Mr. Gale's motion, Jack said in part:

> Mr. President, I should like the privilege of seconding this motion. In considering this matter, it seems to me that we should be guided by the facts. The present hospital plant consists largely of old buildings, some dating back to 1861, each good in its time, but, taken as a whole and measured by present standards, they are not at all well planned nor equipped. This makes it impossible to render the best service to the present number of patients at the minimum cost. Furthermore, many of the buildings constitute a serious fire hazard . . . Many in this community and the surrounding territory entrust those dear to them to our hospital, and all expect perfection and infallibility on the part of the staff, professional and otherwise. Under these circumstances, it is certainly not fair to handicap our doctors and hospital employees unnecessarily with an obsolete plant, nor is it to our own best interests to do so. The hospital has served the community for over three-quarters of a century and, aside from a few generous individuals, the community has contributed comparatively little toward the improvement and enlargement of an institution to which it looks in times of need. An efficient, modern workshop is certainly due our skillful doctors and surgeons for their splendid care of us all in the past and to enable them to render the best possible service in the future. Under these circumstances, I feel it an honor to second Mr. Gale's motion and to do what I can to further the project.

It was voted that the finance committee recommend to the board of directors that "subscription books be opened forthwith to receive contributions to the hospital building fund; also that as soon as possible an organization be established for the purpose of raising not less than $4,000,000."

During the months following Jack's summons to Washington in May of 1940, he could naturally spend very little time on the hospital matters. But even during that period when he was working "full throttle" for the National Defense Commission, the need for the new hospital was never far from his thoughts, and his determination that the hospital should be built remained steadfast.

Toward the end of November 1941, Jack was urged to assume once more the chairmanship of the building committee of the hospital. On December 3 he wrote Mr. Goodwin as follows:

> I should be glad to take over the supervision of the present building program at the hospital, providing you felt the following was in order:
> 1. Re-establish a small building committee.
> 2. Give complete authority to this committee to finish the building as per the present plans and specifications for a sum not to exceed an agreed upon amount.
> 3. Any items involving additional expense over the agreed upon sum to be approved by the Executive Committee prior to making commitments.
>
> The building committee should, of course, have a set of the latest plans and specifications together with copies of the various contracts for reference. A financial statement should also be available as of the date the committee takes over the work, together with a list of approved extras.
>
> The building committee should have the following information:
> 1. A copy of the latest plans and specifications.
> 2. Copies of all contracts.
> 3. Financial statement, including contract cost, total of extras, present total cost, total of expenditures to date broken down into major items.
> 4. Completion schedule.
> 5. Provision for priority building permit and insurance.

Plans for the first unit of the hospital's complex of buildings were in their final stage, and building materials had not yet been restricted. It was, therefore, possible to go ahead in constructing the "South Building," which was the hospital's maternity wing. It would also house the out-patient department.

On July 30, 1942, the Hartford Courant carried the following notice:

> George J. Mead, vice chairman of the National Advisory Committee for Aeronautics, and a member of the board of directors of the Hartford Hospital for several years, was named chairman of the hospital executive committee Wednesday at a meeting of the board. He succeeds James L. Goodwin, who has served in that capacity since 1931, who resigned because of ill health and pressure of other business. Dr. Mead was formerly vice president of the United Aircraft Corporation and one of the original group of founders of the aircraft industry here. He served recently as head of the aircraft procurement office of the National Defense Commission and last year was elected to a term as member of the corporation of the Massachusetts Institute of Technology.

A letter to Jack, dated July 17, 1942, from James L. Thomson, chairman of the finance committee of Hartford Fire Insurance Company, is a heart-warming example of the friendship and respect which his colleagues felt for him.

> I do want to let you know how much we are pleased that you have accepted the chairmanship of the executive committee.
>
> Your great interest in the hospital and your knowledge and ability especially fit you for such an important position. I am sure I do not know what we would have done if you had refused. Your acceptance reflects great credit on you for your unselfish attitude in assuming a civic duty so important to all the citizens of Hartford.
>
> At yesterday's meeting of the executive committee we took appropriate action, and it was felt that the matter was of such great moment that we would call a special meeting of the board of directors within the next few days to confirm the action taken by the executive committee.
>
> From all the accounts I hear that the opening of the new wing went off very nicely and was a decided success. I was very sorry not to be present . . . and that I was unable to rearrange my schedule. . . .

I will also quote a letter from Frank D. Layton, president of Hartford Fire, dated September 18, 1942, following Jack's first report as chairman of the executive committee. This letter from another able business man points up the meticulous care with which Jack approached every task he undertook.

> Due to the fact that I was obliged to leave right after the hospital meeting—to go to another meeting which I had promised to attend—I did not have opportunity to chat with you personally following adjournment.
>
> I do wish to say, however, that, with the other trustees, I was tremendously impressed by your concise but comprehensive and businesslike report and realize more than ever that the hospital and community are fortunate in having the benefit of your services as chairman of the executive committee of the Hartford Hospital.
>
> It was fine of you to take on the responsibilities of the job, and it is apparent, even at this early stage, that you are going to make a success of it despite the exceedingly difficult conditions prevailing in the present situation.

Construction of the main building of Hartford Hospital naturally had to be postponed, due to shortage of labor and materials, until the end of the war. Completion and refinement of plans went forward, however. The tall building, as it was called, was to be thirteen stories high and built in the form of a flat capital "H" with the crosspiece sticking out beyond each of the uprights. This building would include staff quarters and conference rooms, operating rooms, laboratories, X-ray rooms, offices, and the main kitchen. The school for nursing class rooms and facilities for the care of all except maternity and out-patients would be housed there.

The maternity wing was completed and opened in July 1942. It quickly demonstrated the value of a well-planned, up-to-date building. Patients (and volunteers) as well as staff rejoiced in its efficiency and gleaming cleanliness. In the Hartford Times Friday, July 10, 1942, there was a wonderful picture of Jack presenting the keys of the new maternity building to Dr. Wilmar M. Allen, director of Hartford Hospital, as both stand in front of a huge American flag. This was part of the dedication ceremonies which took place at that time. A statement by Mayor Spellacy is as follows: "The new unit will help Hartford maintain its proud distinction of standing at the very top among cities of the country with a low rate of infant mortality. Ten years ago," he noted,

"Hartford was at the bottom of the list with a high rate of mortality."

The newspaper article goes on to say:

> Workers in the hospital's $5,000,000 building fund campaign, directors, corporators, medical and surgical staff members, women's auxiliary and hospital volunteers officials, city and state officials and representatives of other Connecticut hospitals attended.
>
> Dr. Howard W. Brayton, staff president, said that the growing demands of the community could not be met without the new hospital's being built and paid tribute to the "invaluable service" rendered by volunteers as increasing numbers of doctors and nurses are called into military service.
>
> Other speakers reviewed the 82-year-old history of the hospital and Dr. Wilmar M. Allen, director, who accepted the hospital for the administrative staff, noted that more than 23,000 patients had been admitted to the hospital during the past 12 months.
>
> Speakers included William H. Putnam, dedication committee chairman; the Rt. Rev. Frederick G. Budlong, Episcopal bishop of Connecticut, who pronounced an invocation; Dr. H. Gildersleeve Jarvis, chairman of the medical and surgical staff's building committee; George J. Mead, chairman of the directors' building committee; Rabbi Abraham J. Feldman, a trustee of Mt. Sinai Hospital; the Most Rev. Maurice F. McAuliffe, Roman Catholic bishop of Hartford and president of St. Francis Hospital, who pronounced a benediction.
>
> Mr. Mead noted that although the new structure was the largest single addition ever made to the hospital, it was the smallest unit of the new building program.
>
> Rabbi Feldman said that the new hospital will stand as a monument "to those who at all times have faith in our community, faith in America, faith in the future, and confidence in the blessing of our God."

Consideration of Jack's schedule during the months in which he worked and traveled for the National Defense program—May 20, 1940 to February 6, 1941—shows why his health reserves were completely used up. A vicious attack of flu laid him low in February and effectually halted any further traveling, at least for the time being. This illness culminated in an extensive and somewhat dangerous sinus operation which took place in May of '41. He came through the ordeal well, and it brought some relief from the almost constant headaches and respiratory troubles that had plagued him.

He could naturally not visit the companies that had contracted to produce the war materiel, but he continued his work for the board by extensive correspondence with key personnel of the various companies, and with many in the armed forces, as is evidenced by the large file of letters received and sent during those months. A letter from Brig. General Oliver P. Echols dated June 2, 1941, meant much to Jack, as his answer shows.

Dear George: I have been wondering how you are getting along. I hear conflicting reports. First I hear that you are quite well and preparing to return to Washington, and then again I hear that you are still having considerable difficulty with your sinus trouble. I certainly hope that the latter is not correct.

As you have seen in the papers, we finally struggled through with the Fleet-Ford-Douglas deal, after many months of argument and hard work on the part of all concerned. The North American deal is in the mill and ready for signature, except for the fact that there is a strike imminent in the North American plant and Kindelberger will sign nothing until this matter is settled. We are still working with Martin and hopeful of eventually getting him signed up.

Suppose you have read in the paper about the additional big bomber program which has been superimposed on the other. This means we have little time for play around here as you can well imagine.

Hope you will soon be well and return to the N.A.C.A. work here. We need your advice and counsel on a number of matters. Have missed you a great deal during these last few months. (signed) Oliver P. Echols

Dear Oliver: . . . I am intensely interested in what has happened during my long absence and feel very badly to be laid up when there is so much to be done. I gather from the papers that our Ypsilanti plan is now going through, which no doubt pleases Mr. Sorensen mightily. Outside of that, I have heard nothing further about the 500-a-month heavy bomber program.

It does not sound as though the procedure in Washington is getting any simpler. Almost every week, I learn of some other channel through which the work must flow, and well do I know what that means in slowing down the job. Germany recognized to begin with the necessity for clean-cut divisions of responsibility and placing

> an able man in charge of each, with complete authority over that portion of the job. England has been forced to follow suit and yet we do not seem to learn this vital lesson. Too many cooks may not spoil the broth, but they surely can delay it unconscionably, which in this instance is just as bad.
>
> One of the happiest experiences I had in Washington was in making your acquaintance and in working with you, which I particularly enjoyed. It will be a pleasure indeed if the future holds an opportunity for further association. Meanwhile many thanks for thinking of me. I do hope you are getting some time off in which to keep fit and make life worth living. The latchstring is always out and I should be delighted to see you. This mountain air can do wonders for a fellow even over a weekend! There is a good airport at Concord only an hour's drive from here. . . . (signed) George J. Mead.

General Knudsen also wrote Jack in June of 1941 urging him to return to Washington and continue his work on what was now the War Production Board. However, Jack maintained that he was an engineer, not a production man, and that the work he was fitted to do on Knudsen's board was completed. Though deeply involved in helping the free world combat the axis powers by providing desperately needed war materiel for the allies, it should be remembered that America was not technically at war at this time and had hoped to avoid being drawn into the conflict.

Then, on December 7, 1941, came the dawn attack on Pearl Harbor by 100 Japanese fighting planes. The attack lasted less than two hours, but when it was over, five American battleships and many smaller vessels had been sunk. Over 200 Navy planes and nearly 300 Army planes had been destroyed. There were over 2,000 of our soldiers, sailors and marines dead, 1,200 wounded, and 1,000 missing. The horror of that day's events and subsequent declarations of war are so clearly etched in the memories of all Americans who were living at that time that I need not dwell on it here.

Young Jack phoned us that night. He was so deeply shocked by the sneak attack that he couldn't think through what his plan of action should be. We suggested that he go ahead with his studies for the present and decide by the end of the term whether or not he should complete his sophomore year before entering his country's service.

Suddenly this war, in which our role had been that of helpful friends, became *our* war. Our world changed completely overnight. Many of our friends as well as we ourselves had sons who would soon be joining the armed services. Parents plunged into all types of war work. Many of us rationed ourselves on gasoline and vital foods long before the government required us to do so. Nearly all able-bodied Americans mobilized themselves into one gigantic task force to help the war effort in every way possible. Young wives went into industry to release their husbands for the service. Grandmothers took care of children to release the mothers for industry. Those of us who had no grandchildren worked as volunteers in the hospital, the Red Cross, or both. A fully awakened America braced itself to resist the foes which beset us on the east and west.

At the beginning of February 1942 General Knudsen wrote Jack on behalf of Air Secretary Lovett, urging him to return to Washington as Lovett's assistant to help expedite the Air Corps' production program. Now that the United States was actually at war, Jack felt that he should accept this additional opportunity for patriotic service, even though he did not think he was well fitted for the assignment. Knowing the inevitable delays that would be inherent in such a task, due to the lack of responsibility and authority being centered in one person, he stipulated certain conditions as the only ones under which he could accept an assignment of such magnitude. Therefore, on February 6, 1942, Jack wrote General Knudsen as follows with a copy of the letter to Secretary Lovett.

> It is my understanding from our discussions last week that you and Air Secretary Lovett are primarily concerned with expediting the Air Corps' production program. Subsequently I have talked with a few men whose judgment and knowledge of the conditions I value and have reached certain definite conclusions regarding the task. In my opinion, the only way a material improvement can be made is by placing the sole responsibility and authority for the job in the hands of one person and through the maximum simplification of the procedure required to do the work. I should, therefore, be willing to undertake the responsibility only under the following conditions:
>
> 1. Control of all phases of the Air Corps production except the determination of types and quantities and the procurement of

funds, which should continue to be functions of the Chief of the Air Corps.

2. Direct charge of a production division of the Air Corps to be composed principally of existing departments of the Materiel Division and adequately staffed with such officers and others as I may select.
3. Ruling by Mr. Nelson of the War Production Board that it is the duty of the proper divisions of that board to provide such materials, machinery, labor agreements and other aids as are necessary to carry out the authorized program.
4. Agreement to the proposed setup by any other branches of the government which may now perform functions that would be taken over by the production division.
5. Appointment as Assistant Secretary for Air in charge of production, reporting to Air Secretary Lovett.

I have discussed the possibility of returning to Washington with my physicians and have had a check made this week by a specialist in Boston. It is their joint opinion that I am physically able to carry the load providing I follow a routine which has been found essential in my case. To do this would not seriously interfere with my duties as far as I can see. However, I should want this situation to be thoroughly understood by my immediate superior and agreeable to him.

My experience with the initial stages of the aircraft program has made me thoroughly aware of the magnitude of the task you propose. Because of this and due to the vital importance of saving all possible time, I know the absolute necessity for a simple, direct-acting and readily introduced setup such as I have proposed. Normally I should not care to undertake this job, feeling as I do inadequate for such a responsibility. However, if it is felt that I can be helpful in the capacity outlined during the emergency, you may count on me to do my best.

Jack was pretty sure that those who had the say-so would not accept his terms. He knew all too well how dear to the heart of governmental officialdom red tape is, even in time of war. He was right. They did not agree to his terms.

A letter from Igor Sikorsky of Vought-Sikorsky Aircraft, and Jack's reply are of interest here.

Dear George: On Tuesday, June 9, I was present at a dinner given by the Polytechnic Institute of Brooklyn in honor of General Knudsen. In his speech outlining the progress of the aviation industry in the United States, General Knudsen mentioned you as being the person who greatly assisted in this expansion. As far as I can recall, your name was the only one he mentioned out of the whole industry, and I feel, therefore, that it is my pleasant duty to inform you about this.

Our work here is progressing very well, and the place has expanded tremendously. We recently delivered to the American Export Airlines their large flying boat, which has already made a few trans-Atlantic crossings, the first of which established a record for commercial airliners by reaching Ireland from New York in less than 17 hours.

Our helicopter development is also proceeding very successfully. We can now state that a truly practical flying helicopter has finally been produced, because our machine was able to fly to an altitude of 5,000 feet and was able to proceed under its own power from Bridgeport to Dayton, Ohio.

With pleasant recollections of our meetings in the past, and with kindest personal regards to yourself and Mrs. Mead, I am . . . (signed) Igor Sikorsky.

Dear Igor: Your thoughtful note was most welcome. It is cheering to know that General Knudsen should mention my small part in the early stages of the aircraft program. I had only known him through reputation, but became quite fond of him during our association in Washington. He certainly backed me up on most everything I wanted to do, which was a big help in those trying times. It seems to me the industry has covered itself with glory and I certainly take a great deal of satisfaction in the way it has gone to town. The automobile industry will, I feel, give a good account of itself before long and I am sure can teach us a good many valuable lessons about mass production. Presumably the aircraft industry can teach it a trick or two about light materials, which will more or less even the score.

Congratulations on the performance of the trans-Atlantic flying boat. I am delighted that you at long last had an opportunity of carrying through what must have been a cherished project of yours. This will go a long way in educating the public to large aircraft, which might easily revolutionize transoceanic transportation in the future. No doubt, this will bring about the development of large passenger-carrying craft such as you have dreamed about for years.

I am delighted to hear of the progress being made with the development of the helicopter. Such equipment would seem to have a very definite place in modern warfare and I hope your efforts will be crowned with some substantial business from the armed forces. It seems to me you have done a remarkable job in perfecting the helicopter in such a short period. Whenever you can take any time off, you had better fly north for a bit of a vacation. We should be delighted to see you and still have our landing field adjacent to the house.

My session in Washington seems to have taken a good deal more out of me than I at first appreciated. For this reason, I have been forced to be more or less inactive for some time, all of which makes me glad that I had the opportunity of being in on the beginning of the production program. . . . (signed) G. J. Mead"

On November 12, 1942, Vice Admiral S. M. Robinson, chief of the Office of Procurement and Material for the Navy, wrote Jack as follows:

We are most anxious to obtain your services and your intimate knowledge of the aircraft industry in connection with the prosecution of the war effort. . . . I desire to assure you that there is a real need for your service.

I am enclosing a brief outline of your proposed duties and responsibilities. This matter has been taken up with the various people concerned such as the Secretary of the Navy, our Bureau of Aeronautics, and Mr. C. E. Wilson of the War Production Board, and I can assure you that all are in accord with the necessity of this position and the great contribution which you could make in this capacity to the war effort. . . .

Proposed Duties of George J. Mead

1. Head of Aeronautics Production Division of the Office of Procurement and Material; as such will render all possible assistance to the Office of Procurement and Material in an effort to carry out its responsibilities as set forth in General Order No. 166.
2. Represent the Office of Procurement and Material in expediting production of aeronautical material. This will be done through the Bureau of Aeronautics.
3. Study and make recommendations on coordinating the aircraft program with the balance of the Navy war effort programs, with special reference to the Shipbuilding and Ordnance programs to see that the setup for production of the

Aircraft program is such as to minimize or eliminate any adverse effect.

4. Develop and implement ways and means of removing obstacles to the Aircraft production program including coordination of information from design sections with production units, also simplifications of design and material and limitation of changes.
5. Represent the Navy with units of the War Production Board that are interested in problems that affect production of aircraft, and with the production program of the Army to coordinate aircraft production activities.
6. Make or have made field surveys insuring intimate knowledge of production difficulties.
7. Attend meetings in conjunction with various bureaus and the War Production Board to develop and remove causes of delay in production.
8. Keep advised through reports of Planning and Statistics Division as to current status of production in the material bureaus. Assist in coordinating production among the material bureaus.
9. Represent the Office of Procurement and Material as a member of the Executive Agency of the Aircraft Board.

This "outline of proposed duties and responsibilities" which Vice Admiral Robinson enclosed would have kept TEN assistants on the run. Even part of these responsibilities would have involved a prohibitive amount of traveling, and Jack therefore had to decline. On November 17 he wrote Admiral Robinson a courteous note ending with, "I greatly appreciate your thinking of me in this connection, and I am sorry indeed that I cannot have the privilege of working with you. With best wishes and many thanks . . ." Jack did not so much mind giving up the great honor that this particular job represented, but he was deeply grieved that poor health prevented his serving his country in a capacity which, in spite of his modest estimate of himself, he knew he could have done well.

The following month there was an exchange of correspondence between Jack and Harold S. Vance, chairman of the board of the Studebaker Corporation, which shows the high regard which men in the industry all over the country had for Jack's advice and sound thinking. Jack wrote Mr. Vance on December 15, 1942, and I will quote parts of the letter:

> Our former boss, now General Knudsen, spent the evening with me Sunday and had some nice things to say about your war effort. I gather that the change in signals, although delaying you at the onset, has not prevented your doing an excellent job with the Wright engine. This makes me think of our first meeting in the Treasury when you were looking for some way to get into the aviation field. It strikes me you are in it with both feet now.
>
> . . . As far as I can see, the original Defense Commission gang did a pretty good job and there is no need to apologize for our efforts in those early days. . . . I am very happy to have had a part in it when you were there.

Mr. Vance's reply to Jack on December 28 read in part as follows:

> Quite apart from our engine manufacturing activities, we have undertaken an engineering job for the Army Air Forces. Briefly, it is the design and development of a liquid-cooled aeronautical engine of substantially larger size than anything now in existence. Mr. Cole, our vice president in charge of engineering, Mr. James, our chief engineer, and Mr. Tilley, a special engineer who is devoting all of his time to this project, are very anxious to have the opportunity to lay before you their plans and ideas and to secure your advice thereon. Colonel Page of the research section of Wright Field has given his hearty approval of the idea that we should seek your advice and help in this matter. . . .
>
> General Knudsen was in South Bend in September. He told me that in the preceding six months he had visited more than 400 plants and had been on the road most of the time. I am sure that he must take a great deal of satisfaction out of the knowledge that our present war production is the result of what you did in 1940 and 1941, even though this fact is not generally appreciated.

In Jack's reply of December 31, he offered to meet with the gentlemen involved in order that they could discuss the problems in connection with the water-cooled engine.

In the foregoing pages, I have tried to portray the conscientious precision and attention to detail with which Jack approached every task he undertook. The fact that his fellow engineers, industrial executives all over the country, and those high in the armed services turned to him for counsel and help in solving problems incident to the national emergency brought him real satisfaction. The words of Dr. Baxter when he conferred on Jack the degree of doctor of science—"He is in the front line of his country's defense"—were more true than he realized when he wrote the citation.

Chapter XIX

Research Laboratory at Cleveland

Even though circumstances prevented Jack's accepting the post envisioned by Vice Admiral Robinson, there still lay before him one more vital contribution to the war effort, and to the overall progress of aviation. Jack, Dr. Hunsaker, and Dr. Vannevar Bush had been working together on N.A.C.A. matters. A research laboratory to be built at Cleveland, Ohio, which included a huge wind tunnel as one of its main features, had been in the thinking and planning stage for some time. The wind tunnel was a tremendous idea in every sense of the word. In this vital adjunct to the laboratory, all sorts of flight conditions could be simulated for full-sized airplane engines. It would be impossible for one who was not an engineer to estimate the total importance of such a tunnel, the largest in the world at that time. Those in charge of procurement of all types of planes in World War II were determined to anticipate and overcome in advance every flight emergency they could think of, and they were also determined that the most up-to-the-minute designs would characterize the planes from the standpoint of speed, dependability, maneuverability, and strength.

In a letter to Jack dated December 24, 1941, Dr. Hunsaker said in part: "Victory (Secretary of the N.A.C.A.) phoned this evening to tell me that the Emerson Company of Cleveland have been selected as contractors for both buildings (that is, the laboratory and the wind tunnel) and have agreed on a fee of about 4%. They are first-class people and have a force available from a job they are finishing up." Then on January 4, 1942, another letter stated: "The contract is signed for the Cleveland laboratory buildings for completion in one year at a cost-plus fee." On June 12 Dr. Hunsaker reported further: "The Cleveland Laboratory is going ahead faster now that we have priority raised from A-1-b (Air Lab) to A-1-a. The contractor is getting his steel after a slight delay. We'll get the tunnel steel also . . . Yes, the aircraft program is booming, and trouble may come in six months for lack of alloy steel (nickel) for engine forgings, ball bearings, etc. We had a meeting on this yesterday. The lease-lend, tank, and ordnance people take too much nickel. I have protested to Nelson about this. . . . The Navy is putting battleships (which are not far advanced) on low priority to conserve steel for more urgent work. Armor takes a lot of nickel."

Some comments in a letter from Jack to Dr. Hunsaker, dated October 8, 1942, are interesting here, as they show the way his mind went straight to the core of a problem.

> I have felt for some time that the continual development of existing designs was at least as essential as the development of entirely new types, simply for the reason that improvements are thus made available more rapidly to the fighting forces. The real trouble is that—at least heretofore—no one in either service with sufficiently broad experience, good judgment and complete authority has been given charge of changes and the final determination as to whether they are vital, necessary, or simply desirable. Changes originate generally from one of three sources, namely, the service users, production, or from research and development testing. This last source must be intelligently directed and very active if the best equipment is to be made available. Whatever the source and almost regardless of the necessity, each change should be tried out

before being introduced into production, and this takes a certain amount of time. . . .

A vital change, such as installing rear guns in the bombers two years ago, would no doubt have to be made regardless of the effect on production, but I believe there are very few occasions when this will be necessary if the design has been properly developed before being put into large-scale production. The chief engineer of a commercial company can and does handle design improvement changes pretty successfully without interrupting deliveries. If the services had an opposite number, these two men could be relied on, I am sure, to make the best compromise between deliveries and the most thoroughly developed equipment. . . .

It is my present intention to attend the corporation meeting on the 14th. Would you, by chance, be in Boston at that time? If so, I should like to talk with you on several matters, including the above, if you will let me know your schedule. Cary joins me in sending best wishes to Lady Alice and yourself.

In another letter to Dr. Hunsaker dated December 22, 1942, Jack said in part:

The gas-turbine research, as proposed by the Institute's committee on this subject, seems eminently desirable. I would certainly agree that, having explored the matter as far as possible on paper, some life-size—or at least scale—models of the essential components be tried out together. Thanks to the work already done in this field, there seems no longer any great question of the system working, but simply as to what the efficiency might be. If the efficiency is good and substantiates the calculations, then it would be in order to check the other important matter, namely, the weight per horsepower of the complete system. . . . There can be little question that this sort of fundamental research is going on. On the other hand, I doubt whether such a revolutionary change in propulsion could be developed in time to be of use in this war. . . .

The nearest I have come to Washington was a visit from General Knudsen about ten days ago. He was passing through Hartford and gave me a ring, which was very nice of him. Apparently he is well satisfied with the plans made two years ago. It was gratifying to me to learn of our progress and his satisfaction. . . .

It sounds as though you had a fine meeting recently of the N.A.C.A. and I was sorry that I could not be there. I am naturally interested to know how the laboratory is progressing in Cleveland and whether you are able to do any research work in the aerodynamic laboratory. I am afraid that most of our facilities are tied up in what you might call "service" engineering jobs on current models. It is a shame that industry hasn't its own aerodynamic tools in order to free ours for forward-looking work.

Presumably you will be getting home for the holidays and can have a real family reunion and catch up on what your children have been doing. Mary returned from Connecticut College last Wednesday and Peyton from Hotchkiss. Both seem delighted with their respective college and school, and their marks indicate they are making good progress. Jack didn't go back to Princeton this fall but went into the plant to take a course in the service department preparatory to going into the Air Corps . . . The two little boys are fine and growing fast . . . Cary joins me in sending best wishes to Lady Alice and yourself. Please remember me to Van when you see him. I surely do miss all of you with whom I was most intimate in Washington.

Dr. Hunsaker's reply on December 29 gives some specific examples of some of the research which was being carried on even before the completion of the research laboratory and the "tunnel."

Keenan has been working with Pratt & Whitney on the general problem of exhaust gas recovery and has turned up an attractive combination of *engine, compressor* and gas *turbine* in which substantial savings in fuel are possible at the expense of increased power plant weight. . . . What needs to be done is to set up (at Cleveland) a set of E, C AND T and find out how to adjust them to work together. I am asking Keenan, E. S. Taylor, and Soderberg to propose to N.A.C.A. to undertake the engineering work to draw up a scheme for Cleveland to install. First, Keenan must see John Lee or Leonard Hobbs of Pratt & Whitney to get clearance from any obligation to them.

There will be some experimental gas turbines running in 1943, but the compressor of adequate capacity needs looking into further. The Elliot Company of Pittsburgh, Allis Chalmers, de Laval, and others have developments in hand.

I was glad to hear you had a report from General Knudsen as to how production was going. The recent changes in the War Production Board look good. . . . I was sorry you could not attend the December 17 N.A.C.A. meeting and the luncheon party for Orville Wright with General Marshall and Admiral King. It went off well and did some good . . . I think we are keeping up our end on fundamental research and will be able to do more as Cleveland becomes equipped. . . .

Dr. Hunsaker, in answering my recent letter to him asking for permission to quote in this book from his various letters of 1939 to 1942, made the following significant observation.

> I was interested in the June 12, 1942, proposal to get the engine research at Cleveland to undertake an exhaust driven gas turbine to drive a compressor for the high-altitude engine. This exhaust driven turbine did a lot to lead the way for the propulsion gas turbine eventually replacing the engine. George (Jack) had a start on gas turbines before we knew about British or German efforts toward jet propulsion.

A remarkable letter to Allen W. Morton (Koppers Company in Baltimore) from Sam Heron (Ethyl Corporation in Detroit), a friend and associate of Jack's of many years standing, dated December 11, 1944, gives some interesting insights into the varied problems that had to be dealt with in the months preceding our entry into World War II. Some paragraphs on the first page of this letter deal with one detail of the enormous task that confronted the War Production Board and also shows Jack's foresight in anticipating a need and dealing with it. The second page shows the inter-relation of the National Advisory Committee for Aeronautics, the War Production Board, and the Research Laboratory at Cleveland. I am, therefore, quoting most of the letter, as well as parts of the letters which it evoked.

> The appointment of Mr. Stettinius as Secretary of State reminds me of a very pleasant piece of unexpected courtesy for which you were responsible but which was covered by a letter signed by Mr. Stettinius. The facts of the case were as follows: In 1940 Mr. Stettinius held a high position in the Council of National Defense and you were his assistant. I held a minor position in the aircraft section under Mr. George Mead who reported to Mr. Knudsen (as he then was). In any case, Mr. Stettinius became interested in the problem of the adequacy of supplies of petroleum products for aircraft use and approached Mr. Mead in the matter of appointing a suitable government committee to deal with this matter.
>
> Mr. Mead was able to report to Mr. Stettinius that a committee

had already been set up about a month before to deal with the matter. Mr. Stettinius asked for a memo discussing the membership of the committee and the qualifications of the members. Mr. Mead passed on to me the request for a memo which I prepared and forwarded to Mr. Mead with covering letter but with no signature on the memo. A week later I received a personal note from Mr. Stettinius thanking me for the memo and while I appreciated his kindly touch in being willing to sign the document, nevertheless I knew that the instigator was yourself.

In any case, Mr. Stettinius apparently regarded the committee as a potentially satisfactory instrument for the purpose he had in mind. Whether he, you, or somebody else first had this idea does not matter; the fact is that someone in the Defense Commission realized the importance of petroleum products for aircraft and the 100-octane program has clearly shown the importance of the picture which one of you was able to visualize.

In 1939 Mr. Ames, chairman of the N.A.C.A., retired and the President appointed Dr. Vannevar Bush as chairman and George J. Mead as vice chairman. Dr. Bush (I believe) charged Mr. Mead with accelerating aircraft engine research in the United States. Mr. Mead decided that facilities were inadequate and took action which finally culminated in the Aircraft Engine Research Laboratory of the N.A.C.A. at Cleveland, Ohio.

When Mr. Mead's plans for the new laboratory were completed and sent to Congress, he decided that the N.A.C.A. aircraft engine committee should be reorganized. Mr. Mead also decided that the N.A.C.A.'s subcommittee on petroleum products for aircraft use should be reorganized. Mr. Mead privately stated that petroleum products had shown that they could contribute largely to aircraft performance and that since the petroleum industry by and large were the only people who knew about the manufacture of such products, the industry must be considerably represented on any such committee. I happen to know definitely that Mr. Mead's proposal of petroleum industry representation on a government committee was received with considerable amused derision in government circles and the view expressed that any such committee would inevitably result in one vast sales Congress.

In any case, Mr. Mead decided to risk the sales Congress and appointed the subcommittee about May 20, 1940, with Professor Walter G. Whitman (then of the department of chemical engineering at M.I.T. and since 1941 assistant chief chemicals bureau, War Production Board). In any case, Mr. Mead's view was borne out since whatever the committee has done, it has not proved to be a sales Congress. In fact, the committee, with almost its original membership, is still functioning, and whatever its reputation, I may say guts rather than sales is considered to be its principal characteristic. In regard to the committee and its membership, I cannot resist a malicious comment. Mr. Mead proposed Major J. M. Doolittle (now Lieutenant General), then director of aviation, Shell Oil Company, as a member, and the orthodox government circles in Washington bitterly objected on the grounds that Doolittle was a salesman! The politicians always ask one to consult the record. Mr. Mead will not ask this but he hardly need be afraid to have it consulted.

I set out to thank you for your well-concealed Southern courtesy and have ended up by attempting to be an historian.

Some paragraphs of Mr. Morton's reply to Sam Heron, a copy of which he sent Jack, are interesting and delightful and are quoted below.

. . . I remember several discussions relative to the petroleum industry and particularly in connection with aviation gasoline. Eventually all of this was channeled through Robert E. Wilson, who became head of the petroleum section of the industrial materials division. Bob Wilson and I became quite intimate during my sojourn in Washington, and I soon came to admire and respect him very much.

I am inclined to believe the incident you refer to occurred before Bob Wilson came down to Washington, as in the early days I was the recipient of most of Ed Stettinius' mail and also a buffer for many of his visitors. As a result I was overwhelmed with ideas and spent much time searching to find out to whom I could refer them. I remember very distinctly a conversation I had with Ed Stettinius about the necessity of having an inventor's council or something, as I had my desk filled with letters from various inventors throughout the world, and when Dr. Vannevar Bush was finally appointed, he may not realize it, but Allen Morton sent him the most astounding bunch of mail under Ed Stettinius' signature.

Well, I do appreciate your nice long letter and your very thoughtful remembrance, but I cannot accept the responsibility of having had a good idea, for fear it perhaps did not originate with me, though I may have been the medium of passing it along. If ever you have the chance to read Ed Stettinius' book on Lend-Lease, the first part of it gives a wonderful chronological history of the few years preceding Pearl Harbor.

Jack's letter of December 21, 1944, to Sam Heron, acknowledging the copy of the letter to Mr. Morton, is really an expression of his philosophy, namely, "if circumstances make it impossible to carry on your life the way you have been trained to do, don't waste your time, but use your abilities in some way that circumstances do permit."

> The copy of your letter to Morton reached me and brought back memories of many things I had almost forgotten. You are a good one to talk of giving credit where credit is due. You, and you alone, made the suggestions as to a petroleum coordinator and a fuels committee. History shows how good your selections were. All I did in the matter was to convey them to Stettinius in person and discuss them with him.
>
> As you say, it is amusing, if it weren't so serious, to look back at the difficulties we had in establishing any sort of a 100-octane program. I am certainly grateful to you and the others of our small band who gathered in Washington in the spring of 1940, as I feel what we did then laid the groundwork for filling the subsequent colossal demands made on the aviation industry. I think we all may take some real satisfaction from the way the job has gone ahead and the fact that the principles laid down so long ago have continued to guide our war effort in this field. I particularly appreciated your counsel and willingness to help in those days. You were a tower of strength in handling the fuel situation and contributed a lot to the engine program as a whole, as well as to what we should do in the new engine laboratory at Cleveland. I am sorry that I wasn't well enough to carry on through the war, but I am awfully glad I had a chance to do something for a short period. This war has certainly been a vindication of the two-row, air-cooled, radial engine and of the two-speed, two-stage supercharger, so that I feel the work done here was not in vain. Leonard, Andy, and Parkins have certainly carried on a long way since my day and deserve a great deal of credit that I hope they get at the proper time.
>
> Do let me know when you come to Hartford again, as I should very much like to see you. You will laugh when I tell you that I am busy on the administrative side of our hospital and concerned with a new building program. These matters on the face of it seem pretty foreign to my upbringing. However, I find the work very interesting and the principles required in handling them pretty much the same as in any other business. I certainly would be interested to sit down with you and hear some of the interesting things you have been doing. . . .

Then, Sam's reply to Jack, dated December 27, 1944, shows the warmth of his friendship. I wish I had had more opportunities of seeing Mr. Heron during Jack's aeronautical years. He was surely a loyal and devoted friend.

> . . . I am glad to hear that you are well enough to carry on with your hospital activities. This as an occupation for you does not seem amusing to me, as it is a very well worth-while job and to get somebody with business-like instincts to handle it is not too easy.
>
> In regard to Washington and 1940, I don't know whether my idea in regard to writing the letter to Morton was good or not, but anyhow I did it. You will forgive me if I disagree vigorously with you in regard to the question of where credit is due. I will take fifty percent of the credit for the membership of the fuels and lubricants subcommittee, but the idea of such a committee was very definitely yours and not mine. Firstly, I very definitely remember your bringing the subject up with me long before I had any thoughts on the matter and offering your view that it was no use having a petroleum committee composed of engine men and government people, none of whom knew anything about petroleum manufacturing.
>
> I will take credit for Doolittle with the admission that the selection was based both on technical and political grounds. Anyhow, your idea of a committee was a very sound one, and it is still the most powerful committee on aviation petroleum products. I don't think it has a shred of legal authority for half the things it does, and its power comes from the fact that it is unbiased and takes care not to raise a rumpus unless the situation really warrants it. I believe Hunsaker is very proud of the subcommittee and states that it is the only N.A.C.A. committee that tells the Army and Navy what to do and makes them like it.
>
> I agree with your remarks anent Leonard, Andy, and Parkins who have contributed to a very sound engineering policy which has produced a lot of good stuff and has not given any targets for investigations. It seems to me that Pratt & Whitney and Rolls-Royce are the fair-haired boys of the engine industry in this war, and in this connection I would remark that Packard have done a magnificent job under circumstances which often must have been the reverse of easy. . . .

It was hard for Jack during these war years not to be active in the work for which he was trained and in which he knew he was needed, but he channeled his abilities into the work for the hospital with vigor and enthusiasm. As chairman of the building committee, he kept a careful eye on everything connected with the building plans and fund-raising for the new hospital; and as chairman of the executive committee, he evaluated every detail of the administration of the existing organization. This was no sinecure because the mounting needs of the armed services for doctors and nurses kept depleting the professional personnel. All areas of hospital service were reduced drastically. Nurses' aids, who took a fairly extensive course, were of inestimable value, actually functioning as nurses; and another group of volunteers, of which I was a member, worked under the reduced corps of nurses. We were given a shorter course of training and were only taught to carry out such duties as making hospital beds, giving baths and backrubs, and caring for patients coming out of anesthetic. Then, of course, we fixed flowers, gave nourishments, answered the phone, and ran errands.

Charlie and Billy were too young to be fully aware of the gravity of the days we were living through. Their gaiety gave us a lift when the casualty lists mounted, when planes were shot down, when ships were sunk by submarines, when the papers were filled day after day with tragic accounts of bombings of innocent, defenseless people. We were grateful to have our days so filled with work that when night came, sheer weariness brought sleep.

Mary was as happy at Connecticut College for Women as anyone could be during those years, and Peyton was doing well at Hotchkiss. Young Jack was going through the service school at United Aircraft in the hope of preparing himself to be useful in the service more quickly, once he got in. He would leave the house around six in the morning to join his "ride" to the plant. In the afternoon he often reached our gate just as I got off the bus following my work either at Red Cross or the hospital, and we would plod up the hill together. That hill seemed very long and steep after our strenuous day.

Toward the end of the service course at the plant, the trainees were sent on field trips around the country to get actual experience in servicing airplane engines. One of these field trips took him to Louisville, Kentucky, where aunts, uncles, and cousins rolled out the red carpet for him. They did everything they could think of to make his off-duty hours enjoyable. One young cousin arranged a double date with a schoolmate of hers and my brother William's son, who was almost the same age as our Jack. In a letter to me soon after that evening, young Jack said, "I had a couple of dates while I was in Louisville, one of which was super. Her name is Katherine Wathen and she is, as of now, my number one girl." As he had only recently turned twenty, I wondered if Katherine really was *the* girl. I also wondered if she, at seventeen, was ready to make up *her* mind. And I wondered what her family thought of this young New Englander who had quite literally dropped from the sky. Anyway, I kept that letter just in case, and three years later I was glad I had, as I was able to share it with our first daughter-in-law.

When July came, Harry Bergstrom joined the Navy, and a month later our Jack donned a sailor's uniform. He could not become a pilot because he did not have 20-20 vision, so he became an aviation machinist mate. If he couldn't fly for his country, he would at least do all he could to help those who could fly. He was sent to Newport for boot camp and then immediately to Jacksonville, Florida.

In the fall of 1943 a particularly virulent form of virus pneumonia struck Hartford, and people went down like nine pins. In October Jack, Senior, was one of the victims. The previous year he had been elected to the board of trustees of Connecticut College. Following his return from their October meeting, he said that his chest hurt and he thought he was coming down with a hard cold. Both lungs were involved, and for nearly a month he was desperately ill, battling for breath. Penicillin had just been discovered but was available only in limited quantities. Dr. Keefer, who controlled the supply, came from Boston to decide whether the new drug would help. He decided it would not, and all he could suggest was to continue giving Jack plenty of fluids, and oxygen when he could tolerate it. There was so little that could be done for him that those weeks were one long nightmare. At last the disease ran its course, and he began to improve, but a long convalescence lay ahead of him.

Suddenly he realized that young Jack's twenty-first birthday was coming soon. The only thing Jack, Senior, could think of to mark this milestone was for me to go to Jacksonville and spend the day with him. I protested that I couldn't leave him so soon after such a severe illness, even for three days. But he and our doctor friends "cooked it up" between them and made me go. Jack maintained that by the time I had to leave, he would no longer need nursing, and this was the only thing he could do for his son as he came of age.

Though I didn't want to leave my husband, I was glad I had gone, as it was the only special observance we could think of to show young Jack how much he meant to us. Idamae Hobbs gave me a box of luscious toll house cookies to take to her birthday pal, and another friend had given me an hilarious book about military service for him. I can still see him munching those cookies and chuckling over that book as we took turns reading it aloud. There was a pang that Jack, Senior, couldn't be there too, but our sailor said that his Dad have given him a big gift in loaning me to him for his birthday.

Jack, Senior, was finally able to come downstairs for Christmas. That in itself made it a happy day. We had another cause for rejoicing in that Jack's English friend, William Farren, had come to America on aviation business, and he was able to be with us for Christmas. He was now "Sir William," having been knighted for his design of a marvelous airplane. He said when he wrote us about the honor he had received, "It makes no difference; I still do the washing up." It was grand to have him with us. It made a shining oasis for Jack after the long dull period with none of the "shop talk" he loved. Jack's mother was happy now too, after her weeks of anxiety. Having one of her compatriots to share our Christmas was an additional happiness for her. Once more we had been brought safely through deep waters, so this was Thanksgiving and Christmas rolled into one.

Jack needed some fresh air and sunshine but was cautioned to avoid the rigors of New England winter weather, so he was pretty much house-bound until he was able to go south. We spent the children's 1944 spring vacation at Ormond Beach, Florida. There, the sunshine, moderate temperatures, and salty breezes did their beneficent work, and he came home renewed and ready to conquer any problems in connection with the hospital that might present themselves.

One morning during the summer of 1944 in New Hampshire, we were just getting dressed when we heard a joyous, "Hello, is anybody home?" Could it be? It was! There was young Jack at our window at the bungalow. We ran to unhook the screen door of the porch to let him in. To this day, I can see Jack, Senior, shaving lather all over his face, his razor still in his hand, hugging his boy and pounding his shoulders. We were so excited we could hardly come to earth. Young Jack had, after getting as far as Boston, come up on the milk train. He had, of course, sat up all night and was so sleepy he could hardly keep his eyes open through breakfast. But a short nap revived him, and we made the most of the time he could be with us.

Meanwhile, his feeling for Kathie had deepened. It seemed to be the real thing. We had exchanged a few letters with her, and naturally we all wanted to meet each other. So, in the fall we arranged for her to come for a visit. Young Jack could not be there, which made that visit less enjoyable for her, but she overcame her diffidence and met us all with such winsome charm that we could understand young Jack's love for her. He still had to convince Kathie's father (her mother had died several years before) that he was the right husband for her, but he seemed to feel hopeful.

The spring of 1945 brought hope to all the allies that the end of the war was in sight. Christmas of 1944 had been a time of sorrow on both sides of the Atlantic, following the terrible fighting and heavy casualties of the "Battle of the Bulge." None of us who were living then could forget the agony of those days following December 16, when the Germans had found a weak spot in the allied lines near the Ardennes Forest and had swept forward fourteen miles in one day.

Air-borne troops and American tank forces cut through the German lines and stopped their advance near the river Meuse, and within a week the allies had regained all the ground lost in the offensive. The battle had been won, but many brave young lives had been lost. After that final offensive, the German resistance was never as fierce. There were no more major setbacks for the allies in the European theater of the war.

Jack, Senior, worked hard that winter on all phases of the hospital work, administration as well as building plans. Then once more we went to Florida for the children's spring vacation. We rented a little house at Hobe Sound. None of us cared for hotel life, and the little house meant we could have a real family vacation. Kathie's father allowed her to visit us, and during this visit young Jack could get a few days' leave. This gave them a chance to see each other under more informal circumstances, which was good. Kathie stayed on for ten days or so after Jack had to go back to Iowa where he was then stationed, and we got really close to each other during that time. Mary and she were almost of an age, and having always wanted a sister, Mary was thrilled that Jack was providing her with one whom she could love wholeheartedly.

Several weeks later Mr. Wathen allowed Kathie and Jack to announce their engagement, but no date was set for the wedding. Service overseas was still ahead of young Jack, and we all felt they should not be married until he was safely back home again.

Germany's surrender on May 7, which was ratified on May 8, seemed almost like a miracle. V.E. Day meant also that our efforts could be more concentrated in the Pacific. Jack believed that V.J. Day would not be too many months away, and he bent every effort to complete plans, get bids, and be ready to sign a contract for the hospital before the war was over. As the days passed and the end of the war in the Pacific seemed close at hand, Jack urged purchase of building materials for which we had priority once the war should end. He was especially insistent that we order the steel before the price went up. Ceilings had been on so many things for so long that he knew prices would jump the minute the ceilings were lifted.

On August 9 the Hartford Courant reported that John O. Enders, president of Hartford Hospital, had announced that at a special meeting of the board the recommendation of the executive and building committees had been accepted, and the board had voted to proceed with the building program totaling $6,500,000. This provided for a cost of a million and a half more than the estimates of some years previous had indicated. Some thought had been given to reducing the program, but Dr. H. G. Jarvis, chairman of the building committee from the medical and surgical staff, and Dr. Wilmar Allen, director of the hospital, maintained that they could not reduce the program any further (they had eliminated three floors) without seriously jeopardizing the efficiency of the new hospital building. Quoting from the same article in the Courant:

George J. Mead, chairman of the executive committee and chairman of the building committee, under authority of the board of directors, has signed a contract with the George A. Fuller Company of Boston and New York, low bidders, to act as general contractors for Hartford Hospital. The work of clearing the site will start immediately, and it is hoped that the foundations may be completed before winter. A priority application was filed with the War Production Board, and it is expected that materials will be made available more or less as required. The entire program will require two years, if materials can be secured.

The building committee in charge of the project consists of Norman B. Bertolette, Ostrom Enders (in service), George J. Mead, chairman, Barclay Robinson, and Dr. Robert L. Rowley.

Jack's foresight in filing for priority on materials made all the difference in getting the hospital built on schedule, and his insistence on buying the steel ahead of time saved several hundred thousand dollars on that one item.

Five days later, August 14, came V.J. Day. The horror that such a thing as the atom bomb had been discovered and used over-shadowed to some extent the joy over the conclusion of the war. But it *was over,* and now there would be no more casualties among either our enemies or our own service men.

On September 11 the ground-breaking for the "high building" took place. The article stated, "This building, at an estimated cost of $6,500,000, will be joined to the $2,000,000 south building completed in 1942. The new thirteen-story hospital, plus the south building, will have a capacity of 820 beds and 180 bassinets."

The fact that the number of patients admitted, treated, and discharged annually had increased in two years from 23,000 to well over 25,000 pointed clearly to the need for the expanded facilities, and for proceeding with the construction of the new hospital as rapidly as possible. The building committee could take real satisfaction in having worked out the major details of the plans and specifications and having submitted them to able contractors well ahead of time, so that when the moment for action arrived, they were ready to go ahead.

The site was cleared as quickly as possible. Shovels and bulldozers went to work, and soon a great hole two floors deep and the size of a city block yawned, ready to receive the foundations.

Those of us who had seen the model of the hospital could envision the spacious white building, fifteen stories high from the basement to the storage rooms and pharmacy on the thirteenth floor. What we could not see was the thought and care that had gone into those plans, so that every bit of space in those fifteen floors would be used to the best advantage and would be coordinated with other well-planned space. We would have to wait two years to see the basement—the heartbeat of the building where most of the machinery was housed. The gleaming, stainless steel kitchen and bake shop, equipped with every known labor-saving device to facilitate the preparation and serving of food, the butcher shop and storerooms, all of which were deemed a chef's paradise, were all in the future. Two years would have to pass before we could see the airy lobby on the main floor, the auxiliary store, information desk, staff offices, business office, emergency and accident rooms, library records section—all the facilities for carrying on the business of the hospital which was like a small city. On the second floor there would be the nurses', staff, and employees' dining rooms and the main cafeteria, as well as the hospital switchboard.

The plans called for the location of laboratories, X-ray, and therapy departments, and other aids to diagnosis and treatment of the sick on the third floor, and for the location of the fourteen operating rooms and recovery room on the fourth floor.

The floors from five through twelve, where private and semiprivate rooms would be located, were perhaps easier to visualize, but we would have to wait to see the attractive home-like atmosphere which would characterize the rooms.

The building was to be high rather than long. The layout of all space was designed with an eye to efficiency and step-saving. The pneumatic tubes for messages and the vertical conveyor system were a great innovation. These systems, simply by turning dials, would carry messages and supplies to their designated floors in less than four minutes. Hartford Hospital would be one of the first hospitals in the country to install such conveyor systems.

As the steel skeleton climbed ever skyward and the splendid building began to take shape, our hearts and imaginations soared with it. Here was being enacted before our eyes the fulfillment of a dream, giving ever more convincing promise of the completed structure. One editorial remarked that this building would be a monument to the vision, the courage, the concern for the community, and the generosity of Hartford's citizens who were making this dream a reality.

Meanwhile, the conclusion of the war made a difference in the plans for Kathie's and Jack's wedding. It now seemed unlikely that he would be sent overseas, and we therefore felt it would be arbitrary for us to insist that they wait to be married until he finished college and graduate school and established himself. Though young Jack had not had a chance to prove himself professionally, he had worked hard and faithfully at school and college and in the service. We all felt that, given the necessary education, he would do well in his chosen field, which was engineering. He had certainly proved his love for Kathie through these three years of steadfast devotion. Kathie had proved herself true as steel and had spent the time, that might have been gay and carefree, keeping house for her father and preparing herself to be a capable wife.

The decision to make it possible for them to be married in October 1945 was not arrived at immediately. There was much correspondence back and forth and many phone calls. We insisted that Jack should finish college and think in terms of graduate school. We urged them to think over very honestly whether or not they were willing to live the sort of life that would be necessary while Jack was a student. He did not want to go back to Princeton. He had had enough of bigness in the Navy, and if he transferred to a smaller college, it would probably mean an extra year, as some credits would be forfeited in the change. Inasmuch as he would be released from the service within a few months and was planning to go to a small college soon afterwards, the date for the wedding was set for October 23 in St. Anthony's Episcopal Church in Louisville. Jack asked Peyton to be his best man, and Kathie asked Mary to be one of her bridesmaids.

Early in October, Jack, Senior, came down with a severe case of bronchitis, and after the dreadful case of pneumonia just two years before, Dr. Witter put his foot down firmly and decreed that there would be no trip to Louisville for him. We were heartsick. It seemed too cruel that he should miss his son's wedding, but none of us would have been willing to have him risk a repetition of those awful weeks in 1943. Fortunately he was well enough for me to leave him by the time I needed to go. Young Jack was still in the service and had only one week's leave, so he reached

Louisville only two days before the wedding. Mary and Peyton both managed to get there in time for the rehearsal, though transportation was still a problem. Our dear friend, Dr. Guthrie Speers, minister of the Brown Memorial Church in Baltimore, came "to substitute for Jack, Senior." (We found later that he had had to sit up all night as there was no Pullman space available.)

There had been a few panics ahead of time, but they were dealt with, and the wedding was tender and beautiful. Kathie's minister invited Guthrie to take the betrothal part of the service, which was thoughtful of him and meant a lot to young Jack. They looked so young and so exalted as they took their vows. I added my own silent prayers to those of the ministers that they would always be true to each other and that their love for each other would grow deeper with the passing years.

And so our second daughter came to us. She could not have been closer if she had been our very own. With each year that has passed, the bond between us has grown stronger.

Christmas of 1945 was a time of true happiness. The war was over. Kathie and Jack were happily married. Mary was doing well at Connecticut College. Peyton would soon complete his freshman year at Williams, having started in July to take the accelerated course. Charlie and Billy were growing fast both mentally and physically. Following the ground-breaking for the hospital, construction was going well. So it seemed that many things that were vital to us were falling in place.

I knew there was a pang in Jack's heart at the thought that he was not engaged in anything connected with aeronautics, so the gift which, above all others, gave him joy was contained in a small box which Leonard and Tilly gave to him on Christmas Eve. There was such an air of mystery as they presented this box, that we all watched breathlessly as Jack opened it.

On first examination, the steel disc about an inch thick did not seem to have such tremendous significance, but then as we looked closely at it, we saw that etched on it was a tiny Wasp engine together with this interesting bit of aeronautical history:

1925 — 1
1945 — 375,627

The signatures of Leonard, Tilly, Andy, and Wright Parkins were also etched into the medal. These were the four men who had worked most closely with Jack through his years at United Aircraft, although Andy was the only one who had been there from the beginning.

The fact that such an astounding number of Wasp engines had been manufactured in twenty years gave ample proof of the soundness of the concept and the remarkable engineering which lay behind this production record. Of all the medals Jack received, and all the honors that came to him in his whole life, this medal meant the most, because in this small three-inch disc was summed up not only one of the major achievements of his life, but the loyalty and affection of those four close associates. It is doubtful if even they, who had planned and executed this gift with such care and forethought, realized the lift which this tribute gave to Jack.

Chapter XX

The Close of a Career

Jack had recovered from the attack of bronchitis which had struck him down in the fall of 1945, and he got along fairly well through the weeks preceding Christmas; but after the first of the year, each time a very cold spell or a blizzard struck, a fresh onslaught of some respiratory trouble would lay him low. After the third such attack within a few weeks, Dr. Witter, backed by Gilder, put it to Jack straight. If he wanted to be a good husband and father and live out his normal life span, he must arrange to spend the cold months of the year in the South. To Jack's statement that he could not lead an idle resort life for half the year, the doctors insisted that he didn't have to be in Hartford in order to be useful. He had proved that he could *think* anywhere, and the mail and telephone could convey the results of that thinking to those who needed it.

Jack was never one to seek advice and then not follow it, but this was a hard blow. He, who loved the cold sparkling air and snowy expanses, would look at stretches of hot sand. He, who loved to climb mountains on snowshoes, partly because doing so meant overcoming a few extra difficulties, would be doing his walking on flat roads or beaches. Going south for the winter months would mean he would have to resign from the chairmanship of both the executive and building committees of the hospital, because he was never one to hold a position of trust without being able to do the work it entailed. For ten years he had struggled to make the dream come true which had had its inception during the time of waiting while Gilder worked to save the life of our three-weeks' old baby. Now, just when the dream was on its way to becoming reality, when he would have loved to watch every detail of the new building, he must relinquish the reins. He did not mind having the completion of the hospital take place under the leadership of someone else. But he had longed to carry through this project which would be of such benefit to patients and such service to the doctors who had done so much for us during the twenty years we had lived in Hartford.

The doctors' suggestion presented a problem to our family life also. Interruption to Charlie's and Billy's school life militated against their records, so that even if they went to school in Florida, the time away would count as if they had been absent. They were too young for boarding school. How would I manage to be a mother to them and a wife to Jack during the winter months? Jack, in the midst of his own disappointment, told me not to worry. We would work it out somehow. The main thing was to remember that the boys needed the security and happiness of one parent at home, and he reminded me that the company plane flew south frequently, and he was sure that I would often be a welcome passenger.

Through Dr. George St. John, the former headmaster of Choate School, who had a house in Hobe Sound, Florida, we found a little house on the ocean which was poorly planned but which Jack remodeled attractively. It was fun to watch the evolution of the collection of rooms, which had been strung together without much thought, into an inviting six-room house which we named "Casamar." Good weather while the remodeling was going on was cause for gratitude, as doors and windows were often lacking for a while, and occasionally some walls. It was, however, an absorbing interest for Jack. The problems it presented kept his mind busy, and he was therefore happy. The St. Johns put us in touch with a dear woman named Luanna Holmes who came every day but Sunday. She couldn't do enough for us, and when I had to go back to Hartford, she really outdid herself in her efforts to make Jack and the friends who visited him comfortable.

Emmy and Ray Walsh were among the staunch souls who visited Jack that first winter while the house was going through its transformation. That was true friendship. Visiting in "Casamar" during its period of transition was not exactly a vacation.

By mid-March the remodeling was almost complete. At Jack's suggestion, I went down a week before spring vacation began, to help him with the final touches which would change the little house into a home. When Mary, Charlie, and Billy joined us, they were delighted and could hardly believe it was the same house they had seen earlier. It was a happy vacation in spite of the fact that Peyton, after completing his freshman year in February at Williams, had been called into the service. He joined the paratroopers, which was not as much of a worry as it would have been had the war still been going on, but it was not the branch of the service calculated to give parents peace of mind.

Young Jack was released from the Navy in the late spring, and he and Kathie spent some weeks looking around at small colleges. They settled on Haverford, just outside of Philadelphia, and he was accepted. Their first apartment was awful, I gathered. They never let me see it, but they soon found one that was nicer on the third floor of a house that had been made into three apartments.

Jack, Senior's, prediction that I would be invited to ride down on the company plane from time to time proved to be accurate, and I had several visits at "Casamar" before the final one that spring of 1946 when Jack and I drove home together. Jack called it an ancestral pilgrimage, and he planned it so that we could visit several of the places in Virginia where my forebears had lived before my parents had moved, first to North Carolina and then to Kentucky. This trip was a thrill for him as well as for me. The houses along the James River and around Richmond were lovely beyond words. Now, they were no longer just names. It was a delight also to follow the spring as it unfolded on our trip and watch the world come back to life.

We had seen many gorgeous sights on our way north, but our own home with the younger boys to welcome us was the best of all. Jack was glad to see how much had been accomplished on the hospital building. The steel frame was all complete with Old Glory flying proudly from the top.

May 18, 1946, was a grand milestone in our lives as we celebrated our 25th wedding anniversary. There had been so many emergencies, illnesses, partings, and anxieties in the preceding years that our silver wedding day took on especially deep meaning. Kathie and Jack as well as Mary and Peyton came to be with us. Charlie and Billy were at home, and Mary and George Houston, who had had such a big part in helping us find our happiness, joined us. The Hobbses, Tillinghasts, and Chatfields, also came. The Houstons were soon to move to Mexico for a few years. One of their treasures was a beautiful silver and crystal epergne which they wanted us to enjoy. Filled with lilies of the valley, it graced our lovely table which was covered with an exquisite cloth that Mamma had given us on our linen anniversary. We felt very festive and gay as we toasted Kathie's and Jack's recent marriage and their 25th wedding anniversary which would come a year before our 50th.

The gift which the children and I gave to Jack was a simple little silver box which could be used in various ways, with all our signatures and the date engraved on it. Jack's gift to me was an exquisite pin which he had designed and had made for me. It was a lily of the valley—our wedding flower—made of platinum with moonstones for the florets. His forethought and understanding of my feeling about these flowers would have made it a highly valued treasure, even without its own grace and beauty.

Young Jack worked on the farm in New Hampshire that summer during the day and studied math equally hard in the evenings as a self-imposed refresher course. This gave us a chance to see more of Kathie, to come closer to her and enjoy her.

One more unique pleasure that came to us in August was a visit from Neva and Alexander James. Neva was Jack's cousin Heather's daughter. They were on their way from England to British Columbia where they planned to make their home. Both had endured untold trials during the war, "Zander," as we called him, having been captured at the fall of Singapore and been in a terrible prison camp for forty-two months. They loved the New Hampshire place. He particularly loved the vegetable garden where he worked indefatigably. We had been so deeply concerned about all the English cousins throughout the war that it was a joy to have these two with us, for even a little while.

One afternoon the phone rang, and a very much puzzled telegraph operator said, "Mrs. Mead, this seems like a funny message for you, but I am sure I took it correctly. It says, 'Fell out of aeroplane this afternoon, landed safely, no strawberries. Love, Peyton.' Does that make sense to you?" So I told him that Peyton was a paratrooper and that I had asked him to wire me when he took his first actual jump from a plane so I could rejoice with him. I told the operator the strawberry part meant that the harness of his parachute had not scraped or lacerated him. "Gee, no kidding! Don't you want to send him an answer?" So I told him I did indeed, but his Dad and I would write out a good one and call him back.

A day or so later we received a letter from Sally Noyes whom Peyton had been dating more and more constantly the past two or three years. In the letter she shared some of Peyton's comments about his jump. He said among other things that a parachute jump from a plane was like falling off a log. I was glad he thought so, but it didn't seem that way to me.

September came, and with it the necessary return to Hartford. As was our custom, Jack stayed on at the farm while I got the younger boys settled in school once more and Mary back to Connecticut College. Then I returned to the farm for *our* vacation. We always planned on the second week in October when the air was crisp, the sun warm, and the countryside aflame with the glory of autumn in New England. This year, as usual, we visited all our favorite spots, climbed a few mountains, and best of all on the warmer afternoons paddled the canoe far out into the lake, allowing it to glide along noiselessly so we could hear the loons and wild ducks discussing their winter plans. Sometimes when we were close to shore, we would see a graceful doe and her fawn, but more often we saw them from the house, grazing in the hayfield as unafraid as cows in a pasture.

Winter was late in coming that year, so Jack decided to risk staying in Hartford through Christmas. Peyton had a furlough, Sally joined us from Montclair, Kathie and Jack came from Philadelphia. We were all together, so that Christmas of 1946 was a supremely happy time. Jack, Senior, stayed on until the new year came in so that he could be with the family all during their vacations.

Several times during the winter of 1947 I was invited to fly south in the company plane. I also took one commercial flight in a DC-4, the plane which had been designed in Jack's office the summer of 1935 and which was coming into its own as an airliner.

Following one of my trips to Hobe Sound, when I had hardly unpacked my bag after returning to Hartford, young Jack phoned to tell me that Kathie's father had died in his sleep the night before. Did I think it was all right for him to cut classes for three days so he could go to Louisville with her? I told him, of course he must go with her, and that I would fly down the next day. I was glad I could go. Kathie was now very much alone in the world except for us, and I wanted her to feel that she still had a family besides one aunt and some distant cousins who loved her.

Young Jack needed to go back to Philadelphia after the services as he had some vital tests coming up next day. I stayed over, and Kathie and I traveled back together when she was free to leave. We had quite a trip north. The flight we took was grounded in Washington because New York was blanketed under a foot of snow. We finally got a train for New York. Kathie wired Jack to meet her in Philadelphia, and I wired Harry Bergstrom to meet me at Penn Station instead of La Guardia. It was a long, cold, hungry trip, as neither of us had had any lunch or supper; but when we arrived in Philadelphia, I went with Kathie to the vestibule of the car to wave to Jack as he met her. As I saw him running down the platform, carrying her overshoes, I knew he had already become a mature and thoughtful husband. I was grateful for this, for I knew my second daughter needed extra love and thoughtfulness at this time of sadness.

Eventually the winter ended. Spring vacation came, and once more we had a happy time together as a family at Hobe Sound. Peyton was stationed at Fort Benning, Georgia, and was able to join us for a few days. He had learned to fly, so one day he demonstrated his new skill to us. We had written "Happy Landings" in huge letters in the sand, and when we saw him coming, we waved our towels and wished we had learned to "wig-wag" some gay message to him.

In the spring of 1947 there were two big family events. Mary graduated from Connecticut College, and Charlie graduated from Junior School, the curriculum of which had been extended to cover the sixth grade. Mary had always been a brilliant student, and we had thought she might want to go on to graduate school; but she had at one point put in some weeks teaching kindergarten and enjoyed the children so much that she accepted a position as one of the kindergarten teachers at Junior School when it was offered her. She was pretty excited at the thought that in the fall she would be earning her living. She was a winsome and stimulating teacher, and all the little boys wanted her to wait until they grew up so they could marry her.

Once more, summer in New Hampshire was a time of refreshment and family happiness. "Teaser II" had spent the war years in her cradle, as we could of course not use a boat requiring so much gas. (We had hardly used even the outboard motor boat during those years, even to attend Sunday service on Church Island unless it was altogether too windy and rough to paddle.) Jack, Senior, decided that a smaller inboard boat would be more fun for everybody, and so after a good deal of looking, he ordered a twenty-foot Chris-Craft runabout. "Teaser III" reached us in time for Jack and me to enjoy a few spins in her when I came up in October.

It seemed best for Jack to go to Hobe Sound in November of 1947. We had hoped to repeat the family reunion in Hartford which had been so enjoyable the year before, but Dr. Witter advised him not to wait. The day he was to leave was cold and drear. Much as I hated to see him go, I felt it was wise. It looked as if we were in for a hard winter, and a few weeks' extra separation would be a small price to pay if it could mean good health for him. Still, as we thought about the months ahead, the winter seemed very long and hard to face.

That day at lunch, Jack seemed mysterious. Afterwards, when we were finishing his packing, he pulled a letter from Peyton out of his pocket. In it he told us that he and Sally were engaged, they wanted to announce their engagement in the spring and were planning to be married a year later in June 1949, after she graduated from Mount Holyoke. They hoped, in spite of their being so young, that we would think that was all right, even though he (because of the eighteen months in the service) wouldn't graduate from Williams until 1950. He would also still have medical school, internship, residency, etc., to complete before he could become a full-fledged doctor. We were so happy we couldn't keep our minds on what we had to do, so we both sat down and wrote Peyton how happy his letter made us. One bit in Jack's letter has always stayed in my mind. After speaking of Sally's fineness and lovableness, and of how we had loved her since she was a little girl, he added, "and her parents are two of the finest people I've ever known."

We would not have put any obstacles in their path in any case, but young Jack had developed so wonderfully since his marriage to Kathie, had grown from youth to manhood so quickly, that we were truly grateful that Peyton and Sally had found each other when they also were young, and Peyton would have Sally with him through all those years of training that lay ahead.

The news in that letter helped us make our plans for Christmas. We had been puzzled as to how we could work out a plan so that all the family could be happy. This Christmas would be the first one since Kathie's father's death, and so we wanted to make it as happy for her as possible. Peyton solved the problem for us by suggesting that he spend Christmas with his father in Florida. So we asked Kathie and Jack if they would spend part of the holiday with Mary, Charlie, Billy, and me in Hartford. Then we suggested that Mary, Kathie, and Jack go north on the 26th for a week of skiing. Charlie, Billy, and I would meet Sally in New York and go south together, reaching Hobe Sound for Jack, Senior's, birthday on the 27th. Sally's parents agreed, and everyone was pleased with the plans. Peyton arranged to spend a few days in Montclair with Sally and her parents before going south.

Everything worked fine until about 11:00 a.m. December 26. Then the clouds which had been hanging cold and heavy suddenly started crystallizing into snowflakes. We had reached New Haven when the snow began. In less than an hour, there was a major storm. Cars without snow tires clogged both lanes of the southbound Merritt Parkway. We were blocked close to a Stamford exit for almost two hours. Departure time for the southbound train from Penn Station was getting closer and closer. We thought that if we could get off the parkway, we could catch a train from Stamford to New York, take the shuttle from Grand Central to Penn Station, and so meet Sally as planned. We finally managed to reach the exit and the Stamford railroad station. The station master there phoned Penn Station. By a miracle, the message was relayed to Sally to go ahead and take the train even if we had not managed to get to the Penn terminal. We would come as soon as we could.

The train from New York we were to have taken was probably the only one that left on time that afternoon, and that was about an hour before we arrived. I have always wondered how the station master managed to relay the message to Sally in that milling throng of frustrated people. But he had done so, and so part of our plan worked out.

I phoned Jack, explained our problems, told him there was a train leaving in two hours, and we would phone him from Jacksonville the next day. The train we were fortunate enough to get on turned west at Jacksonville so we had to leave it there and travel some other way to Palm Beach, which was the nearest station to Hobe Sound. In Jacksonville we learned there would be no train until the next day. So just on a faint chance, I phoned Eastern Airlines, and a miracle happened. When I gave my name and asked about a flight, the girl said, "Oh yes, Mrs. Mead, there's a flight in an hour, and we are holding three seats for you and your boys. Your husband phoned us this morning and reserved them." We couldn't communicate with each other, but in spite of this he was watching over us and planning for our comfort and safety. That was almost the most wonderful gift I ever received. What a happy reunion that was! Sally had arrived a few hours earlier. We felt very triumphant and grateful about having managed to get there for his birthday, in spite of the storm and all the other obstacles.

That vacation was perfect, but it was over all too soon. We six watched the new year, 1948, come in, and two days later Sally and Peyton took Charlie and Billy back home, and I stayed on for an extra two weeks with Jack, Senior.

While I was there, an official-looking envelope came for Jack from Washington. The letter it contained said that he was to receive the Congressional Medal for Merit, the highest award attainable to a civilian, "for his outstanding service to the United States." Orville Wright was to receive the same honor at the same time. Having his name linked with that of Orville Wright doubled Jack's joy in receiving this accolade. It would be impossible to gauge the affection and respect that Jack felt for the great man who had forty-five years before proved that it was possible to fly in a machine heavier than air.

As in previous years I "commuted" between Hartford and Hobe Sound, either by train or plane, so that we had two or three little visits between the Christmas and spring vacations. Once when I was in Florida, Jack and I went over to Lake Wales to visit his friend, Henry Crane. Many years had passed since they had seen each other, so they had a lot of catching up to do. They had a glorious time exploring each other's minds and hearing about each other's most recent interests. Mr. Crane had heard that Jack was to receive the Congressional Medal for Merit, and he was enthusiastic in his praise for those who had made the selection. Jack was so happy at being with Mr. Crane I hated to have the day come to an end.

An important milestone that season was the completion of Hartford Hospital and its dedication on March 14, 1948. The hospital fulfilled all Jack's dreams for it. All the features he had insisted on were included and proved their worth even before the dedication. The ceremonies on March 14 were full of dignity and meaning, and the tours of the building, which continued for over a week, were proof of the interest and approval of Hartford's citizens. But, at this climax of over ten years of tireless work and determination, Jack could not be present. He was advised not to come north so early. Here was another disappointment, a big one, but if it had to be, he would not complain. He would make do with a blow-by-blow description of the dedication from Gilder and me, and when he came home, he would see for himself the magnificent building which had evolved from all the dreams and plans and labors of recent years. To Jack it was not simply an efficient, well-planned building. Its potential was what rejoiced his heart. To him it represented less fatigue for doctors, nurses and staff, and better treatment and speedier healing for the sick. I can still picture him as he came bounding into the house from his first tour of the completed structure, his eyes shining and his happiness over the fruition of their plans bubbling over.

The ceremony of conferring the Medal for Merit had to be postponed from the original January date to a time in the late spring. Soon after our anniversary, some problems at the farm called Jack to New Hampshire. It had been a long time since I had visited my mother in Louisville, so, as things were under control in Hartford, I decided to take a flying trip to see her. The night before I was to go, a phone call from my husband electrified me. General Powers and John Victory, secretary of the N.A.C.A., were planning to fly up from Washington the next morning to present the award at a private ceremony. Jack knew I couldn't come, but he wanted me to know. Couldn't come? The very idea! I would be there. "But you are going to see your mother." "I'll go to see her next week. She would be crushed if I failed to witness this greatest honor of your life." "But how will you get here in time? They'll be here by eleven and will have the ceremony immediately, and then right after lunch they will have to return to Washington." "I'll be there. I'll leave soon after 5:00 a.m. and get there before they do." Jack was thrilled. He told me afterwards that he wanted so much for me to be present but didn't see how I could make it.

I spent the rest of the evening undoing all the Louisville plans and getting Charlie's and Billy's things packed so that they too could watch the presentation. What a simple yet moving ceremony it was. I wished the rest of the family could have been there, but anyway, we three did witness the conferring of this, the greatest of all the honors Jack had ever received. Somehow the fact that Dr. Victory and General Powers had flown up to the spot in all the world Jack loved best in order to pin the medal and ribbon on his coat, put the rosette in his buttonhole, and read the citation enhanced its significance to him.

The newspaper account of this momentous occasion read as follows:

> Wednesday afternoon, June 16, a private ceremony was held at the Mead Farm, Center Harbor, when Dr. George Jackson Mead was presented the Medal for Merit. Major General E. M. Powers, Assistant Deputy Chief of Staff for Materiel, representing the Chief of Staff, U.S. Air Force, presented the medal, ribbon and rosette to Dr. Mead on behalf of President Truman, while Mrs. Mead and their sons, Charles and William, proudly watched. Others witnessing the ceremony were Col. M. C. Demler, Chief of the Propulsion Service of the Air Force, of Washington, D.C., Major J. B. Carey, aide to General Powers, and representatives of the news. Dr. Mead's other three children were unable to be present.
>
> Expressing his personal esteem for Dr. Mead and the honor he felt in presenting the medal, which is the highest award attainable

to a civilian, General Powers pinned the medal to Dr. Mead's coat as the citation was read by Dr. John F. Victory, Executive Secretary of the National Advisory Committee for Aeronautics. The citation read as follows:

CITATION
FOR THE MEDAL FOR MERIT
DR. GEORGE JACKSON MEAD

Dr. George Jackson Mead, for exceptionally meritorious conduct in the performance of outstanding services to the United States. Dr. Mead, as Chairman of the N.A.C.A. Power Plants Committee, initiated, planned, and energetically promoted the establishment of the aircraft engine research laboratory at Cleveland, Ohio, which laboratory has become the most advanced installation of its kind in the world. Through his insistence, over objections of others, the altitude wind tunnel at the Aircraft Engine Research Laboratory was made adequate for research and test work on full-size airplane power plants under a wide range of controlled, simulated conditions. Because of the capacity of that tunnel and the availability of the other facilities at the laboratory, the bomber program of the United States was substantially accelerated. Dr. Mead was responsible in large measure for bringing into the airplane engine program the vast engineering potentialities of automotive manufacturers.

Dr. Victory congratulated Dr. Mead on behalf of his former associates. Many aeronautical patents have been awarded Dr. Mead. His many achievements in the field of aviation are highly valuable.

Chapter XXI

Continuing Influence

The summer of 1948 was one in which Jack managed to do something special for each member of the family. Jack and Kathie wanted to drive to California, camping along the way, partly to see our great country and partly to look at several graduate schools. The two Jacks put their heads together and their hands to work to improvise a "camper" out of the small car Kathie and Jack had bought. They devised screens that would fit into the window openings; they removed the back seat so that by putting their feet in the trunk Jack and Kathie could put their sleeping bags on top of air mattresses and sleep comfortably in the car. True, most of the items that traveled in the car by day were sheltered under it at night, but it worked very well, and they had a glorious trip.

Sally and Peyton had decided they would like to start their married life in the canoe house the next summer. Above the part where the canoes and outboard motor boat "lived" there was a screened-in porch about 30 × 35 feet which had been built as a rainy-day playroom. Jack drew a plan to make this porch into an ideal apartment for them, and work was started as soon as they approved the plan. The kitchen was minute, so it was just as well that Sally was so slim.

Mary had always loved good music, so her Dad selected an automatic record player for her, which had a wonderful rich tone. It afforded her many hours of blissful listening. Its voice was rarely silent. Charlie and Billy were now promoted to climbing real mountains, and Jack took them on many climbing trips, one up Mt. Jefferson. He also taught them to water ski behind "Teaser III" which was a thrilling accomplishment for them.

The literary club to which I belonged was to study Canada during the winter of 1948–49. I had worked on the program committee and so was able to get my assignment early. Cape Breton was the topic for my long paper. In August Jack became so intrigued with one of my source books that he suggested we ask Sally's parents to join us in September for a trip around the Cabot Trail on Cape Breton so as to see the glorious views and, as he said, make this a "bang-up" paper.

No urging was needed. Dr. Noyes, alas, could not go, but he thought it would be wonderful for Marjorie to have the trip. He set to work to get her excused from her church duties for the two weeks we planned to be gone. Jack worked out our itinerary on some maps of Maine and eastern Canada and made reservations for us everywhere. We were all thrilled about this tour, only sorry that Morgan couldn't join us in such a delightful expedition.

After returning to our winter homes and making the necessary arrangements for our families during our absence, Marjorie and I drove back to Center Harbor the afternoon of September 14. Jack came to the door to meet us, but though he had been fine when I left him four days before, he now looked pale and drawn. He thought some fall pollens were the culprits, urged us not to worry, and assured us he would be all right in the morning. When morning came, however, he was no better. Jack decided he could not set out with us that day, but he would fly to Sydney on Cape Breton and join us for the return journey. That would mean he would miss Ingonish, the most beautiful part of the whole trip, the description of which had so intrigued him that he planned the tour. Marjorie and I begged him to call off the whole trip. No matter how gorgeous the scenery, and how thrilling our explorations would be, how could we enjoy any of it if we had left him to be ill alone. He was adamant. He had made all those reservations, and he wanted us to use them. He overrode all our objections and phoned Harry Bergstrom and asked him to meet us in North East Harbor, Maine, so we would have a man along.

Our hearts were heavy as we started off that afternoon. The trouble did not appear to us to be hayfever, and we hated to leave, but we knew Jack would be really unhappy if we did not go as planned. We checked by phone each evening, and for a while it seemed that each call found him a little better. Then one night—the one in Ingonish—his voice was so weak I could hardly hear him. We omitted the rest of the trip and got back to Center Harbor as fast as we could. The intervening miles seemed endless.

We reached the farm in the early afternoon and were shocked to see the change those nine days had made. Marjorie didn't feel this was any time to visit, so Harry drove her back to Hartford where she could get a train to Montclair. As they drove off, it seemed that the last link with help for my husband was broken. I knew I lacked the experience needed for the days ahead. I got in touch with Dr. Bovaird in Wolfeboro, whom Gilder recommended. He took some tests but could not make any diagnosis that was satisfactory either to him or us. For ten days we struggled with mounting temperatures, followed by subnormal periods. Dr. Bovaird kept in touch with our doctors at home, and finally Gilder came up. Jack brightened and our spirits lifted when he arrived. Surely now we would find out what the trouble was, and Gilder would know how to get Jack well.

The next morning before breakfast as I looked out of a second-story window, I saw Gilder walking up from the boat house, and there was something about his walk that filled me with apprehension. Gilder urged Jack to go to Hartford where the hospital he had worked so hard to build was ready to help him regain his health. At first, Jack refused; but then, after Gilder had left, I pleaded with him so earnestly that he finally agreed to go. The company plane came up to Laconia to fly him down quickly and easily, and an hour after we left Laconia, he was comfortably settled on the tenth floor of Hartford Hospital. When Jack had worked hard years before to kindle the interest and support of the community, it had not occurred to him that he would benefit from the hospital, but here it was, ready to serve him, ready to make available every test, and employ every known technique to restore his health.

Several weeks of intensive tests and treatments followed, and finally on November 1 the doctors thought they had found the trouble and that an operation could save him. Jack urged me to be sure to vote before coming down next morning, which I did as soon as the polls were open, and I was able to have a few minutes with him before he went into the operating room. Less than an hour after the orderlies wheeled Jack away, and I went upstairs to wait, Dr. Witter came to Jack's room to tell me as kindly as he could the trouble the operation had revealed. As soon as I saw his compassionate face, I knew. The trouble had progressed so far and so fast that the doctors thought he could not live a month.

But there followed three of the most heroic months of his life. He made sure that all details of his affairs were in order. As far as was humanly possible, he planned for our care and security. He even selected his own wedding gift for Sally and Peyton—a car which would be delivered in the spring, but the picture of which he pulled out from under his pillow when they were there during the Christmas holidays. I will not dwell on those months of pain, except to say that his fineness and nobility of character were never more manifest than during that time of weakness. It was as if he must crowd into that short time all the generous and thoughtful acts and all the love for us that would normally have been spread over the next fifteen or twenty years. Just here, I will quote a bit of a letter from my sister, Mary Houston, written shortly before he died:

> All through this time that you have been so ill, I have felt very confident of your restoration to complete health and have been so sure that your courage, together with the skill of the doctors, and Cary's care and devotion, would be able to overcome all the hazards of an unusual and perhaps little understood illness. Cary's letter that came yesterday afternoon saddens me more than I can say, for it tells me that all of you are doubtful of being able to lick this thing. In view of that, I cannot let this time of deep anxiety pass, without trying to tell you a few of the things that I have in my heart.
>
> Ever since that evening when I first met you, and you asked me about Cary, and then later became our beloved 'Misser Mead,' I

have cherished the deepest feeling of love and respect for you, a special closeness, and the highest admiration of your fine personal qualities, and of the brilliance of your mind. George has always said that you had the finest brain for aeronautics in the whole country, and your achievements have filled him with the greatest pride and admiration. These things I knew and rejoiced in, but dearer and closer to my heart, were your sweetness and lovability. Our Stuey understood those qualities, though she was only a baby, and your sweetness to her made me feel sure that my beloved Cary would be safe in loving you and in sharing your life. It has been a full and very wonderful life for you both, and whatever may come, you can remember that and feel very proud and happy.

I am not saying any of this very well, but at least you will know that I love and honor you and am, in spite of what the doctors may say, hoping and praying that you will be restored to health and strength.

There were only brief moments of consciousness during the third week in January, and as, with sinking heart, I watched the shadow creep across his face the night of the 19th, I thought with gratitude of the years we had been permitted to share, and of these months which, in spite of their sadness, had given us a closer, more enduring oneness even than before. The end came peacefully during the early hours of January 20, 1949.

The following day, letters and tributes began to arrive, and detailed accounts of Jack's life and career appeared in newspapers and magazines across the country. A newspaper article from the Hartford Times read as follows:

Flags at United Aircraft Corporation were lowered to half-staff Thursday in memory of the late founder. Mr. Mead's integrity and brilliant engineering were acknowledged by Frederick B. Rentschler, chairman of the board. His statement follows: "All of the personnel of United Aircraft are deeply shocked in the passing of George Mead, a name which will always be legendary in our company. Personally, I feel that I have lost a loyal devoted friend of many years' standing. George Mead was not only a co-founder of Pratt & Whitney Aircraft Company and its successor, United Aircraft Corporation, but directed the design and development of the first Wasp engine. That power plant revolutionized both American military and transport aviation and heralded American leadership in this field for the first time in the middle twenties.

"Mr. Mead was one of a very few aviation leaders who helped lay the solid foundation of our aviation industry and permitted it to emerge with the dominant world's air force which was such a vital factor in World War II. . . . We in United humbly acknowledge his contribution to our company and to aviation. Our Pratt & Whitney Aircraft Division particularly has been deeply stamped with and will always reflect George Mead's personal integrity and brilliant engineering leadership."

An account in one of the local papers stated:

Testimony to the engineering accomplishments and public career of the late George J. Mead . . . came from many associates here and through the nation. Leaders in the aircraft industry and government paid tribute to Mr. Mead as "the outstanding aviation engine designer of this generation."

This same news account commented that General Knudsen, under whom Jack had served as director of the air section of the National Defense Council, was no longer living, but a telegram of tribute was sent by Knudsen's former deputy, John D. Biggers of Toledo, Ohio. The article said:

Mr. Biggers is president of the Libbey-Owens-Ford Glass Company. He said, "I am grieved to hear of the passing of my good friend George Mead. His was a fine and lovable character, and he rendered great service to our country during the critically important days of preparation for World War II. General Knudsen and I found him invaluable in planning and carrying into execution the aircraft production program. He not only had indispensable knowledge in this field, but his high integrity and tireless devotion to duty made his services of great importance to his government in time of need."

This same newspaper article contained the following from Dr. Jerome C. Hunsaker, then chairman of the National Advisory Committee for Aeronautics.

George J. Mead was the outstanding aviation engine designer of this generation. His creative work resulted in the American air-cooled engines which were ready to be produced for the war in immense numbers.

From S. Paul Johnston, director of the Institute of the Aeronautical Sciences, came this statement:

> The officers and members of the Institute have learned with profound regret of the passing of George Jackson Mead. He was a founder member of the Institute and served on its first council. He was elected honorary fellow for 1938, the Institute's highest award. During the war . . . he added to his contributions as a great engineer an outstanding performance as an American citizen.

William H. Putnam, president of Hartford Hospital and chairman of the board of trustees of Connecticut College in New London, paid tribute to Jack's service to both institutions when he said:

> George J. Mead brought to the Hartford Hospital and its problems the ingenious mind which he had given to the field of aeronautical engines . . . .
>
> Mr. Mead was formerly chairman of the executive committee of Connecticut College for Women in New London, was a trustee of the college, and he did much for the college welfare. It was a great privilege to know him and work with him.

The February 1949 issue of U.S. Air Services carried a long article about Jack's life and career, which concluded with the following:

> During all his years in aviation, Dr. Mead sidestepped through inherent modesty all forms of personal publicity, continuing without cessation to work on fundamental problems. He was a truly great man, his insight enabling him to choose the most important problems to be solved, and his knowledge and industry enabling him to solve them . . . to be with him, even for a few moments was an education. . . .

Of all the many accolades bestowed upon Jack, it seems fitting to conclude these tributes with excerpts taken from The Choate News issue on February 9, 1949, since it was during his years at Choate that his unusual abilities first became apparent to those outside his family.

> In the death of George Jackson Mead, Choate has lost one of its most distinguished sons. . . . The loss which his family, his school, community, and nation have sustained in his death can be compensated for in part by the value which his life affords as a model for others. Choate is proud of all that Jack Mead accomplished. It is even more proud of the qualities out of which such achievement grew. And most of all, Choate is proud of the modesty and grace with which he wore the laurel.

Our close friends, the Hobbses, Chatfields, and Tillinghasts arranged flowers at the house, planned and provided luncheon for the many devoted friends who came from great distances to attend Jack's service. They also made the church into a garden with the countless sprays—mostly red roses—which were sent as an expression of love and esteem. Dr. Archibald had woven together the passages of scripture we particularly loved, and his short tribute to Jack's victorious life was inspiring. Sally's father gave the prayer, which was the most eloquent and uplifting I ever heard. It has carried me through many hard days.

We laid our dear one to rest in a little cemetery in Center Sandwich, New Hampshire, but learned later there was no way to arrange for care of our lot when we were not there. We, therefore, made our own "God's acre" at the farm on a knoll looking across the lake at the mountains he loved.

Somehow we would have to learn to face life without him. No matter how sorely we needed his wisdom, his help, and his love, we must live our lives in such a way that he could be proud of us. Jack, Mary, and Peyton were grown. They had shown their fineness and maturity in the way they had met the sorrow that had come to them and in their tenderness and consideration of me. But Charlie and Billy were so young, only thirteen and ten. How could I help them develop into the kind of men Jack would want them to be without him to encourage, direct, control, and inspire them? The years ahead seemed to be a long, uphill road.

Then I remembered how my husband loved to climb mountains—loved to overcome difficulties. I remembered that the harder the task he faced, the greater his zest in surmounting it. I remembered how often he had stiffened my spine with some word of encouragement when my steps were flagging. Others had faced, with courage and determination, the same loss I was experiencing.

Whatever happened, I must not fail my husband or the children who had blessed our marriage.

Some day I should like to write a sequel to this book, to tell of the lives of our family in the years following January 1949. However, a short summary of the high points in the life of each one is appropriate here.

Jack graduated from Haverford College in June of 1949, was accepted at both M.I.T. and Johns Hopkins, but chose Johns Hopkins Engineering School and went on to become an able engineer, holding positions of responsibility at both Curtiss Wright and General Electric engine section. He is now a consulting engineer working out of Boston. Jack and Kathie's long-awaited son, Chip (Charles Jackson), was born September 1, 1949, and was followed at intervals of several years by Virginia Randolph, Cary Wathen, and Barbara Hoge.

Our daughter, Mary Mead James, after several years of teaching at Junior School, was asked to found the library at the South Congregational Church in Hartford (our church) and built it up to the point where it comprises worth-while books in all categories, reference books, rare old books and manuscripts, plus a record library and other features. She later also became administrative assistant to the minister of our church and gives invaluable service.

Sally graduated from Mount Holyoke also in June of 1949, and she became Mrs. Peyton Mead at their lovely wedding on June 25. Peyton graduated from Williams in June the following year and was given his first son, Morgan Noyes, as a graduation present. Peyton was accepted at the College of Physicians and Surgeons at Columbia for his medical training and returned to Hartford Hospital for internship and residency. After a year at Memorial Hospital in New York to study special cancer techniques, he became in 1957–58 senior surgical resident at Hartford Hospital and is an esteemed and skillful surgeon. Two daughters, Merrill Fowler and later Carolyn Jackson, were born to Peyton and Sally, followed after several years by George Jackson II.

After two years at Kingswood, Charlie attended Choate where he distinguished himself in many ways and went on to Cornell University. There he met and fell in love with Carol Vieth. Following two years of service in the Marines in the middle of his college years, he and Carol were married on June 20, 1959, at the

Congregational Church at Manhasset on Long Island. It was wonderful to see the four brothers stand together at the ceremony. Carol was a beautiful bride and the wedding was perfect. Following his graduation from Cornell two years later, he joined Xerox Corporation in Rochester as a quality analyst and has gone steadily forward. Their son, Jeremy Stewart, was born on his mother's birthday, October 11, 1962, and was followed by their daughter Betsy (Elizabeth Ellen) two and a half years later, and subsequently by Robert Andrew.

Bill, after graduation from Hotchkiss School, went on to Williams where he met and fell in love with Joanna (Hansy) van Andel, who was living in the home of one of the professors and auditing some courses at Williams. He finally persuaded her that life in America, away from Holland, could be happy, and they were married on December 23, 1958, at the Kloosterkerk in the Hague in a most beautiful ceremony. After graduating from Williams, Bill went on to Harvard Architectural School where he did magnificent work. Jan Willem, their first son, was born in February 1960 and was later joined by Mark Nathaniel and Samuel Aldo. Still later there came three little daughters, Sonya Henriette, Tanya Georgine (after Hansy's mother) and Roanna Margot.

All five of our children have a great deal of their father's creativity which manifests itself in a variety of interesting ways. As time went on, I realized that the years the children had had with Jack had yielded a rich harvest. The imprint of his character, his life, his ideals, was deeper and stronger than I had realized. In a letter written to me after he got back to Williams, Peyton commented on the fact that "even Dad's will was beautiful in the revelations of himself that slipped in here and there." This was true. His thoughtfulness and concern for us all breathed through each page. One fifth of his estate was to be divided among Trinity College, Williams College, M.I.T., and the Hartford Hospital. The bequests to Trinity and Williams were to provide revolving funds for scholarships for gifted students majoring in government, history, or English who needed help in financing their college years. There was provision also for inspiring lectures. For M.I.T. the bequest was similar, except that the scholarships were for exceptional students in engineering; and the hospital bequest was, of course, to assist young interns who wished additional training.

In 1957 United Aircraft announced an award in memory of Jack. The chairman of the board, H. M. Horner, stated in the company paper:

> The outstanding engineering achievement in the company will be recognized beginning this year by the presentation of a medal and a prize of $2,500. The award will be known as the George J. Mead Medal for Engineering Achievement. Members of the engineering staffs of Pratt & Whitney Aircraft, Hamilton Standard, and Sikorsky Aircraft, and the United Aircraft research department will be eligible for the award. . . . George J. Mead, for whom the medal is named, was one of the foremost designers of aircraft engines until his death in 1949. He was one of the founders of Pratt & Whitney Aircraft and the engineering head of the company when it was organized in 1925.

Leonard Hobbs was the motivating force behind this award which was to be given at United Aircraft Corporation's annual meeting to the engineer or engineers who had during the year made the most significant contribution to aviation. Jack Horner and William Gwinn, who succeeded him upon his retirement as chairman of the board at United Aircraft, have been most gracious in inviting me not only to attend the annual meetings of the stockholders, but to participate in presenting the memorial award.

At the annual meeting of United Aircraft Corporation on April 14, 1970, when we were all following the three brave astronauts in Apollo 13 with our prayers and concern on their journey back to earth, it was a heart-lifting experience to witness the presentation of the memorial award to the two young engineers for the development of the sublimator, the instrument used in both life support systems of the Apollo. I will quote from a letter to me from Donald G. Richards, vice president of the engineering division of Hamilton Standard:

> It is my privilege each year to nominate the engineers within this division who I feel are worthy of the George Mead Award for Engineering Achievement. I was, of course, pleased when one of our engineers won the award in 1960, and two of our engineers won the award in 1967, and was particularly pleased when Messrs. Rannenberg and Lovell won the award for 1969.

> We felt that their contribution to the Apollo program was very significant, and it just so happened that as you were participating in the award ceremony, sublimators of the type which they conceived and helped develop were helping the three astronauts on the Apollo 13 mission carry out their inspiring rescue operation.
>
> It must be a source of continuing satisfaction to you to know that your husband was so respected by the corporation that his name is kept before all of our engineers by means of this award. I certainly have considered it an honor to be associated with the event, and I can assure you that our recipients consider it a very, very, great honor. In each case, they have been very worthy individuals, and the type of person we are pleased to help move ahead. . . .

This award seemed particularly appropriate since the N.A.C.A. (National Advisory Committee for Aeronautics), of which Jack had been vice chairman during some of the war years, had become in 1958 the nucleus of a new organization—N.A.S.A. (National Aeronautics Space Administration). Progress in aeronautics had developed to the point where its basic consideration had moved from the realm of air to outer space.

And so, on this Memorial Day, 1970, I will bring this book to a close. It is far from complete, as it chronicles only a few of Jack's more significant achievements, but it is a record of the life and work of one who gave to every task he undertook the utmost of his skill and ability. It tells of one who, because all in the aviation and automotive industry trusted him absolutely, was able to mobilize quickly the country's industrial resources when every moment counted. It tells of a man who, though capable of white hot rage in the face of evil or dishonesty, was free of spite or malice toward anyone. It tells of a man whose loyalty and devotion to his family and friends was unfailing.

His life goes on in many vital ways. Through his creative genius was laid the sure foundation of aviation as we know it today. Through his work for churches, schools, colleges, hospitals, and community, where generous gifts and wise counsel went hand in hand, his help was immeasurable. And most of all, his life goes on through his children and grandchildren in whom the qualities that made him great live on, and through whom they will be transmitted to future generations.

He climbed life's mountains and crossed its streams as he came to them. Wherever there are people who cherish ideals of truth, honesty, faithfulness, and integrity, George Jackson Mead will be remembered with appreciation.

REFERENCES

Chapter

III

(1) Annual meeting paper, Society of Automotive Engineers Journal, "Airplane-Engine Designing for Reliability," by George J. Mead, March 1924

(2) Wright Aeronautical Magazine, "The Radial Engine," 1920

IV

(1) Wright Aeronautical Magazine, Wright Marine Engines, Typhoon Series, March 1924

(2) S.A.E. Magazine, "Some Aspects of Aircraft Engine Development," by George J. Mead, November 1925.

(3) S.A.E. Magazine, November 1925

(4) S.A.E. Magazine, November 1925

(5) Wright Aeronautical Bulletin, "Wright Marine Engine Gold Cup Series," 1924

VI (1) The Pratt & Whitney Aircraft Story, August 1950

VIII (1) The Pratt & Whitney Aircraft Story, page 76, August 1950

XIV (1) "Airplane-Engine Designing for Reliability" (Soc. Automotive Eng. Jour., 1924)

"Wasp and Hornet Radial Air-Cooled Engines" (Soc. Automotive Eng. Trans., 1926)

"The Development of Fixed Radial Air-Cooled Engines" (ibid. 1929)

"Around the Corner in Aviation" (The Technology Review, 1936)

"Power Plant Trends" (Jour. Soc. Automotive Eng. and Jour. of the Royal Aeronautical Society, 1937)

XV (1) N.A.C.A. members during 1940–1942

Dr. Charles G. Abbot, Secretary, Smithsonian Institution

Lieut. General Henry H. Arnold, United States Army, Commanding General, Army Air Forces, War Department

Major General George H. Brett, Acting Chief of the Air Corps, War Department

Dr. Lyman J. Briggs, Director, National Bureau of Standards

W. A. M. Burden, Special Assistant to the Secretary of Commerce

Dr. Vannevar Bush, Director, Office Scientific Research and Development, Washington, D.C.

Smith J. De France, Engineer in Charge, Ames Aeronautical Laboratory, Moffett Field, California

Dr. Robert E. Doherty

Dr. William F. Durand, Stanford University

Major General Oliver P. Echols, United States

Army, Commanding General, The Materiel Command, Army Air Forces, War Department

Clinton M. Hester, Administrator, Civil Aeronautics Authority

Robert H. Hinckley, Assistant Secretary of Commerce

Dr. Jerome C. Hunsaker, Chairman, 1942

S. Paul Johnston, Coordinator of Research

Rear Admiral Sydney M. Kraus, United States Navy; Bureau of Aeronautics, Navy Department

Dr. George W. Lewis, Director of Aeronautical Research

Rear Admiral John S. McCain, United States Navy; Chief, Bureau of Aeronautics, Navy Department, 1942

Dr. George J. Mead, Vice Chairman, 1940

Dr. F. W. Reichelderfer, Chief, United States Weather Bureau

Henry J. E. Reid, Engineer in Charge, Langley Memorial Aeronautical Laboratory, Langley Field, Virginia

Edward R. Sharp, Administrative Officer, Aircraft Engine Research Laboratory, Cleveland Airport, Cleveland, Ohio

Rear Admiral John H. Towers, Chief, Bureau of Aeronautics, Navy Department, 1940

John F. Victory, Secretary, 1940

Dr. Edward Warner, Civil Aeronautics Board, Washington, D.C.

Dr. Orville Wright, Dayton, Ohio

Dr. Theodore P. Wright, Asst. Chief, Aircraft Branch, War Production Board